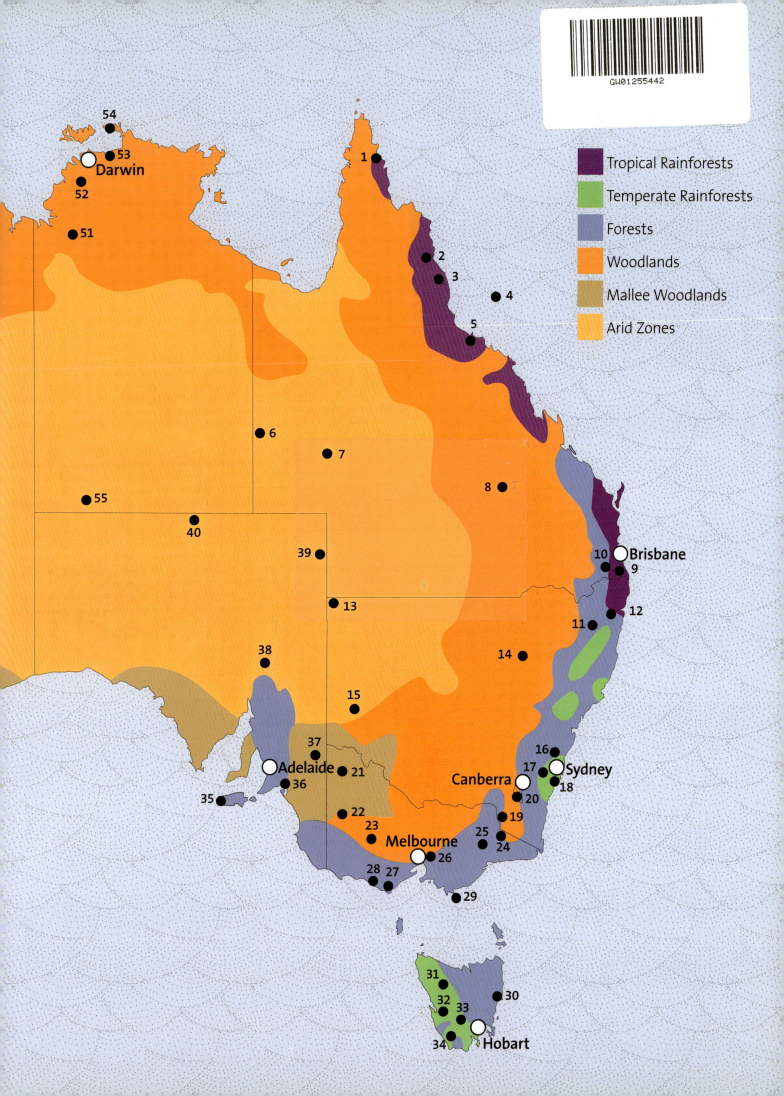

In loving memory of my brother
Scott D. Newton ('Echidna', 1960–2015)

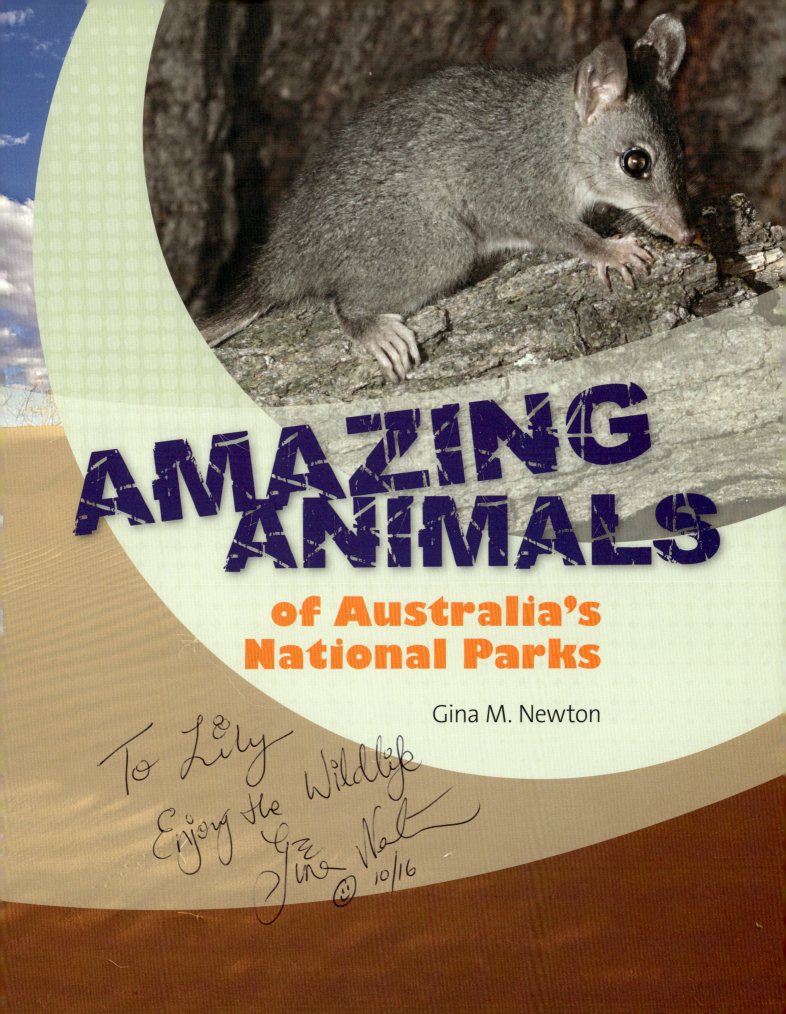

# AMAZING ANIMALS
## of Australia's National Parks

Gina M. Newton

NLA Publishing

His Excellency General the Honourable Sir Peter Cosgrove AK MC (Retd)
Governor-General of the Commonwealth of Australia

### *Amazing Animals of Australia's National Parks*

As Patron of the Foundation for National Parks and Wildlife, I am very pleased to support *Amazing Animals of Australia's National Parks*, an informative and stimulating book published by the National Library of Australia about the unique native animals in our national parks.

Australia has over 700 national parks covering every kind of habitat: woodlands, forests, rainforests, deserts, mountains, wetlands, coasts and oceans. The parks are home to a vast number of species that have adapted to these environments, including fish, reptiles, frogs, birds and mammals—not to mention the millions of different invertebrates.

National parks and other conservation areas play a vital role in protecting habitats and the balanced relationships between animals, plants and their environments that have evolved over thousands of years on our ancient continent.

All of our national parks are actively managed to reduce threats to our rich biodiversity—threats such as feral species (cats, dogs, foxes and Cane Toads, for example) and the effects of pollution, habitat clearing and climate change. But they also exist for people to visit and enjoy, in the process expanding their knowledge about the habitats, flora and fauna of Australia.

In *Amazing Animals of Australia's National Parks*, author and ecologist Dr Gina Newton has drawn on the research and expertise of fellow zoologists and ecologists to introduce us to over 100 animals from 50 parks across all Australian states and territories.

Young readers will find out about Australia's wildlife and the importance of caring for our environment. They will learn about a tree-dwelling kangaroo in Queensland; a frog in Western Australia that resembles a small shell-less turtle; and a bird in eastern Australia that collects and arranges blue objects.

This book is full of fascinating information, sure to make lifelong national park visitors of its readers. I hope you enjoy it as much as I have.

GOVERNMENT HOUSE CANBERRA ACT 2600 AUSTRALIA
TELEPHONE +61(2) 6283 3533 FACSIMILE +61(2) 6281 3760
WWW.GG.GOV.AU

# CONTENTS

| | |
|---|---|
| **Foreword** | 3 |
| **Amazing Animals of Australia's National Parks** | 6 |
| **How to Use This Book** | 8 |

## Woodlands & Grasslands — 10

### Reptiles
| | |
|---|---|
| Common Bearded Dragon | 12 |
| Frill-necked Lizard | 13 |
| Yellow-spotted Monitor | 14 |
| Burton's Legless Lizard | 15 |
| Common Blue-tongue Lizard | 16 |
| Eastern Brown Snake | 17 |

### Frogs
| | |
|---|---|
| Turtle Frog | 18 |

### Birds
| | |
|---|---|
| Emu | 19 |
| Tawny Frogmouth | 20 |
| Galah | 21 |
| Bush Stone-curlew | 22 |
| Barking Owl | 23 |
| Australian Barn Owl | 24 |
| Kookaburra: Laughing & Blue-winged | 25 |
| Fairy-wren: Superb & Splendid | 26 |
| Australian Magpie | 27 |

### Marsupials
| | |
|---|---|
| Wombat: Common & Southern Hairy-nosed | 28 |
| Honey Possum | 29 |
| Rufous Bettong | 30 |
| Spectacled Hare-wallaby | 31 |
| Grey Kangaroo: Eastern & Western | 32 |

## Forests — 34

### Reptiles
| | |
|---|---|
| Common Thick-tailed Gecko | 36 |
| Lace Monitor | 37 |
| Black-headed Python | 38 |

### Birds
| | |
|---|---|
| Black-Cockatoo: Yellow-tailed & Red-tailed | 39 |
| Sulphur-crested Cockatoo | 40 |
| Rainbow Lorikeet | 41 |
| Satin Bowerbird | 42 |

### Marsupials
| | |
|---|---|
| Brush-tailed Phascogale | 43 |
| Numbat | 44 |
| Long-nosed Bandicoot | 45 |
| Koala | 46 |
| Sugar Glider | 47 |
| Common Ringtail Possum | 48 |
| Common Brushtail Possum | 49 |
| Tasmanian Pademelon | 50 |
| Swamp Wallaby | 51 |

### Placental Mammals
| | |
|---|---|
| Little Red Flying-fox | 52 |
| Gould's Wattled Bat | 53 |

## Rainforests — 54

### Reptiles
| | |
|---|---|
| Boyd's Forest Dragon | 56 |
| Northern Leaf-tailed Gecko | 57 |
| Green Python | 58 |

### Frogs
| | |
|---|---|
| White-lipped Tree Frog | 59 |

### Birds
| | |
|---|---|
| Southern Cassowary | 60 |
| Superb Lyrebird | 61 |
| Eastern Whipbird | 62 |

### Marsupials
| | |
|---|---|
| Spotted-tailed Quoll | 63 |
| Striped Possum | 64 |
| Common Spotted Cuscus | 65 |
| Musky Rat-kangaroo | 66 |
| Lumholtz's Tree-kangaroo | 67 |

## Arid Zones — 68

### Reptiles
| | |
|---|---|
| Thorny Devil | 70 |
| Smooth Knob-tailed Gecko | 71 |
| Perentie | 72 |
| Shingleback Lizard | 73 |
| Mulga Snake | 74 |

### Frogs
| | |
|---|---|
| Water-holding Frog | 75 |

### Birds
| | |
|---|---|
| Malleefowl | 76 |
| Major Mitchell's Cockatoo | 77 |
| Cockatiel | 78 |
| Budgerigar | 79 |

### Marsupials
| | |
|---|---|
| Crest-tailed Mulgara | 80 |
| Giles' Planigale | 81 |
| Bilby | 82 |
| Red Kangaroo | 83 |
| Quokka | 84 |
| Southern Marsupial Mole | 85 |

### Placental Mammals
| | |
|---|---|
| Hopping-mouse: Spinifex & Mitchell's | 86 |

## Mountains  88

### Reptiles
Blotched Blue-tongue Lizard  90

### Birds
Wedge-tailed Eagle  91
Gang-gang Cockatoo  92
Crimson Rosella  93
Red Wattlebird  94

### Monotremes
Short-beaked Echidna  95

### Marsupials
Tasmanian Devil  96
Dusky Antechinus  97
Mountain Pygmy-possum  98
Common Wallaroo  99
Yellow-footed Rock-wallaby  100

### Placental Mammals
Dingo  101

## Wetlands & Waterways  102

### Fish
Murray Cod  104

### Reptiles
Freshwater Crocodile  105
Water Dragon  106
Red-bellied Black Snake  107
Pig-nosed Turtle  108
Eastern Long-necked Turtle  109

### Frogs
Banjo Frog: Eastern & Western  110

### Birds
Black Swan  111
Australian Wood Duck  112
Black-necked Stork  113
Purple Swamphen  114

### Monotremes
Platypus  115

### Placental Mammals
Australian Water Rat  116

## Coasts, Oceans & Islands  118

### Fish
Whale Shark  120

### Reptiles
Saltwater Crocodile  121
Green Turtle  122
Flatback Turtle  123

### Birds
Little Penguin  124
Silver Gull  125
Australian Pelican  126
White-bellied Sea-Eagle  127
Hooded Plover  128

### Placental Mammals
Dugong  129
Whale: Humpback & Southern Right  130
Dolphin: Common Bottlenose
 & Indo-Pacific Bottlenose  131
Orca  132
Australian Sea-lion  133
Australian Fur Seal  134

## Little Critters  135
Termites  136
Ants  136
Native Bees  136
Beetles  137
Bugs & Flies  137
Cicadas  137
Dragonflies & Damselflies  138
Grasshoppers, Crickets & Katydids  138
Moths & Butterflies  138
Stick & Leaf Insects  139
Spiders  139
Scorpions  139

**Glossary**  140
**Table of Featured Parks and Animals**  146
**Mammals: Age at Maturity**  150
**Acknowledgements**  151
**List of Illustrations**  152
**References**  155
**Index of Animals**  157
**Index of National Parks**  159

# AMAZING ANIMALS
## of Australia's National Parks

Creeping, crawling, slithering, pouncing, leaping, hopping, running, waddling, fluttering, flying—these are just some of the antics of Australia's 110,000 known species of animals (and there are still twice as many waiting to be described or discovered). In this book, you will meet more than 120 of these amazing animals, representing some of the most iconic, charismatic, devilish and interesting creatures in Australia. And, most of them can be seen nowhere else in the world.

So, want to catch a glimpse of some of these exciting creatures, big and small? Then, besides looking through this book, why not visit one of Australia's many national parks? There are over 700 national parks, with some in every state and territory. National parks are created to protect and preserve Australia's unique wildlife and habitats, and to provide places where people can visit, enjoy and learn more about them. You will find over 50 Australian national parks featured in this book, showcasing a range of different habitat types, from sandy red deserts to snowy mountain tops, from lush tropical rainforests to dry sparse woodlands and grasslands, and from inland wetlands to coastal islands. Each national park may have more than one habitat type, but one type is often the most common. And remember, some animals can only be seen at night.

In general, animals have evolved to live in a particular habitat type, although many species can live across a range of different habitats. For example, the Short-beaked Echidna can live in almost any habitat, including snow. This book is divided into sections according to seven main habitat types. In each habitat section, animals are featured that are likely to be found in that habitat (and the habitat symbols tell you the other types in which they also occur). These Australian animals might be fish, reptiles, frogs, birds, marsupials or placental mammals. There is also a section at the end of the book on 'Little Critters' (insects and arachnids), which account for more than half of all Australia's animal species.

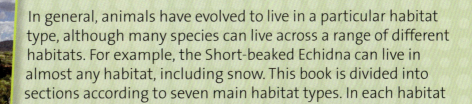

On each animal's page, 'Fast Facts' gives you all the vital statistics, like size, age and number of young. 'Where Does It Live?' tells you where in Australia it can be found and provides details about its home. The 'What's Its Life Like?' section tells you a bit about how the animal moves, behaves, eats and has young, while the 'Interesting Info' section has quirky, fun and fascinating facts—many of which you would never have guessed. At the end of the book, there is a great glossary where you can quickly look up words you may not have seen before.

Whether you read this book from front to back, or dip in and out randomly, Australia's stunningly beautiful national parks and unique native wildlife are sure to AMAZE you!

# HOW TO USE THIS BOOK

**Common Name**
A species may have several common names—only one is used here.

**Scientific Name**

**Habitats Where the Species Lives**

 Woodlands & Grasslands

 Forests

 Rainforests

 Arid Zones

 Mountains

 Wetlands & Waterways

 Coasts, Oceans & Islands

**Abbreviations**

| | |
|---|---|
| M | male |
| F | female |
| y | year |
| mo | month |
| av | average |
| max | maximum |
| ha | hectare (100 ha = 1 km²) |

## Satin Bowerbird
*Ptilonorhynchus violaceus*

### Q&A

**What is it?**
A ground-dwelling songbird considered to be one of the most advanced birds, because it uses tools and 'paints'. The male has glossy blue-black feathers, while females and young males have olive green-brown plumage. Both sexes have lilac-blue eyes.

**Where does it live?**
In wet forests, woodlands and rainforests.

**What's its life like?**
Satin Bowerbirds eat fruits, berries, insects and seeds. Immature males may form flocks with females but adult males are solitary. The male builds a U-shaped bower from twigs and leaves, with two parallel arched walls forming an avenue (35 cm high and 45 cm long) on the ground to attract females. He collects mainly blue objects—such as flowers, feathers, berries, rocks, shells, and bits of plastic or glass—to decorate his bower, and 'paints' its walls with chewed vegetation and saliva. Females may visit several bowers before choosing a mate and mating occurs in the avenue. Females make their nests high in nearby trees or bushes and rear the young alone.

### interesting info

- It takes 6–7 years for males to grow their shiny black feathers. During this time, they practise building bowers.
- Males often rearrange the decorations in their bowers. They sit in the bower and call out to attract females and warn off other males. When a female visits, the male mimics other bird calls to impress her and performs an energetic and noisy dance that includes giving her something blue.
- Males steal each other's decorations, especially blue plastic bottle tops and the blue tail feathers of Crimson Rosellas.

42

- Main Range NP
- Wollemi NP
- Namadgi NP
- Dandenong Ranges NP

**Fast Facts**
- 27–35 cm
- 43–55 cm
- 170–290 g
- up to 26 y
- 1–3 eggs

**List of National Parks**
Just a few of the national parks where the species may occur. It may occur in many more—see the table on pages 146–149.

**Distribution Range**
The coloured areas show where the species is likely to live.

## Conservation Status

 The species is endangered or critically endangered

 The species is vulnerable or near threatened

 The species is not listed as threatened or is of least concern

 A black dot means that the species, or a subspecies, is threatened in a particular area

### Note about Conservation Status
Conservation status is determined by a scientific assessment of the risk of extinction to a species. Status can range from 'Least Concern' (the species is not considered at risk), to 'Near Threatened' and 'Vulnerable' (there is some concern and threats are apparent), to 'Endangered' and 'Critically Endangered' (the species is under considerable threat and in serious risk of becoming extinct), through to 'Extinct'. Official listing can occur at the international level (IUCN Red List), national level and/or state/territory level, and is recognised by law in Australia.

# Brush-tailed Phascogale
*Phascogale tapoatafa*

### Q&A

**What is it?**
A small, arboreal marsupial, also called the Tuan. Its black, bushy 'bottle-brush' tail is as long as its body and has bristles up to 4 cm long.

**Where does it live?**
In dry, open forests and woodlands, in tropical and temperate coastal regions of the mainland. This species nests in large, living trees.

**What's its life like?**
Brush-tailed Phascogales are fast, agile hunters. At night, they spiral up tree trunks and run along branches, feeding on insects, spiders, small vertebrates and eucalyptus flowers. By tearing off bark with their long claws, sharp teeth and dexterous forepaws, they capture hidden prey. During the day, individuals rest alone in one of their many nests in their home range. When it's very cold or food is scarce, several share a nest to increase their chances of survival (communal nesting). Females have more young than they can accommodate on their 8 teats (called supernumerary young) so only the fittest survive. When weaned, young males move many kilometres away but females stay close by.

- Main Range NP
- Dandenong Ranges NP
- Walpole-Nornalup NP
- Tone-Perup Nature Reserve

### Fast Facts
- M 34–49 cm / F 31–45 cm
- M 175–311 g / F 106–212 g
- M 11–12 mo, F 3 y
- up to 8 joeys
- M up to 100+ ha / F 2–70 ha

### interesting info
- This phascogale can leap up to 2 m between trees. Its back feet have ankles that can rotate a bit so it can easily climb up or down trees.
- When frightened, they drum their forefeet.
- Their nests are lined with bark, feathers, fur and even poo—the poo stops other animals, like Sugar Gliders, from stealing their nesting spots.
- The male is unusual because it dies after its first mating season. It's the largest mammal that does this.
- Threats include old trees being cut down, habitat areas becoming too small, feral predators and rainfall that's too low.

43

### Fast Facts about the Species

- length
- height
- wingspan (the distance from one wingtip across to the other)
- weight
- lifespan (how long the animal lives for in the wild)
- number of young in a year
- home range or territory (the area in which the animal usually lives and feeds, and that it sometimes defends)

### Glossary Words
Each page has a selection of words that you may not know underlined in red. Look up the glossary at the back of the book to find out what they mean.

# WOODLANDS & GRASSLANDS

**Woodlands and grasslands or 'the Bush'—widely spaced, medium to short trees with shrubs, herbs and grasses in the undergrowth (tropical, temperate and semi-arid)**

Woodlands are the second largest habitat type in Australia after the arid zone. They are more open than forests. The trees are spaced more widely apart and tend to be shorter but with spreading canopies. Most woodlands are dominated by eucalypts (gum trees) and acacias (wattles), but some also have melaleucas (paperbarks) or casuarinas (she-oaks).

Carnarvon NP (Queensland)

Karijini NP (Western Australia)

Grampians NP (Victoria)

Warrumbungle NP (New South Wales)

Wilsons Promontory NP (Victoria)

Litchfield NP (Northern Territory)

Yanchep NP (Western Australia)

Woodlands let in more light than forests and their undergrowth has a wide variety of shrubs, herbs and grasses. In winter and spring, the undergrowth can be full of colourful wildflowers.

Mallee woodlands have short eucalypts, usually less than 10 m high, with multiple trunks that are adapted to frequent fires. They occur in southern semi-arid regions with fairly reliable rainfall. Savanna woodlands grow in the tropics and have very open tree canopies and grassy understoreys due to the hot, dry conditions and frequent fires.

These national parks have examples of woodlands and grasslands where the animals in this section occur. The animals may also occur in other habitats and in other national parks.

# Common Bearded Dragon
*Pogona barbata*

## Q&A

**What is it?**
A semi-arboreal dragon lizard with a large triangular and spiny head. It has an impressive beard of dark scales and spines that can be erected. It's also called the Eastern Bearded Dragon. In the east, this is the most commonly seen of Australia's eight bearded dragon species.

**Where does it live?**
Along the eastern coast, in woodlands, grasslands and frequently in trees. The Common, or Eastern, Bearded Dragon is often seen foraging at roadsides or perching on fence posts, in farmland or urban areas.

**What's its life like?**
Adults eat mainly plant matter like flowers, fruits, berries and leaves, and a small number of insects. Juveniles eat mainly insects. The Common Bearded Dragon is most active during the day and often basks in the sun to warm up—it's a thermoregulator. Its body gets darker as it soaks up heat. When too hot, it seeks shelter in a burrow or rock crevice, or climbs a tree for shade. In very cold weather, it may hibernate, entering a state of torpor. When breeding, females scoop out shallow holes in the ground, lay their eggs there, then cover them up. The eggs take 45–80 days to incubate.

- Warrumbungle NP
- Grampians NP
- Carnarvon NP

## Interesting info

- All dragons have eyelids and a fringe of scales like 'eyelashes' to protect the eyes.
- Before shedding their skin, sometimes dragons' eyes bulge out.
- When defending itself, the Common Bearded Dragon erects its beard and opens its mouth, which is bright yellow inside. It can also camouflage itself and has strong body spikes for protection.
- The male is very territorial and only lets females and juveniles into its territory. To keep out other males and to attract females, it sits on a perch and communicates by arm-waving and head-bobbing.

## Fast Facts

- 50–60 cm (M larger)
- 600 g
- 10–15 y
- 10–20 eggs (1–3 clutches)

# Frill-necked Lizard
*Chlamydosaurus kingii*

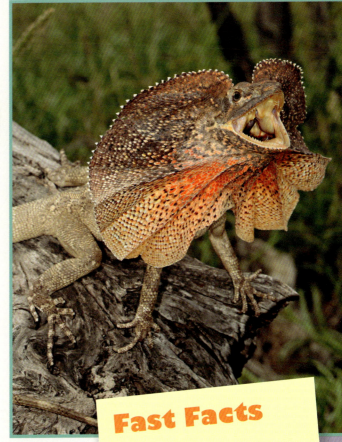

- Carnarvon NP
- Litchfield NP

## Q&A

**What is it?**
The Frill-necked Lizard, or Frilled Dragon, is one of Australia's most iconic reptiles and one of the largest dragon lizards. It has a spectacular neck-frill. It's bipedal, which means that it can run upright on its hind legs. Its tail is long, about 2/3 of its total length.

**Where does it live?**
In the hot, humid woodlands and forests of tropical northern Australia. It's arboreal, living in the tree canopy, mostly 2–3 m from the ground.

**What's its life like?**
The Frill-necked Lizard devours insects and spiders, and occasionally eats smaller lizards. From a tree, it scans the ground for prey up to 40 m away and moves quickly down to ambush them, then returns to the canopy, all in less than 5 minutes. When fighting or threatened, a Frill-necked Lizard hisses and strikes a scary pose by standing on its hind legs, opening its yellow mouth and fanning out its orange-red neck-frill. Males fight for territory and for females. Females lay eggs in underground nests and the gender of hatchlings depends on environmental temperature. When hatched, the young are fully formed and can hunt and use their frill immediately.

### Fast Facts
- up to 95 cm (includes tail 65 cm)
- up to 900 g
- up to 20 y (captivity)
- 4–25 eggs

### interesting info

- The Frill-necked Lizard uses camouflage. It can lighten or darken its colour to match the background habitat.
- The Frill-necked Lizard can run slowly like other lizards, as well as fast, upright with its hind legs akimbo.
- Frill-necked Lizards change trees often — it doesn't matter what kind of trees they are.
- This lizard is more active in the wet season than in the dry season.
- The frill is up to 30 cm across and helps keep the dragon's body at the correct temperature.
- Predators include snakes, eagles, owls, Dingoes, and feral foxes and cats.

# Yellow-spotted Monitor

*Varanus panoptes*

## Q&A

**What is it?**
A very large black and yellow spotted monitor, or goanna, with a flattened tail and a dark stripe running through the eye. It's the deepest nesting reptile in the world. It's also known as the Argus or Floodplain Monitor.

**Where does it live?**
In a wide range of habitats across northern Australia, including woodlands, grasslands, riparian and river floodplain habitats, and coastal beaches. It spends most of the time on the ground and in burrows.

**What's its life like?**
This monitor feeds on invertebrates like scorpions, locusts and spiders, and on vertebrates such as small mammals, reptiles and other monitor species. Carrion also forms a large part of the diet. Like other monitors, it flicks out its sensitive forked tongue when searching for a meal. It's great at finding and digging up food. Yellow-spotted Monitors build complex burrow systems (warrens) with nests at the end of spiralling tunnels up to 3 m deep. Females lay eggs in the tropical wet season. Deep nests help keep the humidity and temperature right for egg incubation. Warrens are shared by several individuals (males and females) indicating social interaction, which is unusual for lizards.

○ Carnarvon NP
○ Karijini NP
○ Litchfield NP

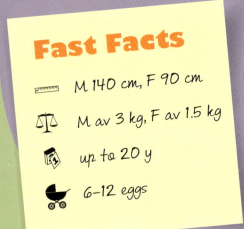

### Fast Facts

- M 140 cm, F 90 cm
- M av 3 kg, F av 1.5 kg
- up to 20 y
- 6–12 eggs

## Interesting info

- There are about 30 monitor species in Australia.
- **The Yellow-spotted Monitor can 'tripod'. This means that it stands on its hind legs and tail when searching for prey or to make itself look bigger when it's threatened. If disturbed, it runs fast along the ground and up a nearby tree.**
- **Monitors eat anything they can find. They are particularly good at finding the eggs of marine and freshwater turtles.**
- **Lots of Yellow-spotted Monitors in northern Australia are killed after they eat Cane Toads, which are poisonous feral pests.**

# Burton's Legless Lizard
*Lialis burtonis*

## Q&A

**What is it?**
A large legless lizard that's one of Australia's most widespread reptiles. Burton's Legless Lizard has a long, pointy, wedge-shaped snout. Legless lizards are often mistaken for snakes as they have no forelimbs and only small flaps for hind limbs.

**Where does it live?**
In dry habitats—woodlands, forests, sandy deserts and rocky outcrops—but not at high altitudes. It prefers low vegetation and likes to burrow under loose leaf litter or just under the soil surface, which may help it control its body temperature (thermoregulation).

**What's its life like?**
Burton's Legless Lizard is a lizard- and gecko-eating specialist, and sometimes eats dragons and small snakes. It suffocates prey by gripping it and then swallowing it head first. This is possible because of its flexible jaw, recurved teeth and hinged skull. It's a visual and ambush predator, relying on good eyesight to detect prey's movement while it stays hidden. Vertical pupils help focus on prey from a distance. Its eyes can retract, to protect them while it struggles with prey. Unlike most other lizards, it may wiggle its tail to attract prey (caudal luring). Females lay eggs under rocks, logs or leaf litter and often share a nest with other females.

- Carnarvon NP
- Warrumbungle NP
- Yanchep NP
- Karijini NP
- Litchfield NP

## Fast Facts
- 75 cm
- 150 g
- up to 7 y (captivity)
- 2 eggs (1-3 clutches)

## Interesting info

- Legless lizards are a type of gecko. They can squeak and they use their tongue to clean and moisten their eyes.
- A legless lizard isn't like a snake: it usually has a broad tongue, not a forked slim one; it usually has ear openings, unlike a snake; it can drop its tail, but a snake can't; and its tail is much longer than its body, while a snake's tail is short.
- The colours and patterns of Burton's Legless Lizards help camouflage them and are different in different locations; e.g. stripes are good camouflage in spinifex grass.

# Common Blue-tongue Lizard
*Tiliqua scincoides*

## Q&A

**What is it?**
The best-known lizard in Australia and one of the largest skinks in the world. There are four other blue-tongue lizard species in Australia. All have large smooth scales, a triangular head, flattened striped bodies, small legs and pointed tails.

**Where does it live?**
In many habitats across eastern and northern Australia, except for alpine and rainforest areas. At night, the Common Blue-tongue seeks shelter in logs or among leaf litter. It's also sometimes found in suburban backyards.

**What's its life like?**
After a morning bask in the sun, the Common Blue-tongue forages for flowers, fruits and slow-moving prey like snails, slugs and certain insects. Its teeth and jaws are strong so it can crush the hard shells of snails and beetles. During cold weather, it buries itself deep in its shelter and is inactive. Its predators include birds such as kookaburras and raptors; large snakes such as the Eastern Brown, Red-bellied Black and Mulga; and feral cats and dogs. Sometimes in urban areas, it's killed by eating snails poisoned with snail bait, and by sunbaking on roads. Watch out when mowing the lawn as Blue-tongues often hide in long grass!

- Carnarvon NP
- Warrumbungle NP
- Wilsons Promontory NP
- Grampians NP
- Litchfield NP

## Interesting info

- **The Common Blue-tongue looks fierce by hissing and sticking out its big blue tongue and showing its pink mouth.**
- There are several main types of Australian lizard — geckos (around 200 species), legless lizards (50 species), dragons (80 species); monitors (30 species); and skinks (430 species).
- **Except for monitors, if a lizard loses its tail, the tail can regrow (autotomy).**
- This lizard is bred in captivity and sold as pets in some states, but you aren't allowed to catch them in the wild.

## Fast Facts

- 80 cm (av 45 cm)
- up to 1.2 kg
- 10–15 y
  20–30 y (captivity)
- 10–25 live young

# Eastern Brown Snake
*Pseudonaja textilis*

### What is it?
One of the most commonly encountered snakes. Its mouth-lining is pink and its body colour varies with location, from tan, to grey, to dark brown, with a cream to yellow or orange belly. The juvenile has a dark patch on the head and may have bands along the body. Its scientific name means 'false cobra'. It's also called the Common Brown Snake.

○ Carnarvon NP
○ Grampians NP

### Where does it live?
A variety of habitats along the eastern coast but prefers dry environments. It doesn't occur in rainforest or alpine regions. When inactive, it shelters beneath logs, rocks or artificial materials (like sheets of iron or building materials). It thrives in agricultural regions and on the fringes of cities or towns.

### What's its life like?
The Eastern Brown Snake is active by day and, in warmer weather, by night. It's a big hunter, eating rats and mice, frogs, reptiles, small birds and eggs. It's often attracted to buildings on farms that harbour rodents. It hunts by sight, smell and movement, and subdues captives with venom and constriction. When attacking prey, it winds its body into an S shape, spreading its neck and striking rapidly and repeatedly with its mouth open, like a cobra. Predators and threats include raptors, feral cats, other snakes, people and cars. Females lay eggs in a soil crack burrow, which is often defended until the hatchlings emerge.

## Fast Facts
- up to 2.2 m (av 1.5 m)
- up to 2.4 kg
- up to 10 y
- 10–35 eggs

## interesting info
- Eastern Browns usually flee from danger. But, if they can't, they're fast and will bite. People shouldn't try to catch or kill these snakes as their bite can be deadly.
- In spring, most snakes killed on roads are males because, after winter, they start moving around earlier than females.
- Males fight to win females and may wrestle each other for up to an hour.
- If Eastern Browns bite each other, they don't die because they're immune to their own venom. They're also immune to the venom of Mulga Snakes, their predators.

# Turtle Frog

*Myobatrachus gouldii*

Yanchep NP

## Q&A

**What is it?**
One of the most fossorial (spends most of its time underground) of Australia's frogs. It looks like a little turtle without its shell and also a bit like a sumo wrestler. It has a small, distinct head with tiny black eyes and a round pink body with short limbs.

**Where does it live?**
In burrows in the sandy soils of south-western WA, in coastal plains and woodlands with dense scrub and relatively high rainfall. It prefers banksia woodlands and often lives close to termite colonies.

**What's its life like?**
The Turtle Frog stays mostly underground. Its burrow is 1–2 m deep and protects it from water loss and the sun's heat. The sandy soils filter rainfall from the surface, keeping the frog moist. It prefers termites but also eats other small insects, and feeds either underground or on the surface. After heavy rain, males come to the surface to call for mates. The male leads the female into his burrow where they stay together for several months before they mate. There is no tadpole stage, with young froglets hatching directly from the egg, inside the burrow—a strategy to cope with a dry environment.

## interesting info

- The Turtle Frog burrows headfirst with its front feet, not with its back legs like most burrowing frogs. Its feet have claws but no webbing or toe pads, as it doesn't swim or climb trees.
- It has the biggest egg of any Australian frog species—7.4 mm in diameter.
- The Turtle Frog waits a long time between courtship and mating. This is unusual for frogs. It might be waiting until conditions are good for the new froglets.

## Fast Facts

- 3–7 cm (F larger)
- 4–10 g
- unknown
- up to 40 large eggs

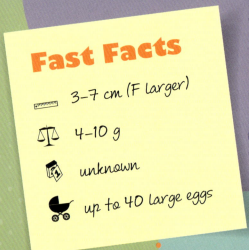

# Emu
*Dromaius novaehollandiae*

### What is it?
Australia's tallest native bird. The Emu has straggly feathers and a bare blue neck. It doesn't fly but, as the only bird with calf muscles, it's built for sprinting, which is also helped by its tridactyl (three-toed) feet.

### Where does it live?
In grassland plains, open woodlands and scrublands, from the desert to the coast. It used to live in Tasmania but became extinct in the 1860s, soon after European settlement.

### What's its life like?
Emus live in pairs or in groups of 30 to hundreds when food is plentiful. As omnivores, they eat grass, flowers, seeds, fruit, insects, snails and grubs. They swallow large stones (gastroliths) to help grind up food in their gizzard. Emus may move hundreds of kilometres to find food and water. They pair up in summer and breed in winter, except during drought. The male builds the nest, incubates the eggs and cares for the chicks for 18 months (so he misses the next breeding season). Predators include Dingoes and Wedge-tailed Eagles. If attacked from above, the Emu runs in a zig-zag pattern; if attacked on the ground, it kicks with its powerful legs.

- Carnarvon NP
- Warrumbungle NP
- Wilsons Promontory NP
- Grampians NP
- Yanchep NP
- Karijini NP
- Litchfield NP

## interesting info

- Apart from the Emu, some other birds that can't fly are the Ostrich, the Cassowary and the Kiwi.
- Emus can run fast—up to 50 km/hour—with a three-metre stride. They can also swim.
- Emus make several calls—booming, grunting and drumming. Booming is created in a neck sac and can be heard up to 2 km away.
- Two dwarf emu species from Kangaroo Island and King Island were made extinct by sealers around 200 years ago.
- Overall, the numbers of Emus have increased since Europeans came to Australia.

## Fast Facts
- 1.5–2.1 m
- 30–50 kg
- up to 20 y / up to 40 y (captivity)
- 5–24 eggs (av 9)

# Tawny Frogmouth
*Podargus strigoides*

## Q&A

**What is it?**
A large-headed and stocky owl-like bird that's not an owl. Its plumage varies from grey to brown and is camouflaged to look like a tree branch. The wide bill is tipped with tufts of bristles.

**Where does it live?**
In woodlands and forests, in any climate. It's active during the night and rests during the day.

**What's its life like?**
Tawny Frogmouths mate for life and pairs share all nest and chick-rearing duties. In arid regions, they breed when there is heavy rain. They hunt by perching on low branches, watching and gliding down to pounce on prey. They eat similar food to kookaburras, but hunt during dusk and night rather than in the day like kookaburras. Prey includes insects, spiders, rodents, reptiles and frogs. The Frogmouth bashes large prey against the tree that it's perching in, to kill it before eating. Predatory birds, snakes and native and introduced mammals prey on the Tawny Frogmouth and its eggs. Other threats include habitat loss, fires, cars and exposure to toxic pesticides in food.

- Carnarvon NP
- Warrumbungle NP
- Wilsons Promontory NP
- Grampians NP
- Yanchep NP
- Karijini NP
- Litchfield NP

## interesting info

- The Tawny Frogmouth is not a raptor and uses its bill to catch prey, but raptors, like owls, use their strong legs and feet.
- The Tawny Frogmouth can sit completely still with its bill pointing up. Its plumage makes it so well camouflaged that it looks like part of a tree, making it almost invisible.
- When threatened, the adult gives an alarm call, which signals to its chicks to remain absolutely still.
- It uses different calls. You can hear its warning screams for kilometres.
- In winter, it goes into a type of torpor to save energy.

### Fast Facts

- 33–53 cm
- 65–98 cm
- 280–350 g (M larger)
- up to 14 y
- 2–3 eggs

# Galah
*Eolophus roseicapillus*

## Q&A

**What is it?**
An often noisy, pink and grey cockatoo. The male has brown eyes and the female has red eyes.

**Where does it live?**
In any open country with suitable trees and waterways, and in urban centres. It's absent only from the driest deserts and the thickest forests. Due to landscape changes since European settlement, it has spread towards the coast and has replaced the Major Mitchell's Cockatoo in part of its inland range.

**What's its life like?**
The Galah feeds mainly on the ground, eating seeds, nuts, berries, roots and insects. Its hard, rough tongue moves food around inside its bill and mouth. It lives in pairs or in small to very large flocks. Adults are generally sedentary, moving around only locally, while young birds are nomadic. In harsh times, large flocks travel long distances for food. The Galah matures at 4 years and mates for life, sharing egg incubation and care of the young. The pair nests in a tree hollow, lining the nest with gum leaves and wood stripped from the entrance. If one of the pair dies, the other may take on a new mate.

- Carnarvon NP
- Warrumbungle NP
- Wilsons Promontory NP
- Grampians NP
- Yanchep NP
- Karijini NP
- Litchfield NP

## Fast Facts

- 34–38 cm
- 75 cm
- 270–350 g
- up to 30 y / over 60 y (captivity)
- 2–5 eggs

## interesting info

- In light rain, Galahs are often seen doing a 'rain dance', hanging upside down from branches or wires with their wings spread out.
- Mates show affection by preening the feathers on each other's faces.
- In the wild, Galahs will occasionally breed with Major Mitchell's Cockatoos, Cockatiels, Sulphur-crested Cockatoos and Corellas.
- The bill keeps growing but the Galah keeps it trim by chewing on wood and hard seeds.
- Galahs have a reputation of being 'silly', but in fact they're very intelligent. In captivity, they can learn to say words.

# Bush Stone-curlew

*Burhinus grallarius*

### What is it?
A large, slim, ground-dwelling bird with long, gangly legs, large yellow eyes and prominent white eyebrows.

### Where does it live?
In open forests and woodlands, on the edges of rainforests and along waterways. This bird is now most abundant in the tropical and subtropical north of Australia.

### What's its life like?
The Bush Stone-curlew is mainly nocturnal and its eerie call, *wer-loo, wer-loo*, can be heard through the bush, especially at dusk and night-time. It eats frogs, lizards, snails, insects and small mammals, and hunts alone or with a mate. It takes all its food from the ground. During the day, it's inactive, relying on its plumage as camouflage, to hide from predators. It has an unusual courtship dance, where it stretches out the wings, neck and tail and marches on the spot, calling loudly. The female lays her eggs in a scrape on the ground near logs, and both parents incubate the eggs and care for the young.

- Carnarvon NP
- Grampians NP
- Yanchep NP
- Karijini NP
- Litchfield NP

## interesting info

- When disturbed, these birds crouch down or freeze like statues, so that predators, like raptors, can't see them. But, this doesn't work well with predators that smell their prey, like Dingoes and goannas.
- Bush Stone-curlews have disappeared from many habitats south of the Great Dividing Range, probably because foxes and cats have killed them. It's also because their habitat has been cleared. These birds need fallen trees for camouflage and nesting.
- In the south, Bush Stone-curlews are occasionally seen on golf courses and in cemeteries (where they probably sound like ghosts!)

**Fast Facts**

- 54–60 cm
- 60 cm
- 85–105 cm
- 550–750 g
- up to 30 y
- 1–3 eggs

# Barking Owl
*Ninox connivens*

- Carnarvon NP
- Grampians NP
- Karijini NP
- Litchfield NP

## Q&A

### What is it?
A medium-sized, grey-brown and white owl with piercing yellow eyes. Its call sounds like a dog barking and it has an alarm call that sounds like a woman screaming.

### Where does it live?
In open woodlands and forests with large trees for nesting and roosting. It often lives near wooded rivers and wetlands, and likes gum trees (eucalypts) in the south and paperbark trees (melaleucas) in the north.

### What's its life like?
A visual hunter at dusk and dawn, the Barking Owl catches prey from the ground, in trees, on the wing and on the surface of water. It prefers to eat mammals such as rabbits and sugar gliders, but will also take birds, mice, bats, possums, lizards, insects, frogs and fish. It can catch and eat birds as big as cockatoos and ducks. These owls mate for life and have a feeding range of 1,400 to 2,500 ha. The Barking Owl nests in hollows of old, living eucalypt trees, on a bed of wood debris that it collects. The female incubates the eggs and the male provides the food.

## Fast Facts

- 35–45 cm
- 85–120 cm
- M 425–740 g
- F 380–710 g
- up to 16 y
- 2–3 eggs

## interesting info

- Early settlers thought the Barking Owl's calls belonged to the 'bunyip', a scary mythical creature that lived in swamps and billabongs.
- In the south-east, the numbers of this owl have really declined. This is mainly because many large trees have been cut down. Gum trees have hollows good for nesting only when they're 100–200 years old.
- The Southern Boobook Owl is similar to the Barking Owl, but it's browner with white markings around its eyes like goggles. It's the smallest and most common owl in Australia.

# Australian Barn Owl

*Tyto alba delicatula*

## Q&A

**What is it?**
A medium-sized brown and white owl with a white heart-shaped face. It's also known as the Eastern Barn Owl.

**Where does it live?**
In open grasslands and woodlands, and farmlands. The Australian Barn Owl sometimes roosts in caves or on rocky islands offshore. It's rarer in Tasmania. The Barn Owl, *Tyto alba*, is the most widespread land bird around the world, occurring on every continent except Antarctica.

**What's its life like?**
Australian Barn Owls mate for life and nest in hollows in trees, caves or cliffs. Males and females roost separately when not breeding. They're not territorial but they do have a feeding range in which they catch rodents, small birds, bats, reptiles, frogs and insects. Before mating, the male brings the female gifts of food. These birds hunt in total darkness, using sound. While hovering, the disc of feathers around its face directs sounds to its ears (which are at different levels on each side of the head), so it can pin-point (triangulate) the location of prey. If food is scarce, the young may starve in the first year while learning to hunt.

- Carnarvon NP
- Wilsons Promontory NP
- Grampians NP
- Yanchep NP
- Karijini NP
- Litchfield NP

## interesting info

- Of all animals, this owl eats the most rodents (mice and rats), so it's great for pest control around farms. Some farmers put up nesting boxes to encourage it to stay. When there are plagues of rodents, Australian Barn Owls breed a lot, but, when the rodents have gone, many starve to death (boom-and-bust cycle).
- The structure of this owl's flight feathers allows it to fly silently.
- **Although it can't move its eyes, it can turn its head 180 degrees, without moving its body.**
- Australian Barn Owls can fly long distances, even across the ocean.

### Fast Facts

- 30–40 cm
- 70–100 cm
- 310–360 g
- av 5, up to 20 y (captivity)
- 3–6 eggs

# Kookaburra: Laughing & Blue-winged

*Dacelo novaeguineae* and *Dacelo leachii*

## Q&A

**What are they?**
Large, stout kingfishers with a big head and bill (about 10 cm long). The Laughing Kookaburra (LK) or 'laughing jackass' has brown wings and a brown eye-stripe, and the Blue-winged Kookaburra (BWK) or 'howling jackass' has blue wings and no eye-stripe.

**Where do they live?**
In woodlands and open forests with clearings, tree-lined watercourses, coastal swamplands and farmlands. A native of the eastern mainland, the LK was introduced into south-western Western Australia in 1897, Tasmania in 1902 and Kangaroo Island in 1926. The BWK is tropical and subtropical in distribution.

**What are their lives like?**
Both species often live in territorial groups consisting of a dominant pair (that mate for life) and helpers. The young stay for about four years and help the parents with incubating eggs and feeding new chicks. Both species breed over spring and summer. Nests are in tree hollows up to 20 m above the ground or in holes in riverbanks, termite mounds or even haystacks. Kookaburras are carnivorous, wait-and-pounce hunters. They perch and watch, swooping on unsuspecting prey like insects, reptiles, frogs, crustaceans and small mammals. They bash prey against a tree to kill it before eating it. Kookaburras may plunge into water when hunting or bathing.

- Carnarvon NP
- Warrumbungle NP
- Wilsons Promontory NP
- Grampians NP
- Yanchep NP
- Karijini NP
- Litchfield NP

## Fast Facts

- LK 40–48 cm
- BWK 38–40 cm
- 66–80 cm
- up to 455 g (av LK 310 g, BWK 300 g)
- up to 15 y
- up to 20 y (captivity)
- 2–4 eggs

## Interesting info

- The LK is the world's largest kingfisher. Its call is famous—*kook-kook-kook kook-ka-ka-ka*, followed by chuckles. The BWK's call consists of barking *klock-klocks*, followed by cackling screeches. These calls are used mainly to warn other birds to stay away from their territory.
- Up to 12 adult BWKs feed the chicks at one nest.
- Like many other carnivorous birds, kookaburras vomit pellets of indigestible bits, like bone or fur.
- While both are kingfishers, BWKs often eat fish, but LKs rarely do.

# Fairy-wren: Superb & Splendid

*Malurus cyaneus* and *Malurus splendens*

■ Superb

≡ Splendid

○ Carnarvon NP
○ Warrumbungle NP
○ Wilsons Promontory NP
○ Grampians NP (Superb only)
● Yanchep NP

## Q&A

**What are they?**
One of Australia's favourite small songbirds. The male Superb Fairy-wren has a blue head and nape, while the male Splendid Fairy-wren is all blue. Females of both species are brown but the female Splendid has a blue tail. Male fairy-wrens can also have brown 'eclipse' plumage when they are immature or not breeding.

**Where do they live?**
In woodlands and forests with plenty of undergrowth for shelter. While the Superb occurs in the wetter south-eastern corner of the continent, the Splendid lives in drier inland and western regions.

**What are their lives like?**
Fairy-wrens are energetic little birds that live in groups of 3–12. The group consists of a mated pair and helpers who are females and non-breeding males (although both the male and female of the bonded pair will often mate with other birds). All the birds in the group defend the territory and care for the young. The dome-shaped nest, made from dry grass, twigs and spiders' webs, is built in low bush or spinifex grass, or higher up in trees, such as paperbarks or mulga. Fairy-wrens eat insects, seeds and fruit. While the Superb has adapted well to urban environments in the east, the Splendid hasn't done so in the west.

## interesting info

- A breeding male may steal females from other males (this is called kleptogamy)—he flies into his neighbour's territory, carrying a flower petal as a gift for a female. If he isn't chased away, he tries to mate with her.
- Sometimes males sing their 'predator warning' songs when there aren't any predators around, to make females come close to them for protection.
- Fairy-wrens normally hop, but they can trick predators by running with the head and tail lowered so they look like a mouse.

## Fast Facts

- 11–14 cm
- 12–16 cm
- 7–13 g
- up to 10 y
- 2–5 eggs (av 3)

# Australian Magpie
*Cracticus tibicen*

### What is it?
Australia's best-loved large songbird. It has a pointed, black-tipped bill. The species has a variety of black-and-white plumage patterns.

### Where does it live?
Wherever there's a combination of open grassland and trees. The Australian Magpie is only absent from deserts and the densest forests. It nests and roosts in treetops, but forages and feeds on the ground in grass or bare soil.

### What's its life like?
Australian Magpies have a complex social structure. They often live in small groups (tribes of 2–20) within a permanent territory, which they constantly defend against other magpies, physically and with song. Others may form flocks with no territory—these birds often don't breed. Pairs may bond permanently or not, with breeding in winter or spring. Females build shallow nests in the treetops (5–15 m off the ground) and rear the chicks. The tribe guards and cares for the fledglings, including by swooping on people. Magpies find insects and grubs by listening for the sounds they make when moving, even underground. They also catch frogs and lizards to eat.

- Carnarvon NP
- Warrumbungle NP
- Wilsons Promontory NP
- Grampians NP
- Yanchep NP
- Karijini NP

## interesting info

- Magpies have several calls, like warbling, duetting and carolling. They use most of these calls to defend their territory.
- Magpies are called 'policemen of the bush', because their alarm calls alert other animals to predators in the territory.
- Magpies are good mimics and like to play. They sometimes hide food (called caching) under leaf litter to eat later.
- Some urban magpies become friends with humans.
- Magpies were introduced into New Zealand about 150 years ago. Now they're pests there, but they only live for six years.

## Fast Facts

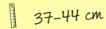

- 37–44 cm
- 65–85 cm
- 220–350 g
- up to 30 y
- 2–5 eggs

# Wombat: Common & Southern Hairy-nosed

*Vombatus ursinus* and *Lasiorhinus latifrons*

Common

Southern Hairy-nosed

## Q&A

### What are they?
Barrel-shaped grazing marsupials and among the largest burrowing animals in the world. Unlike the Southern Hairy-nosed Wombat (SHNW), the Common Wombat (CW) has a naked snout and small ears. The CW is grey to brown, while the SHNW is grey to tan. The closely related Northern Hairy-nosed Wombat (*Lasiorhinus krefftii*) is critically endangered, with only 200 left.

### Where do they live?
The CW inhabits woodlands, grasslands and forests of cooler, south-eastern Australia, from snowy mountain tops to the coast. CW subspecies are smaller and occur in Tasmania and on Flinders Island in Bass Strait. The SHNW occurs in more arid, open woodland scrub and mallee of WA and SA.

### What are their lives like?
Wombats spend a lot of time underground. At night, they forage for grass and other plants, travelling up to 3 km. Burrows protect them from heat, cold, rain, predators and bushfires, and can be up to 20 m long. Networks of burrows, called warrens, have several entrances and nesting chambers, and are built over generations. Wombats are solitary, but may share a warren. They communicate by scent marking and leaving piles of poo to mark their territories. Their poo is often cubic (helps it not to roll off rocks or logs). Wombats have a backwards-facing pouch (so it doesn't fill with dirt when digging) and carry joeys for 6–10 months.

Wilsons Promontory NP

Common

Southern Hairy-nosed

## Interesting info

- Unlike Koalas, wombats have big brains and are playful and quick to learn.
- A wombat can dig 2 m of burrow in a night with its powerful limbs. It uses its 'bulldozer' head and body to compact the soil.
- **Its rump can crush predators against burrow walls.**
- Over short distances, wombats can run as fast as 40 km per hour.
- **The teeth of wombats never stop growing.**
- SHNWs sometimes don't drink water for 3–4 months.
- **Poisonous weeds, a skin condition called mange, habitat loss and cars threaten wombats.**

## Fast Facts

- up to 120 cm
- 19–39 kg
- up to 15 y / up to 34 y (captivity)
- 1 joey
- 1–82 ha (overlapping)

# Honey Possum
Tarsipes rostratus

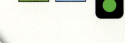

• Yanchep NP

### What is it?
A tiny, mouse-like marsupial with a long pointed snout. It has three dark stripes down the centre of its back and weighs much less than a house mouse. Its Noongar Aboriginal name is Nyuarilpirangar (or Noolbenger), meaning 'the one who squeezes tight into blossoms'.

### Where does it live?
Only in banksia-rich sandplain heaths of south-western WA. This area has a high winter rainfall and a diversity of nectar-rich plants like banksias, grevilleas and eucalypts.

### What's its life like?
The Honey Possum has no teeth and is totally nectivorous. It climbs shrubs to reach flowers where it uses its long, mobile, brush-tipped tongue to feed on nectar and pollen. It forages in the evening and early morning, darting from blossom to blossom. The Honey Possum serves an important ecological role as a pollinator of its food plants. It's solitary and sleeps most of the day among vegetation, curled into a ball. When food is scarce, it enters a state of torpor, dropping its body temperature. Females have a well-developed pouch with 4 teats and breed 2–3 times a year. They also carry dormant embryos, like kangaroos.

## Fast Facts
- 135–195 mm (F larger) (includes tail 70–105 mm)
- 7–16 g
- M 1 y, F 2–3 y
- 2–3 joeys + 4 dormant embryos (2–3 litters)
- M 0.8 ha, F 0.14 ha (overlapping)

## interesting info
- Honey Possums are the only survivor of an ancient marsupial group.
- When resting, it curls up so it doesn't lose its body heat.
- Instead of claws, it has fingernails and toenails, like a monkey, and can climb up several metres by gripping branches.
- The Honey Possum can hang from its strong, long and slender prehensile tail.
- The Honey Possum gives birth to the lightest of all mammalian young, at less than 4–5 mg, but the male's sperm is the largest of any mammal.

# Rufous Bettong

*Aepyprymnus rufescens*

### Q&A

**What is it?**
A medium-sized marsupial with reddish-brown and grey fur, a silvery belly and a hairy muzzle. It's also called the Rufous Rat-kangaroo.

**Where does it live?**
In open woodlands or forests with sparse or grassy understoreys and deep soils. Rufous Bettongs avoid dense undergrowth. They sometimes hang out in trios, a male with two females.

**What's its life like?**
The Rufous Bettong builds a dome-shaped nest, with a single entrance, out of woven grass, often hiding it against a log, tree or grass clump. It carries bundles of nesting material with its partly prehensile tail. During the day, it rests in the nest and emerges half an hour after sunset to feed. Bettongs browse on herbs and grasses and dig up roots and tubers with long foreclaws. Often, they consume entire plants—flowers, seeds, roots and leaves. They also eat invertebrates and underground fungi. Breeding occurs throughout the year, with males pairing up with 1–3 females. Single joeys are in the pouch for 4 months and at foot for another 2 months.

○ Carnarvon NP

## Interesting info

- The Rufous Bettong spits out balls of chewed up fibre—called a bolus—that it can't digest.
- To find enough food, this bettong may travel 2–4.5 km a night.
- Nests help protect it from predators, and individuals usually have 5 or 6 nests, about 100 m apart.
- Females are larger than males and both can make loud growls and grunts.
- Rufous Bettongs used to live in south-eastern Australia but foxes killed them and the habitat was cleared. Now they're extinct there, but they still live in the north-east.

### Fast Facts

- 65–89 cm (includes tail 31–41 cm)
- 1.3–3 kg
- 4–12 y (av 6 y)
- 2–3 joeys (1 in pouch, 1 at foot, 1 dormant embryo)
- 45–110 ha (M larger)

# Spectacled Hare-wallaby

*Lagorchestes conspicillatus*

## Q&A

● Karijini NP
● Litchfield NP

### What is it?
A small kangaroo and the most recognisable hare-wallaby. It looks like it has spectacles, thanks to the red-orange rings of fur around its eyes. It also has a grey 'moustache' below the nose and a white stripe across the hips.

### Where does it live?
Across northern Australia, including topical grasslands, tall desert shrublands, open woodlands and forests. In much of northern Australia, its range overlaps with stock grazing land. A large population lives on Barrow Island (BI) off WA.

### What's its life like?
The Spectacled Hare-wallaby eats mainly grass, and some herbs and shrubs. It selects the best, succulent morsels with its front paws but, in very dry conditions, it survives on fibrous desert plants. Well adapted to dry conditions, it doesn't need to drink water and gets moisture from its food. It also produces limited and highly concentrated urine. This wallaby is solitary and nocturnal, making shallow 'hides' under bushes or among grass tussocks where it shelters to avoid the daytime heat. Breeding occurs throughout the year and the single joey leaves the pouch at 5 months. If the joey dies, the mother has a dormant embryo waiting to activate.

## Fast Facts

- 76–102 cm (includes tail 37–53 cm)
- 1.5–4.7 kg
- up to 6 y / 9 y (captivity)
- up to 3 (+ 1 in pouch + 1 dormant embryo)
- 8–10 ha (BI) / 180 ha (mainland)

## interesting info

- Hare-wallabies are fast over short distances, zig-zagging all over the place when they are alarmed. They can also hop high. When moving slowly, they use all four legs.
- The Spectacled Hare-wallaby is common in northern areas. Since the 1980s, it has disappeared from the desert areas of central Australia because of foxes, cats, drought and fire.
- Aboriginal people used to burn the desert habitat in central Australia in patchy patterns. Spectacled Hare-wallabies could survive this sort of fire but they can't survive the huge hot summer wildfires that happen today.

# Grey Kangaroo: Eastern & Western
*Macropus giganteus* and *Macropus fuliginosus*

## Q&A

**What are they?**
Large kangaroos, with males second in weight after male Red Kangaroos. Grey Kangaroos have finely haired muzzles. The Eastern Grey (EG) is silver-grey and has a dark eye ring and pale face. It's called a Forester in Tasmania. The Western Grey (WG) is browner with a woolly coat, dark face and black ears.

**Where do they live?**
In dry, open woodlands, including mallee scrub, with grassy understoreys, and in open forests along the eastern and southern coasts. The WG's range is drier, with half the annual average rainfall of the EG's range. The two species overlap in the south-eastern corner of Australia. Both are also commonly found in highly modified habitats like farmland, plantations and golf courses.

- Carnarvon NP
- Warrumbungle NP
- Wilsons Promontory NP
- Grampians NP
- Yanchep NP

**What are their lives like?**
Eastern Greys form mobs of up to 50, while WGs form smaller groups of up to 20. Male Greys establish dominance hierarchies by sparring and kickboxing and may be solitary. Females tend to stay in areas where they were born and around female relatives. Females mate mainly, but not exclusively, with dominant males. Grey Kangaroos tend to breed seasonally in the south, but year round elsewhere, depending on the abundance of food and water. Joeys are independent at 18 months. Greys serve an important ecological role as grazers, eating mainly grass, but they can also browse on shrubs. Threats include Dingoes, foxes, eagles, habitat loss, cars and culling by humans.

## Interesting info

- Male kangaroos are called 'bucks' and females are called 'does'.
- Male WGs have a strong smell and are called 'stinkers'.
- Greys communicate by clucking, coughing and foot-thumping when alarmed.
- Greys differ in their reproductive biology—the Western has no dormant embryos, and shorter gestation periods and pouch times.
- Grey Kangaroos may swim to avoid predators, and large males can kill or drown dogs.
- In south-western WA, WGs sometimes eat poisonous plants, but the poison doesn't hurt them.
- The EG's record speed for hopping is 65 km/hr.

## Fast Facts

EG 139–339 cm (includes tail 43–109 cm)
WG 138–323 cm (includes tail 43–100 cm)

M 18–72 kg, F 17–42 kg

EG 6–10 y (max 18 y)
WG 9–13 y (max 20 y)

1 in pouch, 1 at foot, 1 dormant embryo (EG only)

20–1,400 ha

# FORESTS

**Forests, also called 'the Bush'—tall, straight trees forming a single dense canopy, often with thick undergrowth (tropical to temperate, dry and wet)**

The trees in forests grow closer together than the trees in woodlands. In forests there is a single dense canopy, unlike rainforests, which have complex canopies of several layers.

Many of Australia's forests are dominated by eucalypt (gum) trees. Forests often occur in hilly and mountainous areas wherever there is sufficient rainfall and nutrients to support the growth of large trees. Some Australian forests have breathtakingly giant trees. For example, Mountain Ash gum trees in Victoria and Tasmania are the tallest flowering plants in the world, reaching 90 metres or more.

Dandenong Ranges NP (Victoria)

Main Range NP (Queensland)

Freycinet NP (Tasmania)

Tone-Perup Nature Reserve (Western Australia)

Walpole-Nornalup NP (Western Australia)

Judbarra/Gregory NP (Northern Territory)

Namadgi NP (Australian Capital Territory)

Wollemi NP (New South Wales)

Australian forests that have understorey shrubs with small, hard leaves adapted to drier conditions are called dry sclerophyll forests. There are also wet sclerophyll forests that have understorey plants with broad, softer leaves, including tree ferns, which are suited to higher rainfall regions.

Forest floors are covered with leaf and bark litter and fallen logs. These provide essential shelter, nesting material and food for many wildlife species. Australia has lost nearly 40 per cent of its forests since European settlement, with much of the remaining forest broken up into patches because of land clearing.

These national parks have examples of forests where the animals in this section occur. The animals may also occur in other habitats and in other national parks.

# Common Thick-tailed Gecko
## *Underwoodisaurus milii*

**Q&A**

**What is it?**
A purplish, plump gecko with white to yellow spots, a large head, skinny legs and a carrot-shaped tail with 5 or 6 white stripes. It's also known as the Barking Gecko as it squeaks when disturbed. The large prominent eyes show that it's active at night.

**Where does it live?**
Across southern mainland Australia in dry terrestrial habitats such as forests, shrublands and rocky outcrops. This gecko often shelters under rocks or logs, or in shallow burrows (its own or those of other animals).

**What's its life like?**
Common Thick-tailed Geckos forage at night in open spaces, on rocky outcrops or among low vegetation. They eat insects, spiders, scorpions, and smaller geckos and lizards. They're more tolerant of cold climates than other gecko species which is why they're common in southern Australia. These geckos often shelter in groups. They mate in spring and early summer. Each female lays two eggs in a shallow nest dug in the soil or in a rock crevice. She lays clutches of eggs about one month apart. Hatchlings are quite large at 5 cm long.

- Main Range NP
- Wollemi NP
- Walpole-Nornalup NP
- Tone-Perup Nature Reserve
- Dandenong Ranges NP

## interesting info

- These geckos are popular pets.
- When threatened, the Common Thick-tailed Gecko stands up on all four legs, arches its back and waves its tail. It lunges at its enemy while making a loud wheezing bark.
- Like all geckos and most skinks, it can drop its tail when attacked. It can grow a new tail, which isn't patterned like the original one.
- The tail stores fat and a big tail means the gecko is healthy.
- All geckos have clear scales over their eyes, which they lick to keep them clean and moist.

### Fast Facts

- 12–15 cm
- 15–30 g
- up to 20 y (captivity)
- 2 eggs (up to 6 clutches)

# Lace Monitor
*Varanus varius*

## What is it?
The second largest Australian monitor. It's powerfully built with a tail that is much longer than its body. Its scaly skin has broad blue-black or yellow bands, scattered with cream spots. These bands fade with age. It has strong curved claws for climbing and digging. It's also called the Lace Goanna.

- Main Range NP
- Wollemi NP
- Namadgi NP
- Dandenong Ranges NP

## Where does it live?
In forests and woodlands of eastern mainland Australia. While Lace Monitors forage on the forest floor for food, they prefer living in the safety of trees. In winter, they shelter in tree hollows or under logs or rocks.

## What's its life like?
A carnivore, the Lace Monitor eats insects, reptiles, birds and mammals. It commonly raids birds' nests, such as those of the bush turkey, for eggs, as well as garbage bins in parks and camp sites. It also feeds on carrion. The Lace Monitor can gorge on food and then go for many weeks without feeding. It leads a solitary life except during the breeding season. The female lays eggs in termite mounds (on the ground or in trees) to take advantage of the constant temperature inside the mounds. After 9 months, hatchlings scratch their way out and immediately fend for themselves, although sometimes the mother returns to dig the mound open for them.

### Fast Facts
- up to 2.1 m
- up to 20+ kg
- up to 40 y (captivity)
- 4–14 eggs

## interesting info
- Australian monitors are often called goannas.
- Like snakes, a monitor has a forked tongue, which it flicks in and out to 'smell' the air with an organ, called Jacobson's organ, on the roof of its mouth. Many animals, including other reptiles and some mammals, have a Jacobson's organ, which helps them find prey or mates.
- The skin of monitors looks pebbly because their scales don't overlap. The scales of many other lizards and snakes do overlap.
- Monitors become fatter with age, so older animals can be quite big and round.

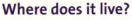

# Black-headed Python
*Aspidites melanocephalus*

## Q&A

**What is it?**
A distinctive python with a shiny black head and neck. Its muscular, striped body ends in a short tail. Its body colour varies across Australia, from grey to brown in the west, to orange and yellow in the east. The body pattern can fade with age.

**Where does it live?**
Widespread in the tropical north, in dry forests, woodlands and rocky escarpments. The Black-headed Python shelters in rock crevices, under logs, in termite mounds and in burrows that are abandoned or that it has dug itself. Although it can climb trees and swim, it's hardly ever found up trees or in water.

○ Judbarra/Gregory NP

**What's its life like?**
Black-headed Pythons hunt mainly other reptiles like lizards, geckos, dragons and small monitors. They also eat snakes, including venomous species, but luckily they're immune to even the most toxic venom. Occasionally, they take small birds and mammals. They are considered to be a more 'primitive' type of python, because they don't have the heat sensing pits on the mouth that other pythons have. These pits wouldn't be useful for detecting its cold-blooded reptilian prey. Black-headed Pythons are non-venomous and subdue prey by using constriction and suffocation. As important predators of reptiles, they play a key role in ecosystems in northern Australian. Dingoes, raptors and humans are its main predators and threats.

### Fast Facts
- up to 2.5 m (av 1.5–2 m)
- up to 10 kg (captivity)
- 20–30 y (captivity)
- 5–10 eggs

## interesting info

- All pythons are non-venomous and kill their prey by constriction (they squeeze their prey to death).
- Instead of warming up outside in the sun, where it might be attacked by predators, the Black-headed Python often sticks only its head out of its burrow. The black head and neck help to absorb heat, warming up the entire body.
- If disturbed, Black-headed Pythons hiss loudly, but usually don't bite. They have strong jaws though, so a bite would hurt.
- In warmer weather, they're active at night. In cooler weather, they're active during the day.

# Black-Cockatoo: Yellow-tailed & Red-tailed

*Calyptorhynchus funereus* and *C. banksii*

## Q&A

### What are they?
Large black-cockatoos—the Yellow-tailed Black-Cockatoo (YTBC) with yellow cheek patches and tail-panel and a short crest, and the Red-tailed Black-Cockatoo (RTBC) with a larger, helmet-like crest and red tail-panel. The female RTBC has yellow flecks on her head and body.

### Where do they live?
YTBCs: In eucalypt woodlands (from the coast to the snow) and pine plantations in eastern Australia. They also occur on Kangaroo Island and the Bass Strait islands.
RTBCs: The only black-cockatoos in northern and inland Australia (except for the Palm Cockatoo on Cape York). They prefer open forests, woodlands and river floodplains.

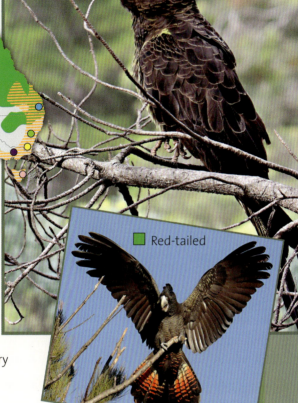

- Main Range NP
- Wollemi NP
- Namadgi NP
- Dandenong Ranges NP
- Freycinet NP
- Walpole-Nornalup NP
- Tone-Perup Nature Reserve
- Judbarra/Gregory NP

### What are their lives like?
The YTBC occurs in pairs or family groups, but flocks of hundreds move from the high country to the lowlands between autumn and winter. The RTBC lives in pairs, small groups or flocks of hundreds or sometimes thousands. Both species feed on seeds from native and non-native shrubs and trees. The YTBC eats pine cones, wood-boring moths and beetle grubs. It listens against the tree for sounds of the grubs moving and shreds off bark with its powerful bill to catch them. Both species nest mainly in tree hollows of old eucalypts (often more than 200 years old). The females incubate the eggs, while the males supply them with food.

## Fast Facts
- 50–65 cm
- 100–110 cm
- 610–900 g (F larger)
- 25–60 y
- 1–2 eggs (1 surviving fledgling)

## Interesting info
- The YTBC's voice is a squeal—kee-ow kee-ow, while the RTBC's sounds like a rusty windmill—kreee-kreee. YTBCs call to each other when they're flying. So do RTBCs.
- Usually only one chick survives. It stays with its parents until the next breeding season.
- Black-cockatoos use tree holes for nests. Usually, only old trees have holes. So when these trees disappear, the black-cockatoos don't nest and their numbers decrease. Their numbers also decrease because bird smugglers take the black-cockatoos, which is against the law.
- Australia has five black-cockatoo species.

# Sulphur-crested Cockatoo
*Cacatua galerita*

## Q&A

**What is it?**
Australia's most recognisable parrot. This white bird has a large grey-black bill and a yellow upswept crest. When excited or alarmed the crest is fully extended over the head, while at other times the crest is flattened. The male has black eyes and the female has red-brown eyes.

**Where does it live?**
Mainly in eastern and northern Australia in tropical and temperate forests, woodlands and grasslands, and tree-lined waterways. This cockatoo was introduced into WA in the early 1900s.

**What's its life like?**
Sulphur-crested Cockatoos live in small groups or in flocks of up to hundreds and feed on the ground or in trees. They eat seeds, berries and insects and their pincer-like bills can cut through the toughest seed shells. When on the ground, at least one sentry sits high in a tree to warn of danger. At dusk, the noise from communal roosting sites can be deafening while the birds jostle for positions. They mature at 6–7 years and nest in high tree hollows or in holes in cliffs. Both parents raise the nestlings, and family groups often stay together. Threats include loss of old trees, the illegal bird trade and cars.

- Main Range NP
- Wollemi NP
- Namadgi NP
- Dandenong Ranges NP
- Judbarra/Gregory NP

## interesting info

- The screeches of Sulphur-crested Cockatoos are sometimes so loud they can hurt your ears.
- The Sulphur-crested Cockatoo is a very intelligent bird. It can learn to say words and can even dance to music! But, it can also damage crops and buildings.
- **This bird's skin produces a powder that waterproofs its feathers (other birds produce oil).**
- All parrots' feet have two toes facing forward and two toes facing backwards. This allows them to hold objects with one foot, while standing on the other. Feet like this are called zygodactylous.

### Fast Facts

 44–55 cm

 103 cm

 700–975 g

 up to 60 y
100+ y (captivity)

 2–3 eggs

# Rainbow Lorikeet
### Trichoglossus haematodus

## Q&A

**What is it?**
A rainbow-coloured parrot with a streaked blue head, orange chest and bright red bill. The juvenile bird has a black beak.

**Where does it live?**
In coastal rainforests and woodlands, mainly on the eastern coast. It's also attracted to suburban gardens. The highest numbers of the Rainbow Lorikeet occur in the tropics and subtropics.

**What's its life like?**
Rainbow Lorikeets often travel in pairs, or join a noisy, fast-moving flock, and sometimes roost communally at dusk. Sometimes they are quite sedentary, moving within the local area, depending on which plants have flowers and fruit. They feed on nectar and pollen, but also eat fruit, seeds and insects. Eucalypts, banksias and paperbarks are a favourite food source and Rainbow Lorikeets play an important ecological role in pollinating these trees. Pairs mate for life and aggressively defend their feeding and nesting areas, even against much bigger birds like Magpies. Females incubate the eggs, while both parents prepare the nest and care for nestlings. Its predators include raptors and snakes.

- Main Range NP
- Dandenong Ranges NP
- Judbarra/Gregory NP

## Fast Facts

- 25–32 cm
- 35–46 cm
- 75–150 g
- up to 20 y
- 2–3 eggs (1–3 clutches)

## interesting info

- The Rainbow Lorikeet has a brush-tipped (hairy) tongue that soaks up the nectar from flowers.
- The male and female look similar, but the male has a broader chest and a squarer head. He displays by puffing himself up and hopping around his partner.
- At tourist shows, large numbers of Rainbow Lorikeets sit on people's arms and heads while being fed.
- Sometimes, these birds become pests and damage fruit crops. In Perth, in the 1960s, they were accidentally released and now take the food and nesting hollows of other native birds there.

41

# Satin Bowerbird
*Ptilonorhynchus violaceus*

## Q&A

**What is it?**
A ground-dwelling songbird considered to be one of the most advanced birds, because it uses tools and 'paints'. The male has glossy blue-black feathers, while females and young males have olive green-brown plumage. Both sexes have lilac-blue eyes.

**Where does it live?**
In wet forests, woodlands and rainforests.

**What's its life like?**
Satin Bowerbirds eat fruits, berries, insects and seeds. Immature males may form flocks with females but adult males are solitary. The male builds a U-shaped bower from twigs and leaves, with two parallel arched walls forming an avenue (35 cm high and 45 cm long) on the ground to attract females. He collects mainly blue objects—such as flowers, feathers, berries, rocks, shells, and bits of plastic or glass—to decorate his bower, and 'paints' its walls with chewed vegetation and saliva. Females may visit several bowers before choosing a mate and mating occurs in the avenue. Females make their nests high in nearby trees or bushes and rear the young alone.

- Main Range NP
- Wollemi NP
- Namadgi NP
- Dandenong Ranges NP

## interesting info

- It takes 6–7 years for males to grow their shiny black feathers. During this time, they practise building bowers.
- Males often rearrange the decorations in their bowers. They sit in the bower and call out to attract females and warn off other males. When a female visits, the male mimics other bird calls to impress her and performs an energetic and noisy dance that includes giving her something blue.
- Males steal each other's decorations, especially blue plastic bottle tops and the blue tail feathers of Crimson Rosellas.

## Fast Facts

 27–35 cm
 43–55 cm
 170–290 g
 up to 26 y
🛒 1–3 eggs

# Brush-tailed Phascogale
*Phascogale tapoatafa*

## Q&A

**What is it?**
A small, arboreal marsupial, also called the Tuan. Its black, bushy 'bottle-brush' tail is as long as its body and has bristles up to 4 cm long.

**Where does it live?**
In dry, open forests and woodlands, in tropical and temperate coastal regions of the mainland. This species nests in large, living trees.

- Main Range NP
- Dandenong Ranges NP
- Walpole-Nornalup NP
- Tone-Perup Nature Reserve

**What's its life like?**
Brush-tailed Phascogales are fast, agile hunters. At night, they spiral up tree trunks and run along branches, feeding on insects, spiders, small vertebrates and eucalyptus flowers. By tearing off bark with their long claws, sharp teeth and dexterous forepaws, they capture hidden prey. During the day, individuals rest alone in one of their many nests in their home range. When it's very cold or food is scarce, several share a nest to increase their chances of survival (communal nesting). Females have more young than they can accommodate on their 8 teats (called supernumerary young) so only the fittest survive. When weaned, young males move many kilometres away but females stay close by.

## Fast Facts

- M 34–49 cm / F 31–45 cm
- M 175–311 g / F 106–212 g
- M 11–12 mo, F 3 y
- up to 8 joeys
- M up to 100+ ha / F 2–70 ha

## interesting info

- This phascogale can leap up to 2 m between trees. Its back feet have ankles that can rotate a bit so it can easily climb up or down trees.
- When frightened, they drum their forefeet.
- Their nests are lined with bark, feathers, fur and even poo—the poo stops other animals, like Sugar Gliders, from stealing their nesting spots.
- The male is unusual because it dies after its first mating season. It's the largest mammal that does this.
- Threats include old trees being cut down, habitat areas becoming too small, feral predators and rainfall that's too low.

# Numbat
*Myrmecobius fasciatus*

### What is it?
A colourful marsupial, red-brown above and paler below, with a dark horizontal eye-stripe. It has prominent white bands on its back and a long bushy tail that can be arched up over the body, carried erect or trailed behind. The snout is pointed and its sticky tongue is half the length of its tail and body combined. It's also called the Banded Anteater.

### Where does it live?
Only 200 years ago, Numbats were found across the southern half of Australia, but by the 1970s numbers were low, restricted to a small area in south-western WA, mainly in Wandoo eucalypt (*Eucalyptus wandoo*) forests.

### What's its life like?
Unlike most marsupials, the Numbat is diurnal. It's solitary and territorial, resting at night in nests in hollow logs or burrows. It's an insectivore, eating 15,000–20,000 termites a day. It finds them by scent, mainly in underground galleries. It catches them on its long sticky tongue and uses its ridged palate to scrape them off its tongue. Females have no pouch—the young cling on to one of four teats. Older joeys are left in a nest or briefly carried on the mother's back. Predators include pythons and raptors and the arched tail may shield against birds-of-prey. Numbats are threatened by foxes, cats, dogs, fire and habitat loss.

○ Tone-Perup Nature Reserve

## Fast Facts
- 34–50 cm (includes tail 14–21 cm)
- M av 600g, F av 480 g
- 5 y
- 4 joeys
- 20–25 ha (defended territory)

## interesting info
- The Numbat is the only marsupial that feeds just on termites.
- When termites finish eating out old Wandoo trees, the trees fall to the ground. These hollow logs provide Numbats with nesting places.
- In winter, Numbats sunbathe a lot.
- When frightened, these animals stand on their hind legs and look around (probably for predators), ready to dash to safety.
- Like all marsupials, Numbats are tiny (2 cm) when they're born. They then climb through the mother's fur to find a teat, which they tightly hold on to for many months.

# Long-nosed Bandicoot
*Perameles nasuta*

### What is it?
The size of a rabbit, with much smaller ears than its cousin, the Bilby. This grey-brown, thick-coated marsupial has a long, thin and almost tubular snout. It has white feet and a short, pointed tail. Unlike some other bandicoot species, there's no pattern of bars across its hindquarters.

### Where does it live?
In wet forests, including rainforests, and woodlands along the east coast. This bandicoot is sometimes seen in suburban gardens, leaving behind small holes in lawns.

- Main Range NP
- Wollemi NP
- Dandenong Ranges NP

### What's its life like?
A nocturnal hunter, the Long-nosed Bandicoot uses its curved claws to dig distinctive conical holes. It sticks its snout into the holes to sniff out insects and the roots of plants. When it's moving about, it sniffs the ground, making high-pitched sounds like a toy trumpet. During the day, it rests in hidden, shallow nests that are lined with grass and leaves and have a closable entrance. It's solitary, apart from mating times. Breeding occurs all year except in winter. Females have 8 teats but have litters of only a few joeys, which they wean at 2 months. Females have several litters, one quickly after the other, suggesting high juvenile mortality.

## Fast Facts
- 43–60.5 cm (includes tail 12–16 cm)
- 520 g–1.3 kg (M larger)
- 2–4 y
- 1–5 joeys (av 2) up to 4 litters
- 2–5 ha (M larger)

## Interesting info
- Joeys are born after only 12.5 days inside the mother. This is the shortest gestation period of any mammal. The newborns climb up into a pouch that faces backwards.
- Bandicoots have coarse, water-shedding outer coats of hair, but soft fur underneath.
- They often sit in a hunched position and use their forepaws to hold food while eating.
- Two toes on the hind feet are joined together, making a 'comb' to remove ticks and mites from their fur. Feet like this are called syndactylous.
- Threats include habitat fragmentation and feral animals.

# Koala
*Phascolarctos cinereus*

## Q&A

**What is it?**
Australia's number one pin-up marsupial, often (incorrectly) called a Koala Bear. It has round fluffy ears and thick, grey waterproof fur. Under the tail area is a tough pad that helps it sit comfortably in trees. Its closest living relative is the wombat.

**Where does it live?**
In wet and dry eucalypt forests and woodlands of eastern Australia. Of the 800 eucalypt species around Australia, Koalas eat the leaves of about 90, but usually eat from less than 10 species in their local area.

**What's its life like?**
Built for climbing, Koalas have strong limbs, two opposable 'thumbs' on each front paw, and rough pads and curved claws on all paws. They spend most of the day resting or sleeping, four hours eating and 20 minutes climbing trees or mating. Koalas are solitary, with a discrete home range. The male has a scent gland on his chest for marking territory. Koalas eat about a kilogram of gum leaves each day. A newborn suckles in its mother's pouch for 6 months and then lives on her back for 4–6 months. Before emerging from the pouch, it eats its mother's 'pap' (special poo) containing the microorganisms needed to digest gum leaves.

- Main Range NP
- Wollemi NP
- Namadgi NP
- Dandenong Ranges NP

## interesting info

- Eucalypt leaves don't provide the Koala with much energy. Perhaps this is why it sleeps so much.
- It has a 2-m long appendix—the longest of any mammal—filled with microorganisms that help digest gum leaves.
- Koalas usually get their water from leaves and dew.
- Millions of Koalas were hunted for their fur early last century and then became extinct in SA.
- Threats to Koalas include habitat fragmentation and loss, dogs, cars, diseases and bushfire.

## Fast Facts

- 60–85 cm (M larger)
- 7–15 kg (Vic) / 4–9 kg (Qld)
- M 10–12 y, F 13–18 y
- 1 joey (2 rare)
- 2–150 ha

# Sugar Glider
*Petaurus breviceps*

### Q&A

**What is it?**
A small, nocturnal 'flying' possum with membranous skin (called a patagium) that joins the fifth finger and first toe and enables it to glide between trees. It has a black stripe from nose to mid-back and a long bushy tail, usually with a white tip.

- Main Range NP
- Wollemi NP
- Namadgi NP
- Dandenong Ranges NP
- Freycinet NP
- Judbarra/ Gregory NP

**Where does it live?**
From open forests and woodlands with little understorey, to dense rainforests in much of eastern and northern Australia where there are eucalypts with tree hollows. It was introduced into Tasmania in 1835. They can occur in suburban and rural settings.

**What's its life like?**
By day, Sugar Gliders sleep in groups in leaf-lined nests in tree hollows. Each group has a dominant male and up to 6 females and their young. The male marks its territory and the other gliders with scent. Juveniles are forced to leave the territory at 7–10 months and many die. When it's cold or food is scarce, the group huddles together for warmth and may enter torpor for short periods. Sugar Gliders are good climbers and vigorously defend food sources, emitting loud 'yip' alarm calls when fighting. They feed on nectar, pollen, insects, flowers and tree gum. Owls, kookaburras, goannas and snakes are their natural predators.

### Fast Facts
- 31.5–42 cm (includes tail 16.5–21 cm)
- 95–170 g (M larger)
- 6–9 y / 12–17 y (captivity)
- 2 joeys (2 litters)
- 0.5–7 ha (defended territory)

### interesting info

- The Sugar Glider can glide 50 m or more. When it's near a tree, it brings in its hind legs and swoops upwards to land on all 4 feet.
- The Yellow-bellied Glider glides the farthest—up to 140 m, while the mouse-sized Feathertail Glider glides the shortest distance—about 20 m.
- The 5 Australian glider species are important in forests because they **pollinate** plants, eat insect pests and become food for owls.
- A nesting box can be a safe place for Sugar Gliders in cities and in the country.

# Common Ringtail Possum
*Pseudocheirus peregrinus*

## Q&A

### What is it?
A common, nocturnal, rabbit-sized possum with small ears that have a white patch behind them. The Common Ringtail's colour varies from grey to red tones. Its prehensile tail tapers to a slender white tip and is often carried curled up in a coil.

### Where does it live?
In forests, woodlands and rainforests, in different types of vegetation, often where shrubs form dense, tangled foliage. In cities, Common Ringtails live close to humans and find food in their gardens but, unlike Common Brushtails, they don't nest in buildings.

### What's its life like?
By day, Common Ringtails rest in spherical nests (dreys) in tree hollows, tree forks or dense undergrowth. Nests have a circular entrance and are lined with grass and bark that the possums carry with their curled tails. Ringtail pairs build and use up to 8 nests in their home range. Family groups nest and forage together, and males help raise young, until the group forces juveniles out. Ringtails are folivores, eating leaves, flowers and fruits of eucalypts and other plants. Leaves are hard to digest, so while in the nest they eat their own soft poo (coprophagia) to digest their food again. At night, their poo is harder and they do it outside.

- Main Range NP
- Wollemi NP
- Namadgi NP
- Dandenong Ranges NP
- Freycinet NP

## Interesting info

- The Common Ringtail makes soft, high, twittering sounds and marks its territories with a smelly liquid from its anal gland.
- It can hold things because each hand has two fingers opposing the other three. Its hind feet are syndactylous (two toes joined together) and have opposing first toes.
- **Common Ringtails live in trees nearly all of the time, but they can walk on the ground and swim.**
- Threats include forest clearing, predators like foxes, cats and dogs, and car traffic. Half of the babies die in their first year.

## Fast Facts

- 60–78 cm (includes tail 30–39 cm)
- 660 g–1.1 kg
- 3–6 y
- 2 (1–2 litters)
- F up to 2.6 ha
  M larger (not overlapping)

# Common Brushtail Possum
*Trichosurus vulpecula*

## Q&A

### What is it?
A common possum with long oval ears, a pointed face, a thick tail and a scary cry. It's one of the largest possums, but its size and colour vary greatly. In the north, it has shorter hair and is a more coppery colour; in the south, it's woollier and is silvery-grey to grey-black.

### Where does it live?
Wherever there are trees, especially in open forests and woodlands. It also frequently lives near humans. Although it's rare in arid central and inland Australia, it's one of the most widely distributed of Australia's marsupials.

- Main Range NP
- Wollemi NP
- Namadgi NP
- Dandenong Ranges NP
- Freycinet NP
- Walpole-Nornalup NP
- Tone-Perup Nature Reserve
- Judbarra/Gregory NP

### What's its life like?
Brush-tailed Possums are nocturnal, spending their days in dens in hollow branches or tree trunks, fallen logs, rock cavities or hollowed termite mounds. In cities, the roof cavities of houses are a favourite. They're mostly arboreal, climbing trees using sharp claws, the opposable first toes of the hind feet and their prehensile tails. They're folivores, with leaves (even from plants that are toxic to other animals) making up most of their diet. Food also includes flowers, fruit and insects. Breeding time varies with location and food, but usually there's one young, which stays in the pouch for 4–5 months, then on its mother's back for another 2 months.

## Fast Facts

 60–95 cm (includes tail 25–40 cm)

 1.2–4.5 g (M larger)

 10–13 y

 1 (1–2 litters)

 0.25–5 ha

## Interesting info

- Many young Brushtails die at 6–18 months old, when they move away from their birthplace.
- Especially in the breeding season, these possums make deep coughs and hisses. They can sound quite scary! They mark their territorieswhi with scent glands. The fur on a male's chest has a red stain because he has a scent gland there.
- Predators include Dingoes, Tasmanian Devils, cats, dogs, foxes, pythons, owls, quolls and monitors.
- Around 175 years ago, Brushtails were taken to New Zealand. They're now a pest there and are hunted for their fur.

# Tasmanian Pademelon
*Thylogale billardierii*

● Freycinet NP

## Q&A

**What is it?**
A small, compact and fluffy, short-tailed wallaby. The Tasmanian, or Red-bellied, Pademelon's blunt face has grey fur on the cheeks. Its body is dark brown to dark grey above and reddish on the belly and ears.

**Where does it live?**
From the coast to the snowy highlands of Tasmania and on the larger Bass Strait islands, among the dense vegetation of wet forests and rainforests. It used to occur in SA and Vic, but is now **extinct** on the mainland.

**What's its life like?**
Tasmanian Pademelons often live close to forest edges. They are mainly nocturnal but can be seen early morning or late afternoon when they venture out for about 100 m to feed in grassy clearings. They're generally solitary but form small groups of about 10 to feed. If disturbed, they scatter quickly. They hold leaves in their forepaws when eating. In snowy country, they use their stout forelimbs to uncover vegetation. To reach feeding areas, they can travel for 2 km along pathways they make through ground vegetation. Joeys spend 6 months in the pouch and 3 months suckling at foot. When a joey leaves the pouch, the dormant embryo starts growing.

## Interesting info

- Males put on weight all their lives and can be twice the weight of females.
- Tasmanian Pademelons are called browsers because half of their diet is made up of leaves (the other half of their diet is grass). Animals that eat mainly grass are called grazers.
- Predators include Tasmanian Devils, Spotted-tailed Quolls and Wedge-tailed Eagles.
- In Tasmania, you often see pademelons that have been killed by cars.
- People are allowed to hunt Tasmanian Pademelons outside national parks and reserves.

## Fast Facts

- 88–111 cm (includes tail 32–48 cm)
- 2.4–12 kg (M larger)
- 5–6 y
- 1–2 (+ 1 dormant embryo)
- 170 ha

# Swamp Wallaby
*Wallabia bicolor*

- Main Range NP
- Wollemi NP
- Namadgi NP
- Dandenong Ranges NP

### What is it?
A wallaby with a brown-black coat and dark 'mask', from eyes to nostrils, and reddish fur around the ears. A beige to white stripe runs along the jaw line. It's also called a Black Wallaby.

### Where does it live?
In thick undergrowth of rainforest or in wet eucalypt forests and woodlands with dense, moist understory. It occurs in both tropical and temperate regions along the east coast. It's expanding its range into drier areas.

### What's its life like?
Other wallabies are grazers, but Swamp Wallabies are mainly browsers and so have different teeth, including molars that have cutting edges. They can eat and digest a wide variety of plants and underground fungi, as well as plants that are unpalatable or poisonous to other animals, like bracken fern and hemlock. They're usually solitary but may form small groups when feeding. During the day, they shelter from predators like Dingoes, which actively hunt juveniles. Swamp Wallabies are active at times, both day and night. Breeding occurs throughout the year with young occupying the pouch for 8–9 months and suckling at foot until 15 months old.

## Fast Facts
- 130–172 cm (includes tail 64–87 cm)
- 70 cm
- 10–22 kg (M larger)
- 15 y
- 1 in pouch, 1 at foot, + dormant embryos
- 16–98 ha (overlapping)

- When the Swamp Wallaby hops, the tail is held out straight behind it and its head is held low. Like all macropods, it can also move slowly on all fours.
- Like many marsupials, Swamp Wallaby mothers can suckle two joeys that are different ages.
- After bushfires, Swamp Wallabies are important because they spread the spores of fungi that trees depend on.
- Swamp Wallabies have been introduced to New Zealand.

# Little Red Flying-fox
*Pteropus scapulatus*

## Q&A

**What is it?**
The smallest megabat and most wide-ranging of Australia's four flying-fox (or fruit bat) species. It has a grey, fox-like head with large eyes and reddish-brown fur on its body and naked legs. Its reddish-brown wing membranes appear transparent in flight, a feature that's unique among flying-foxes worldwide.

**Where does it live?**
In a variety of habitats in temperate and tropical climates, from moist coastal forests to drier inland areas. Responding to food sources, it tends to visit coastal areas in summer and move inland in winter. It roosts in trees and is the only flying-fox to hang in dense clusters.

**What's its life like?**
In spring, groups clump together in trees such as eucalypts, paperbarks and mangroves, usually near water. If food is plentiful, their 'camps' can have 5,000 to one million individuals, with hundreds often staying in the same tree from 2 days to several months. Noisy roosting activities like courting, mating and fighting occur in early mornings and late afternoons, while during the day they rest quietly. At dusk, columns of this nectivorous bat leave the camp to forage on nectar and pollen from flowering plants. It may also eat fruit, leaves, bark, sap and insects. Males and harems of females establish territories, with females establishing new maternity camps after mating.

- Main Range NP
- Wollemi NP
- Dandenong Ranges NP
- Judbarra/Gregory NP

## interesting info

- Numbers of flying-foxes increase when lots of their food plants are flowering.
- Flying-foxes are important because, when they are feeding, they help to pollinate plants and to spread seeds (up to 60,000 per night per individual). But they can also damage trees at their camp sites.
- Threats include habitat clearing, fire, raptors and snakes.
- You shouldn't touch bats as they might have a rare disease called the Australian Bat Lyssavirus.
- One quarter of the world's mammal species are bats.

## Fast Facts

- 19-24 cm
- 310-605 g (M larger)
- up to 1.5 m
- up to 16+ y (captivity)
- 1
- 20-100 km (foraging)

# Gould's Wattled Bat
## Chalinolobus gouldii

### Q&A

**What is it?**
One of the most widespread microbat species in Australia. This flying placental mammal has black fur on its head and shoulders, brown fur on its back, a high forehead, a short snout and fleshy lobes at the corner of its mouth. Like all bats, its wings are made of hairless elastic skin (the patagium) stretched over long finger bones.

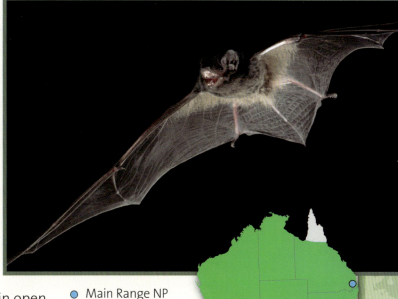

**Where does it live?**
Across most of Australia and on Norfolk Island, in open and dense forests, woodlands, mallee, tall shrublands, farmland and suburban areas. The size of individuals varies with location. It roosts mainly in tree hollows, but sometimes under loose bark, or in old birds' nests, bat boxes or buildings.

- Main Range NP
- Wollemi NP
- Namadgi NP
- Dandenong Ranges NP
- Walpole-Nornalup NP
- Tone-Perup Nature Reserve

**What's its life like?**
Gould's Wattled Bats roost by day, clumping together in colonies of up to 30 or more, often dominated by females. Males tend to roost alone. Active from sunset, these bats forage in and below the tree canopy, catching moths, beetles, bugs, cockroaches and flies—often in their wing-membranes. They have good eyesight but mainly use echolocation to catch insects on the wing. In cold climates, they enter torpor in winter. Humans can just hear some of their high-pitched chirps and buzzing calls. When moving between roosts, mothers can fly with young attached to their teats. Young are independent at 2–3 months. Predators include owls, snakes, feral cats and Pied Currawongs.

### Fast Facts

- 7.6–12.5 cm (includes tail 3–5 cm)
- 7–18 g (av 14 g)
- 30 cm
- up to 8 y (max 12 y)
- 2 pups
- 7–11 km (max 22 km)

### Interesting info

- Bats are the only group of mammals that can really fly.
- Microbats hunt insects and find their way around by making high-pitched sounds (that humans can't hear). These sounds echo back to their large ears and tell them about an object's size and how far away it is. This way of finding things is called echolocation.
- Bats roost by hanging from their feet. But, when giving birth or pooing, they hang right-way-up by their thumbs.
- Australia has about 70 microbat species and 11 megabat (flying-fox) species.

# RAINFORESTS

**Rainforests—'wet' forest with a dense complex canopy, typically with no single dominant tree species and often with multiple layers of trees; sometimes sparse undergrowth; fires are rare (tropical to temperate)**

In rainforests, the trees grow closely together, their leaves forming a thick canopy. There are several layers of tree foliage, with some trees growing under the main canopy layer and others emerging above the main canopy. Little sunlight reaches the forest floor, which is covered in thick decaying leaf litter. Particular types of plants grow there—often ferns, mosses, lichens and some tree seedlings. There are also vines, epiphytes (plants that grow on trees) and stranglers in rainforests. Many of the trees have huge buttresses (large roots above ground) radiating out from the lower trunk.

Daintree NP (Queensland)

Great Otway NP (Victoria)

Dorrigo NP (New South Wales)

Crater Lakes NP (Queensland)

Kutini-Payamu NP (Queensland)

Lamington NP (Queensland)

Mount Field NP (Tasmania)

Southwest NP (Tasmania)

There are tropical, subtropical and temperate rainforests. Biodiversity is highest in tropical rainforests. Rainforests can grow in the highlands or in sheltered valleys and sometimes occur close to the coast (these ones are called littoral rainforests).

Rainforests grow in areas of higher rainfall or in moist pockets of the landscape, along the east coast of Australia and in Tasmania. Tropical and subtropical rainforests occur in Queensland and northern New South Wales, while temperate rainforests occur in southern New South Wales, Victoria and Tasmania. The largest single area of tropical rainforest in Australia occurs in Queensland's Wet Tropics World Heritage Area.

These national parks have examples of rainforests where the animals in this section occur. The animals may also occur in other habitats and in other national parks.

# Boyd's Forest Dragon
*Hypsilurus boydii*

## Q&A

**What is it?**
A well-camouflaged greenish-brown, arboreal dragon lizard with a wedge-shaped head and a very long tail. Its cheeks have large white scales and its head has a large spiny crest. On its throat it has loose yellow skin, which is important for display or defence.

**Where does it live?**
In the rainforest trees of the Wet Tropics in northern Qld. Boyd's Forest Dragon clings vertically to the trunk of thin trees 1–2 m off the ground. It's one of at least two rainforest dragon species in Australia.

**What's its life like?**
The diurnal Boyd's Forest Dragon defends a large territory of 500–1,000 m² and has a few favourite trees to which it regularly returns. An ambush predator, it preys on insects, ants and earthworms, in the trees or by darting down to the forest floor. Unlike other lizards, it does not thermoregulate. Instead, its body temperature conforms to that of the surrounding air temperature (thermoconforms), a good strategy in the thick canopy of a rainforest where not much sunlight gets through the trees. Females lay eggs in shallow holes in rainforest clearings, including on road edges and walking tracks.

- Daintree NP
- Crater Lakes NP

## Fast Facts

- 30–48 cm
- 100–150 g (M larger)
- up to 15+ y
- 1–6 eggs (1–3 clutches)

## interesting info

- **When threatened, Boyd's Forest Dragon often just hides on the other side of the tree trunk.**
- **Juveniles sleep on the ends of flimsy branches in undergrowth and wake up when they feel the vibrations from a predator.**
- **A male's territory usually contains one or two smaller female territories.**
- **The best way to spot this dragon is to look at the sides of trees at about head height while slowly walking through the rainforest—closely examine any large bump as it may be a Boyd's.**

# Northern Leaf-tailed Gecko
*Saltuarius cornutus*

### What is it?
One of Australia's largest geckos. The Northern Leaf-tailed Gecko is arboreal and has a flattened body and a distinctive leaf-shaped tail. It's brown to green with mottled patterning that often looks like lichen.

### Where does it live?
In the rainforest trees of the Wet Tropics of northern Qld, where there is a high level of humidity.

### What's its life like?
The Northern Leaf-tailed Gecko is a master of camouflage and mimics its surroundings so well that it's difficult to spot. It often looks like lichen or rock or bark. The flattened body and tail help it blend in and spines on its flanks help to diffuse tell-tale shadows. Camouflage helps to hide it from predators like owls, rats and snakes, and from prey while hunting. An ambush predator, it eats large invertebrates like spiders and cockroaches. It hunts at night by flattening against a tree, head towards the ground, and dropping onto moving prey. Females lay eggs under bark at the base of a tree, which hatch after 3 months.

## Fast Facts
- up to 23 cm
- 30–40 g
- up to 15 y
- 2 eggs

## Interesting info
- This gecko's scientific name, *Saltuarius*, means 'keeper of the forest'.
- Its tail is about the same size as its head. When attacked, this gecko, like most others, wiggles its tail to distract the predator. If the predator grabs the tail, the tail drops off and the gecko escapes. Later, the gecko grows a new one (autotomy).
- The Wet Tropics has lots of different types of reptiles, with more than 160 species. Australia has about 950 reptile species. Most of them live in WA and Qld.

○ Daintree NP
○ Crater Lakes NP

# Green Python
*Morelia viridis*

## Q&A

**What is it?**
A bright green arboreal python, often with a row of white scales along its back. Its head is clearly defined from the body. Its body is triangular in cross-section with an obvious spine. Females are larger than males.

**Where does it live?**
In rainforest trees of northern Qld. The Green Python rests in a looped coil on a branch or vine in dense foliage, with its head resting in the middle.

**What's its life like?**
The Green Python feeds mainly on small mammals and reptiles. Like all pythons, it's non-venomous and has curved teeth for gripping prey. It often hangs on low branches and grabs unsuspecting rodents from the ground. To catch prey, it holds onto a branch with its prehensile tail, and then strikes out from an S-shaped position and seizes the prey in its mouth. It winds itself around the prey and squeezes it. This 'constriction' causes the prey's chest cavity to collapse, resulting in death. Female Green Pythons lay their eggs in a tree hollow and coil around them to keep them warm until they hatch 6–8 weeks later.

○ Kutini-Payamu NP

### Fast Facts
- 1.5–1.8 m (max 2.2 m)
- 1–2 kg
- 3–12 y up to 28 y (captivity)
- 8–25 eggs

## Interesting info

- Young Green Pythons are bright yellow. Their colour changes to bright green when they're between one and three years old.
- The tip of the tail is a different colour and used to attract prey.
- All pythons have good senses of smell and sight. Most can also feel a prey's heat because they have special pits that lie between their lip scales. These enable pythons to 'see' the heat shadow of warm-blooded prey like mammals and birds.
- When too many trees in their rainforest are removed, Green Pythons can't live there anymore.

# White-lipped Tree Frog
*Litoria infrafrenata*

## Q&A

**What is it?**
Possibly the largest tree frog in the world and the largest frog in Australia. It's also known as the Giant Tree Frog and is usually bright green (and sometimes bright yellow), but can change to bronze-brown for camouflage or when it's cold. It has a white lower lip and large tympanums (external ears). The tadpoles are dark brown with a silvery-cream stripe on each side.

**Where does it live?**
In rainforests and paperbark (melaleuca) swamps of the Wet Tropics in northern Qld. It's arboreal but comes down to breed in pools or swamps. Sometimes it's found in tropical farms or gardens.

**What's its life like?**
The White-lipped Tree Frog hunts most actively on warm humid nights and eats insects, like crickets and beetles, as well as spiders. Its big webbed feet have large specialised toe pads for climbing trees (and walls). In spring or summer, after rain, males call to females from perches 3–4 m above the ground, close to water. Breeding occurs in still bodies of water, where females lay several large clusters of eggs that merge together and float on the surface. Tadpoles feed on aquatic plants and, after 4 weeks, metamorphose into froglets, leave the water and climb onto foliage. Threats to this species include disease, parasites and clearing of its habitat.

## Fast Facts
- M 11 cm, F 15 cm
- 95 g
- 10 y
- up to 4,000 or more eggs

## Interesting info
- **Male White-lipped Tree Frogs have loud barking calls—da-dak, da-dak, da-dak.**
- All tree frogs have horizontal pupils, which help them see at night. Horizontal pupils occur in some other nocturnal animals, such as geckos.
- **Like all frogs, the White-lipped Tree Frog has lungs but also breathes through its skin.**
- The presence of frogs can tell you about how clean the water is in the environment. If there are pesticides and poisons in the water, there won't be many frogs.
- **Habitat loss, pollution and disease cause frog populations to decline.**

- Kutini-Payamu NP
- Daintree NP

# Southern Cassowary
*Casuarius casuarius johnsonii*

## Q&A

**What is it?**
Australia's second largest native bird. The Southern Cassowary is a flightless bird with shaggy black plumage and a blue neck with two dangling red wattles. A brown horny 'casque' (helmet) of up to 17 cm sits on top of its head. Each powerful three-toed foot has a 12 cm-long dagger on the inner toe.

**Where does it live?**
In rainforests of north-eastern Queensland, mainly in the Wet Tropics and Cape York regions.

**What's its life like?**
The Southern Cassowary forages on the forest floor for fruit, fungi and invertebrates, and can eat fruit that's toxic to other species. It eats fruit from 240 plant species and performs the vital ecological role of seed dispersal in the rainforest. The female is dominant and larger than the male. Individuals live alone, except for fathers with chicks. The male builds the nest, incubates the eggs, and rears and feeds the chicks. Chicks leave their father after 9–18 months. Some think the casque's purpose is to protect the head when running through the forest, or to aid in hearing the low rumbling sounds of other cassowaries.

- Kutini-Payamu NP
- Daintree NP
- Crater Lakes NP

## Interesting info

- **The Southern Cassowary is the largest frugivore (fruit eater) bird in the world.**
- It has claws like daggers, which can cause serious injuries.
- **You can tell if a cassowary is nearby by the piles of dung full of fruit seeds and by its three-toed footprints.**
- Southern Cassowaries live in a small area (about 13,000 km²) and there aren't as many as there used to be (about 2,500 or less). They're threatened mainly by habitat loss, feral animals eating their eggs, cars, dogs and hunting.

## Fast Facts

 1.5–2 m
 1.3–1.7 m
 M 55 kg, F 80 kg
 30 y
50 y (captivity)
 3–5 eggs

# Superb Lyrebird
*Menura novaehollandiae*

## Q&A

**What is it?**
Australia's largest songbird and greatest mimic. While the female is plain, the male has an elaborate tail, each side bordered by a long striped feather creating a shape like a musical instrument called a lyre.

**Where does it live?**
In temperate rainforests and wet forests and woodlands east of the Great Dividing Range. The Superb Lyrebird was introduced to Mt Field National Park in Tasmania in the 1930s.

**What's its life like?**
These lyrebirds rarely fly, but can run away fast from threats. They spend hours each day foraging, using their large feet to rake over rotting vegetation on the forest floor. Food includes worms, beetle and moth larvae, spiders and centipedes. They roost in trees at night. Breeding is in winter when food is most abundant. During the mating season, the male and female defend separate territories, which may overlap. The female builds a big dome-shaped nest on the ground, among rocks or in a tree fork. She lines the nest with her own feathers and raises the nestling alone. The chick emits a loud ear-piercing shriek if an intruder enters the nest.

## Fast Facts

- 80–103 cm (includes tail)
- 1 kg
- up to 19 y
- one large egg

## interesting info

- The male Superb Lyrebird is an amazing mimic of other birds' songs, as well as other sounds, such as dog barks, car alarms, motors and chainsaws. Songs can last for 20 minutes.
- In autumn and winter, his songs increase as he rakes up large mounds of leaves. Sitting on top of his mound, he sings and dances to attract females, while spreading his elegant tail over his body.
- The male develops his beautiful tail feathers at 3–4 years of age. These feathers drop out (are moulted) every spring.

- Dorrigo NP
- Mt Field NP

# Eastern Whipbird
*Psophodes olivaceus*

### What is it?
A secretive bird with a call that sounds like the crack of a whip. It has dark olive-green plumage, a black head and crest, and a white patch on its cheek and throat.

### Where does it live?
In wet habitats like rainforests, wet eucalypt forests and dense heathlands, generally near waterways. It occurs in dense vegetation near the ground (undergrowth).

### What's its life like?
The Eastern Whipbird is sedentary, staying in the same area all year around. The male and female form a breeding pair that bond for many years and together they defend a territory of 5–10 ha where they feed with their young. It fly-hops over the forest floor, with its tail fanned, probing rotten wood and tossing leaves aside while hunting for insects and other invertebrates to eat. It rarely flies. The female builds a nest of twigs lined with grass in shrubs or in trees a few metres off the ground. The male feeds the female while she incubates the eggs. He also helps to feed the nestlings.

- Daintree NP
- Crater Lakes NP
- Lamington NP
- Dorrigo NP

## Fast Facts

 21–31 cm

 27–32 cm

 47–72 g

 up to 12 y

 2–3 eggs (1–2 clutches)

- You can easily recognise the call of the Eastern Whipbird in the eastern Australian bush. The male's long whistling call ends in a loud 'whip-crack' that's answered by the female. Depending on where she is, she replies with *choo-choo, weece-weece, awee-awee* or *witch-a-wee*. The two-part call sounds like there's just one bird calling (antiphonal calling). Their song helps them to keep contact with each other while they look for food separately—up to 30 m apart.
- The distribution of the Eastern Whipbird has become patchy in the north due to land clearing.

# Spotted-tailed Quoll
*Dasyurus maculatus*

## Q&A

**What is it?**
The largest marsupial carnivore on mainland Australia. Its tail is covered in large spots and is as long as the head and body combined. It's also known as the Tiger Quoll.

**Where does it live?**
On the eastern coast, from northern Qld to Tas, in rainforests and wet eucalypt forests with more than 600 mm rainfall a year.

**What's its life like?**
Spotted-tailed Quolls spend the day in dens in rock crevices, caves, hollow logs or tree hollows, and forage at night in large home ranges. Equipped with long claws and jaws that open really wide, they are deadly hunters, preying on birds and mammals in trees and on the ground. They kill by biting the back of the neck. As top predators, Spotted-tailed Quolls play an important ecological role in regulating populations of prey species. Quolls communicate by smell and sound. When a female is pregnant, folds of skin on her belly form a pouch over the 6 teats. Predators of quolls include owls, eagles, pythons, Dingoes and Tasmanian Devils.

- Daintree NP
- Crater Lakes NP
- Lamington NP
- Dorrigo NP
- Mt Field NP
- Southwest NP

## interesting info

- Quolls are sometimes called 'native cats'. The Spotted-tailed Quoll is the largest of Australia's four quoll species. It's the only one to have spots on its tail.
- The Spotted-tailed Quoll has special non-slip foot pads that help it to be a good climber.
- Quolls greet each other with nose-to-nose sniffs.
- Its scats are shaped like 'twisted rope'.
- A newborn quoll is the size of a grain of rice.
- The biggest threats are habitat fragmentation, poison baits, and feral cats and foxes that eat the same prey.

## Fast Facts

- M 93 cm, F 81 cm
- M 7 kg, F 4 kg
- 3–4 y
- 4–6 joeys
- M up to 2,600 ha (overlapping)
  F up to 650 ha (not overlapping)

# Striped Possum
*Dactylopsila trivirgata picata*

- Kutini-Payamu NP
- Daintree NP
- Crater Lakes NP

## Q&A

**What is it?**
A black-and-white striped possum with black ears and a bushy tail. The stripes form a 'Y' shape on its forehead. The prehensile tail is much longer than the body.

**Where does it live?**
In tropical rainforests and adjoining forest and woodlands of northern Qld. The Striped Possum is more common in New Guinea.

**What's its life like?**
By day, Striped Possums sleep in leaf-lined nests in tree hollows or in clumps of tree epiphytes. At night, they leap and run through the tree canopy. They make lots of noise, including snorting and shrieking, tearing and scratching at bark, and slurping and chewing loudly. The main diet of the Striped Possum is wood-boring insects, extracted by biting bark with long incisor teeth and pulling them out with its long tongue and long fourth finger. Ants, termites, fruit, leaves, small vertebrates and honey from native bees are also part of the diet. The female Striped Possum has two teats in a well-developed pouch and carries young on her back when they're weaned.

### Fast Facts

- 58.5–61.5 cm (includes tail 34.5 cm)
- 310–545 g (M larger)
- 5–10 y
- 1–2
- 5–21 ha

## interesting info

- Striped Possums find food by drumming on tree branches with their forefeet.
- The fourth finger on each hand is almost twice the length of the other four fingers. It has a hooked claw on the end for getting insects and grubs from behind bark.
- **It gives off a strong and unpleasant smell.**
- Its call is a loud, rolling, guttural gargle.
- **Male Striped Possums strongly compete with each other for females.**
- Scientists still have a lot to learn about these possums.

# Common Spotted Cuscus
*Spilocuscus maculatus nudicaudatus*

## Q&A

**What is it?**
A marsupial closely related to the Common Brushtail Possum. With a round, bare-skinned face and large forward-looking eyes, it looks a bit like a monkey. It has thick, woolly grey-ginger fur and a strong prehensile tail. Its ears are almost invisible. Males have white blotches.

**Where does it live?**
In the treetops of rainforests at the northern tip of Australia on the Cape York Peninsula. It occurs from the coast to the top of the McIlwraith Range at 820 m altitude. It's also seen in palm trees and paperbark trees in the coastal fringe.

**What's its life like?**
Although arboreal, the Common Spotted Cuscus can travel up to 150 m on the ground, which means it can colonise new habitats. It's mainly nocturnal and rests in the tree canopy on a loose platform of leaves and twigs, rarely returning to the same tree the next night. It feeds on fruits, flowers and leaves, but its large canine teeth indicate a partly carnivorous diet. Although this hasn't been seen in the wild, it does eat meat in captivity. It's mainly solitary, but is able to breed year round. The female usually rears a single joey in her pouch for 6–7 months. Likely predators include Wedge-tailed Eagles and Amethystine Pythons.

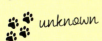
Kutini-Payamu NP

## Interesting info

- The Common Spotted Cuscus has thick fur to keep its body heat.
- When the weather is hot, it pants and licks its bare-skinned feet and face. As its saliva dries up, it cools the animal.
- When it feels stressed, it secretes a substance on the bare skin around the eyes, which stains red when dry.
- The Common Spotted Cuscus is an excellent climber and uses its toes and tail to grip branches while climbing.
- Some individuals are completely white.
- Males are territorial, acting aggressively towards each other.

## Fast Facts

- 66–102 cm (includes tail 31–44 cm)
- 1.5–4.9 kg (F larger)
- 11 y
- 1–3 (av 1)
- unknown

# Musky Rat-kangaroo
*Hypsiprymnodon moschatus*

## Q&A

**What is it?**
The smallest, busiest and most ancient kangaroo. The Musky Rat-kangaroo, or Hypsi, represents a link between kangaroos and possums. It has rich brown fur, a hairless tail and a strong musky odour. Unlike other macropods, it has 5 toes, including an opposable 'big toe' on each hind foot.

**Where does it live?**
In the rainforests of north-eastern Qld in the Wet Tropics World Heritage Area. It occurs from the coast to highlands over 1,200 m in altitude.

**What's its life like?**
The Musky Rat-kangaroo forages on the forest floor in the daytime. It eats mainly fruits but also eats seeds, invertebrates and above-ground fungi. During seasons when there isn't much fruit, it may lose up to a quarter of its body weight and relies on hidden food supplies. It often uses networks of roots and logs as pathways. It has a quadrupedal gait and can use its opposable toes to occasionally climb vines and trees. It's generally solitary and sleeps at night in one of many hidden nests. Unlike other macropods, it has several young but no dormant embryo. Its gestation period is 19 days—the shortest of all macropods.

- Daintree NP
- Crater Lakes NP

## interesting info

- The Musky Rat-kangaroo collects the leaves for its nest with its mouth and forepaws. It kicks the leaves into a pile, which it carries to its nest site with its prehensile tail.
- Musky Rat-kangaroos bury seeds to eat later (called caching). The seeds are hidden from predators like rats, and many of them grow. This is an important way that rainforest plants are spread around.
- When rainforest is cleared, the patches of rainforest left become too small for Musky Rat-kangaroos to live in. So, rainforest seeds aren't spread around by them anymore.

### Fast Facts

- 27–43 cm (includes tail 12–16 cm)
- 360–680 g
- 4–6 y
- 1–4 joeys (av 2)
- F av 1.4 ha
- M av 2.1 ha (overlapping)

# Lumholtz's Tree-kangaroo
*Dendrolagus lumholtzi*

### What is it?
An arboreal kangaroo with a long tail that's not prehensile. It's blackish-brown, flecked with light fur on the lower back and a paler band around its face. Its paws and tail tip are black.

### Where does it live?
In high altitude and lowland rainforests and forests along watercourses, mainly above 300–800 m in a limited region of the Wet Tropics in north-eastern Qld.

### What's its life like?
The Lumholtz's Tree-kangaroo is active on and off throughout the day and night (cathemeral). It sleeps crouched on a branch, with its tail hanging, gripping with its clawed forefeet and balancing with its short, broad hind feet. It's a folivore and has a lower metabolic rate than other kangaroos. Its limited activity includes moving along branches, climbing and jumping between trees. It lives alone or in small groups that include one male. Adult males often fight (but not fathers and sons). It has the longest gestation period of any marsupial—45 days—and joeys spend 2–3 years with their mother. Threats are habitat loss, cars, dogs and climate change.

○ Crater Lakes NP

## interesting info
- Lumholtz's Tree-kangaroo was named after Norwegian explorer Carl Sofus Lumholtz.
- It often comes to the ground, where it walks or runs on all four legs, or hops with its tail held out stiffly.
- It climbs down trees backwards. When it's 15 m or less from the ground, it twists around and leaps to the ground, landing so that its hind feet face away from the tree trunk.
- Tree-kangaroos evolved from ground kangaroos millions of years ago and the two Australian species—Lumholtz's and Bennett's—are the most primitive.

## Fast Facts
- 89–151 cm (includes tail 47–80 cm)
- 5–10 kg (M larger)
- up to 15 y
- 1 joey
- 1–2 ha (territorial)

# ARID ZONES

**The 'Outback'—arid (desert-like) and semi-arid zones, including mallee and mulga shrublands and spinifex grasslands**

Australia is the second driest continent on Earth, after Antarctica. Australia's driest region, the arid zone covers about 70% of the continent. It occurs inland and covers the whole of central Australia through to the western-central coast. The arid zone includes deserts such as the Simpson Desert, the Gibson Desert and the Great Sandy Desert.

The arid zone has low rainfall of 250 mm or less a year. Plants are adapted to arid conditions and include stunted wattle bushes (mulga), stunted gum trees (mallee), saltbushes and spinifex (or hummock) grass. There are also bare areas of sand, stony 'gibber' plains, and rocky ranges.

Cravens Peak Reserve (Queensland)

Sturt NP (New South Wales)

Little Desert NP (Victoria)

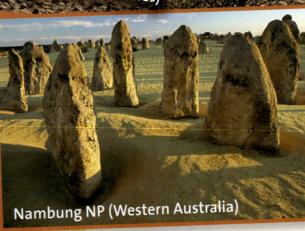

Nambung NP (Western Australia)

Witjira NP (South Australia)

Uluru–Kata Tjuta NP (Northern Territory)

Wyperfeld NP (Victoria)

Rottnest Island (Western Australia)

Kinchega NP (New South Wales)

Diamantina NP (Queensland)

The arid grasslands represent one quarter of Australia's vegetation. They occur in WA, SA, NT, western Qld and NSW. Trees are short (less than 10 m) and grass mounds grow across clay plains and sand dunes. These grass hummocks can be huge and can spread to form circles of 10-m diameter or more.

The arid zone can be very hot by day, but can quickly become cold at night. Surprisingly, it's full of animal life that has adapted to a dry, harsh environment, with most creatures coming out at night to feed.

These national parks have examples of arid zones where the animals in this section occur. The animals may also occur in other habitats and in other national parks.

# Thorny Devil
*Moloch horridus*

- Nambung NP
- Uluru-Kata Tjuta NP
- Witjira NP
- Cravens Peak Reserve

### What is it?
A dragon lizard with fearsome-looking thorns and spines (close-ups of the Thorny Devil have been used in scary movies). In reality, the Thorny Devil is quite docile and doesn't bite. Its jerky motion, with tail held high, makes it look more like a wind-up toy.

### Where does it live?
In sandy regions throughout much of arid inland Australia, such as the spinifex–sandplain desert of the interior and the mallee belt of SA and southern WA.

### What's its life like?
Thorny Devils are ant-eating specialists, using the tongue to feed on 45 ants a minute and up to 2,500 a meal. Trails of ants are the easiest to eat. Thorny Devils have an unusual way of drinking. The thorns and a system of tiny channels between the scales collect moisture from dew, rain or the ground and carry it to the mouth from the back or up the legs by capillary action. Males attract a mate by waving a front leg and bobbing the head. Females lay eggs in a shallow burrow about 30 cm underground. As soon as the hatchlings reach the surface, they start hunting for ants.

## Fast Facts
- 15–20 cm
- 35–90 g
- up to 20 y
- 3–10 eggs

## interesting info

- Thorny Devils are active by day and need protection. They camouflage themselves by changing colour to match their surroundings and by 'freezing' like statues.
- At night the Thorny Devil buries itself in soft sand to sleep, leaving only the spiny head exposed.
- When threatened, it lowers its head so that the spiny knob on the neck looks like another head. Or it puffs up its body with air to appear bigger.
- Thorny Devils often sunbake but, when the sand gets too hot, they run fast on 'tippy-toes' to seek shelter.

# Smooth Knob-tailed Gecko

*Nephrurus levis*

- ○ Uluru-Kata Tjuta NP
- ○ Witjira NP
- ○ Diamantina NP
- ○ Sturt NP
- ○ Kinchega NP

### What is it?
A soft-skinned nocturnal gecko with a small body and a large head with big eyes and earholes. It has a short, paddle-shaped tail that ends in a small round knob.

### Where does it live?
In desert woodlands and spinifex sandplains. The Smooth Knob-tailed Gecko is a ground dweller and spends a lot of time in the safety of a cool burrow. It's a good excavator and can quickly dig a new burrow.

### What's its life like?
The Smooth Knob-tailed Gecko's large jaws allow it to catch and eat large invertebrates and small geckos. It gets enough water from its prey, so it rarely drinks. In the open, owls and snakes can take it, and goannas can dig it up from its burrow. When alarmed, it waves its knob-tail, arches its back to look tall and may lunge with an open mouth. The knob-tail has receptors that sense vibrations and other information about the environment. Like all native geckos, it lays only two eggs but may have many clutches of eggs a year, if conditions are good.

## interesting info
- Geckos are often called the 'night-shift' lizards because they hunt at night.
- All gecko species have five fingers and five toes. Most geckos' digits end in claws.
- In some climbing species, special scales under the digits help them stick to smooth surfaces. In most species that stay on the ground, such as the Smooth Knob-tailed, these scales are bumps that don't grip.
- Geckos don't blink or have tears—they use their tongue to keep their eyes moist and clean.
- Many geckos store fat in their tail to help over winter.

## Fast Facts
- 8–14 cm
- 14–25 g (F larger)
- 10 y up to 18 y (captivity)
- 2 eggs (up to 5 clutches)

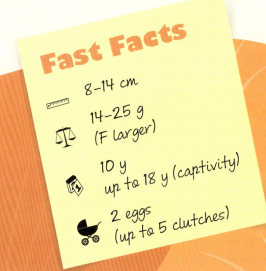

# Perentie
*Varanus giganteus*

### What is it?
The largest Australian lizard and monitor. The Perentie is also the fastest, reaching speeds of up to 30 km/hr over short distances. Although it's big and fast, it's quite shy.

### Where does it live?
In the west of the Great Dividing Range, in arid central and western Australia. It inhabits rocky outcrops, stony gorges and sandy deserts. The Perentie shelters in caves, rocky crevices or in its own burrows.

### What's its life like?
The Perentie is a diurnal hunter and scavenger that travels over wide areas to attack or dig up prey. Its forked tongue picks up scent from the air, relaying it to the Jacobson's organ in its mouth. Perenties eat almost anything they can overpower, including insects, reptiles, birds and mammals. Fortunately, they also prey on rabbits and introduced mice. When threatened, they 'freeze' (lying flat and still) or run. If cornered, a Perentie stands and fights, by clawing, hissing, lunging forward with an open mouth, and whipping with its tail. A powerful digger, it excavates a burrow in a few minutes. The female lays eggs in a burrow, often under a boulder.

- Cravens Peak Reserve
- Uluru-Kata Tjuta NP
- Witjira NP
- Diamantina NP

### Fast Facts
- up to 2.5 m
- up to 20 kg
- up to 25 y
- 6–14 eggs

### interesting info
- Australia has several types of lizards—monitors (goannas), dragons, geckos, legless lizards and skinks.
- Monitor species are all sizes—the smallest is 20 cm and the largest is around 2.5 m.
- **All monitors can swim.**
- Monitors got their name from 'tripoding' behaviour—standing on their back legs and tail to 'monitor' (check) their surroundings.
- **During the breeding season, males fight and wrestle each other, standing on their back legs.**
- Monitors have sharp, backward curving teeth that they use to hold prey, but not to chew it.

# Shingleback Lizard
*Tiliqua rugosa*

### What is it?
A very slow moving, broad-bodied lizard with a blue tongue, a triangular head, a short stumpy tail and large 'pine cone' scales.

### Where does it live?
In dry, semi-arid south and south-west Australia, in open habitats with lots of ground cover, including mallee woodlands, shrublands and coastal dunes. Shinglebacks shelter in tussock grass or leaf litter, or under rocks or logs.

### What's its life like?
In the early morning, the Shingleback sunbakes to warm up before searching for food. Like all reptiles, it doesn't produce its own body heat. During really cold weather, it seeks shelter and stays inactive. It mainly eats plants (and loves yellow flowers) and sometimes catches insects and eats carrion. Predators include large birds, snakes, and feral cats and dogs. The Shingleback lives alone for most of the year, but spends time with its mate each spring. The pair usually mates for life. Unlike most reptiles, there is no egg stage and young are born live and very large at up to 22 cm long and weighing 200 g.

- Nambung NP
- Diamantina NP
- Sturt NP
- Kinchega NP
- Wyperfeld NP
- Little Desert NP

## interesting info

- Like all reptiles, lizards regularly shed their skins. They usually rub the skin off in fragments (snakes usually shed their skin in one piece).
- The Shingleback stores fat in its stumpy tail that it uses during winter hibernation.
- When threatened, it opens its bright pink mouth and sticks out its big blue tongue. It also hisses and flattens itself to look bigger. Its tail is shaped like another head, which confuses predators.
- The Shingleback has lots of common names— Bobtail, Stumpy-tail, Pinecone Lizard, Sleepy Lizard, Double-headed Lizard and Bogeye.

## Fast Facts
- 41 cm
- up to 600 g
- up to 20 y
- 1–3 live young

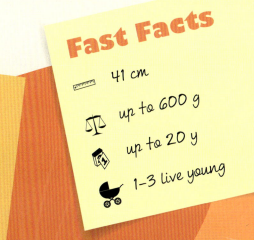

# Mulga Snake
*Pseudechis australis*

### What is it?
A species of black snake, also called the King Brown Snake, and the most widespread of Australia's venomous snakes. It has a thick-set body, a broad head and bulbous cheeks. Its colour varies in different locations, from pale brown to olive to rich red-brown, with a cream to white belly. Scales on its back often have a two-toned colour.

### Where does it live?
Throughout most of mainland Australia, in many habitats, from forests to deserts. The Mulga shelters in soil cracks, hollow logs, grass clumps, or burrows that other animals have abandoned. It is often found in environmentally disturbed areas such as wheat fields.

- Nambung NP
- Uluru-Kata Tjuta NP
- Witjira NP
- Diamantina NP
- Sturt NP
- Kinchega NP

### What's its life like?
Depending on the temperature (it avoids the hottest and coldest temperatures), the Mulga Snake is diurnal or nocturnal. It eats lizards and snakes, including venomous snakes and even other Mulga Snakes. It also eats insects, frogs, birds and mammals. Like all snakes, it swallows its prey whole with the help of jaws that can separate and stretch. The adult has few predators but birds-of-prey can take juveniles. In northern Australia, the number of Mulga Snakes has decreased because they eat Cane Toads, which have deadly toxins in their skin, which kill the snakes.

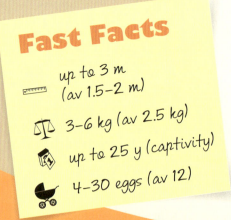

**Fast Facts**
- up to 3 m (av 1.5–2 m)
- 3–6 kg (av 2.5 kg)
- up to 25 y (captivity)
- 4–30 eggs (av 12)

## interesting info

- When a Mulga Snake bites, it injects more venom than any other snake in the world. This snake is also the heaviest venomous snake in Australia.
- Like most venomous snakes, the Mulga only bites when people disturb it. Black snake antivenom is used to treat a Mulga Snake bite.
- **When threatened, the Mulga flattens its neck like a cobra.**
- Mulga Snakes lay their eggs and then leave. When the eggs hatch after 2–3 months, the young must look after themselves.

# Water-holding Frog
*Cyclorana platycephala*

### What is it?
The best known of Australia's water-holding frog species. Its colour varies from grey to brown to green, depending on location. It's a large and robust frog with a very wide mouth and eyes that sit on top of its flattened head. Its feet are fully webbed.

### Where does it live?
In flat, dry inland habitats of the arid zone near seasonal or temporary watercourses. There are three separate populations.

### What's its life like?
Water-holding Frogs survive long periods of heat and drought by burrowing underground and aestivating (being dormant). When its bladder is full, it surrounds itself in a cocoon of mucus and dead skin, which reduces water loss. After heavy rain, the frog comes to the surface, sheds the cocoon, absorbs water, then feeds and breeds in temporary pools, claypans and creeks. Females lay egg masses that spread out on the water surface to get enough oxygen. Tadpoles grow quickly and become very large (6–8 cm). Unlike most other frogs, adults catch prey under water (aquatic insects, tadpoles and small fish), stuffing them into their mouths with their 'hands'.

- Cravens Peak Reserve
- Witjira NP
- Diamantina NP
- Sturt NP

## interesting info
- Water-holding Frogs were a source of water for Aboriginal people living in the desert.
- The urine of many burrowing frog species is mostly pure water.
- Water-holding Frogs can burrow as deep as 1 m or more, where they can remain dormant for up to 5 years or more. They always burrow in backwards, using a bump on each hind foot that is shaped like the edge of a shovel.
- Males call while floating. They have a long drawn-out call—*mawww, mawww*.

## Fast Facts
- 4–7.2 cm
- 70 g but varies (heavier after rain)
- unknown
- up to 3,000+ eggs

# Malleefowl
*Leipoa ocellata*

- Nambung NP
- Wyperfeld NP
- Little Desert NP

## Q&A

**What is it?**
A stocky, ground-dwelling, mound-building bird with large feet.

**Where does it live?**
In arid and semi-arid mallee scrub, low eucalypt woodlands and coastal heaths. It requires sandy or gravel soils and abundant leaf litter.

**What's its life like?**
Malleefowls are sedentary and territorial. They mate for life, but feed and roost apart. For 9 months each year, the male tends a large incubation mound (1.5 m high and 2–5 m wide) that he makes by raking up sandy soil and placing a layer of decomposing leaf litter inside to create heat. Over several weeks, he opens the mound so his mate can lay more eggs. The chicks hatch at intervals and dig to the surface. They immediately lead independent lives. But only a few survive; the rest are killed by predators. Malleefowls feed on insects, seeds and plants and can live without drinking for long periods.

## Fast Facts
- 51–61 cm
- 1.5–2.5 kg
- up to 40 y
- 5–35 eggs (average 16)

## Interesting info

- Malleefowls have excellent hearing and eyesight. When disturbed, they often 'freeze'.
- Their patterned feathers make good camouflage. They can also run away quickly.
- The male keeps the incubation pocket inside the mound at around 33°C. Each day, he opens the mound, sticks his head in the pocket to test the temperature with his sensitive bill and tongue. He adds more leaf litter and sand, or opens it up a little more, depending on his temperature 'reading' and the weather. This heat regulation ability is rare among animals.

# Major Mitchell's Cockatoo
*Lophochroa leadbeateri*

### Q&A

**What is it?**
An attractive pink-washed, white cockatoo with an upswept crest decorated with red and yellow bands. The male has brown eyes and the female has red eyes. It's also called the Pink Cockatoo.

**Where does it live?**
In mallee and mulga woodlands, sandplains and tree-lined watercourses, mainly in the arid and semi-arid interior.

**What's its life like?**
This cockatoo occurs in pairs, family groups or flocks of 20–50. It feeds on the ground and in trees, eating seeds, native melons, roots, bulbs and insect larvae. It's usually sedentary near permanent water, but nomadic in drier areas while searching for food and water. It mates for life, both birds defending their territory and caring for the eggs and nestlings. Major Mitchell's Cockatoos make their nests in hollows, which they line with wood chips and bark, in very old trees like eucalypts or Cypress Pines. Their territories are based on a feeding area of up to 30 km². Known predators are eagles, falcons, foxes and feral cats.

- Nambung NP
- Uluru-Kata Tjuta NP
- Kinchega NP
- Wyperfeld NP

### Interesting info

- This species is named after Sir Thomas Mitchell, a nineteenth-century Scottish explorer of south-eastern Australia.
- Like most cockatoos, it's left-footed. Its tongue and jaw muscles are very powerful.
- It's smaller than a Sulphur-crested Cockatoo but larger than a Galah.
- Unlike other cockatoos, Major Mitchell's Cockatoos won't nest close to each other, so they don't do well when their habitat is broken up into small pieces.
- Cookie, who has lived in a Chicago zoo since 1934, is the oldest Major Mitchell in the world. He's over 80 years old.

### Fast Facts

- 35–40 cm
- 81 cm
- 300–450 g
- up to 50 y
- 80+ y (captivity)
- 2–4 eggs

# Cockatiel
*Nymphicus hollandicus*

### What is it?
A small grey cockatoo with a long tail. The male has a pale yellow face and crest.

### Where does it live?
In open woodlands and grasslands near water in arid and semi-arid country across the mainland.

### What's its life like?
The Cockatiel is a 'dimorphic' bird, meaning that the male and female have different feather colourings and patterns. It mates for life and occurs in pairs or small flocks. It feeds on the ground or in trees. The Cockatiel eats seeds, nuts, berries and grains, and it uses its strong, hooked beak to manipulate and crack open seeds. It is nomadic, moving around to find food and water. In dry times, it flies from inland Australia towards the coast. The Cockatiel breeds whenever there is good rain. It nests high in a tree hollow and the male and female share nest duties. It always enters the hollow backwards, tail first.

- Nambung NP
- Cravens Peak Reserve
- Uluru-Kata Tjuta NP
- Witjira NP
- Diamantina NP
- Sturt NP
- Kinchega NP
- Wyperfeld NP
- Little Desert NP

## Fast Facts
- 25–35 cm
- 30–46 cm
- 80–120 g
- 10–36 years
- 4–7 eggs

## interesting info

- **The Cockatiel is the smallest member of the cockatoo family.**
- When flying, it gives a distinctive *queel-queel* call.
- **It often eats cultivated crops, which makes it unpopular with farmers.**
- It can sometimes reproduce at the age of one, which is unusual for a cockatoo.
- **The Cockatiel can mimic human speech and is nearly as popular as the Budgerigar as a pet bird. Pet Cockatiels have been bred in lots of different colours.**
- It was first recorded during Captain Cook's first voyage to Australia and was then called a Crested Parakeet.

# Budgerigar
*Melopsittacus undulatus*

   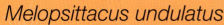

## Q&A

**What is it?**
A small bright green, yellow and black parrot, with a long tail. It has dark spots on its cheeks and throat. The cere at the top of the bill is blue in the male.

**Where does it live?**
In grasslands, mallee and mulga across the interior of mainland Australia, mainly in the arid and semi-arid zone. In drought, this species may retreat to coastal areas.

**What's its life like?**
Budgerigars are nomadic, constantly moving to find water and seeds of native grasses and herbs. They form flocks of tens to thousands, which look like waves when flying. To confuse predatory raptors, Budgies dart across the sky, twisting and turning together, making lots of noise. They nest in hollow tree limbs, stumps or fence posts. Many pairs nest in the same tree. The females are dominant and incubate the eggs. Budgerigars breed when there are heavy rains (which encourage grass growth) and may lay several clutches. This boom-and-bust breeding can lead to population explosions, with the birds dying off as food and water starts to disappear.

- Rottnest Island
- Cravens Peak Reserve
- Uluru-Kata Tjuta NP
- Witjira NP
- Diamantina NP
- Sturt NP
- Kinchega NP
- Wyperfeld NP
- Little Desert NP

## Interesting info

- You can hear Budgerigars before you see them. Their voices are full of musical chirrups, zizzing chatter and rasping scolds.
- Budgerigars have survived the harsh conditions of inland Australia for five million years. They rest during the heat of the day to save moisture.
- **Flocks of 20,000 Budgies have been seen.**
- They're great mimics of human speech and are the third most popular pet in the world, after dogs and cats. In captivity, they're bred in other colours, like blue, yellow, white, mauve and grey.

## Fast Facts

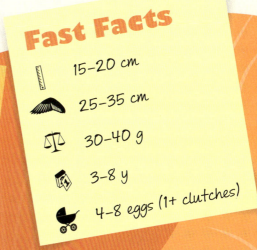

- 15–20 cm
- 25–35 cm
- 30–40 g
- 3–8 y
- 4–8 eggs (1+ clutches)

# Crest-tailed Mulgara
*Dasycercus cristicauda*

○ Witjira NP

### What is it?
A small but aggressive carnivore with a short, flattened tail that has a crest of black hairs along the bottom half. It's also known as the Crest-tailed Marsupial Mouse. It's often confused with the Brush-tailed Mulgara (*Dasycercus blythi*), which doesn't have a crest on the tail.

### Where does it live?
In sandy regions of desert, such as the Simpson Desert, in central Australia. It lives on and around sand dunes that have spinifex bushes.

### What's its life like?
The Crest-tailed Mulgara's complex burrows have multiple entrances with several side tunnels, nests and pop-holes. It lives alone or shares burrows, and marks entrances with urine and droppings. A nocturnal hunter, it preys on insects, spiders and small vertebrates, such as geckos, rodents or birds. Sometimes it's active in the day and may sunbathe at the burrow entrance in winter. Females produce many young but have only 8 teats, so the extra young die. A sedentary animal, it's sensitive to changes in habitat, climate and food resources, and population numbers tend to fluctuate widely. Threats include feral predators, like cats, and feral grazers, like camels, and fire.

## Fast Facts
- 19.5–35 cm (includes tail 7–13 cm)
- M 75–170 g  F 60–95 g
- up to 7 y
- up to 8
- M up to 25 ha  F up to 11 ha (overlapping)

## interesting info
- The Crest-tailed Mulgara is a 'dasyurid'. Dasyurids are carnivorous marsupials and include marsupial mice, quolls and Tasmanian Devils. They have separated toes, whereas most marsupials have the second and third toe joined together. Rather than a pouch, they have a fold of skin surrounding the teats.
- The Mulgara's kidneys are specialised to produce concentrated urine. This is to save water, which it gets mainly from its prey rather than from drinking.
- It's now extinct in New South Wales.

# Giles' Planigale
*Planigale gilesi*

## Q&A

### What is it?
A marsupial carnivore that can fit on the tip of your thumb. It's like a tiny mouse, but with a flattened, triangular-shaped head, small round ears and black eyes. It's also called the Paucident Planigale.

### Where does it live?
In the arid and semi-arid inland of eastern Australia where there are deep, cracked clay soils near permanent water (like lakes) or areas that have periodic flooding, such as river floodplains. Giles' Planigale also likes dense, patchy undergrowth.

### What's its life like?
The numbers of this planigale depend on the depth and closeness of cracks in the soil. Along with vegetation, cracks provide shelter from predators, heat and cold, and places to find food—invertebrates like spiders, cockroaches, beetles, locusts and slaters. It kills prey with quick bites. Giles' Planigale's head shape and broad feet help it to squeeze and climb through the cracks. It finds larger prey, like centipedes, in deeper cracks. Giles' Planigales are most active around dawn and dusk. Females call out to males in the breeding season, and have 12 teats in their backwards-facing pouch. Threats include feral predators, habitat clearing, stock grazing and changed patterns of river flooding.

- ○ Witjira NP
- ● Diamantina NP
- ● Sturt NP
- ● Kinchega NP

## Interesting info

- **Giles' Planigale was named in 1972, after Ernest Giles, a nineteenth-century explorer of Australia's deserts.**
- In Victoria, it was found in 1985 for the first time, near the Murray River.
- **Lots die in their first year (more than 80%).**
- In winter, planigales use torpor (similar to sleeping) and sunbathe to save energy, so they need to find less food. Many small animals living in Australia's harsh arid zone use torpor and sunbathing to save energy.
- **When there is plenty of food, Giles' Planigale stores fat in its tail, which becomes carrot-shaped.**

## Fast Facts

- 11.5–15 cm (includes tail 5.5–7 cm)
- M 9.5–16 g, F 5–9 g
- 1–2 y, 5 y (captivity)
- 6–8 young (1–2 litters)
- free ranging

# Bilby
*Macrotis lagotis*

Diamantina NP

### What is it?
A bandicoot with a delicate build, soft silky grey fur, long ears and a long black-and-white crested tail. It's also known as the Greater Bilby or the Rabbit-eared Bandicoot.

### Where does it live?
In central Australia, on desert sandplains, sand dune fields and stony country with cracking clays. Bilbies prefer sparse ground cover like spinifex (hummock) grass and acacia shrubs. Satellite populations occur in south-western Queensland.

### What's its life like?
The Bilby uses its strong forelimbs and stout claws to dig for food and to make burrows, where it spends the day. It gets its water from food. It uses up to 12 burrows, which can be 3 m long and 2 m deep, with the entrance next to a termite mound, shrub or spinifex tussock. Feeding at night, the Bilby's omnivorous diet includes insects, insect larvae, seeds, bulbs, fruit and fungi. It licks up its food with its long tongue. Bilbies live alone or in pairs, with home ranges that change according to food supply. The female has a backwards-opening pouch with 8 teats, but usually raises only 2 young.

## Fast Facts
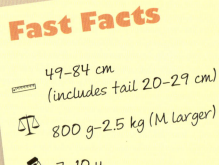
- 49–84 cm (includes tail 20–29 cm)
- 800 g–2.5 kg (M larger)
- 7–10 y
- 1–3 joeys (up to 4 litters)
-  temporary

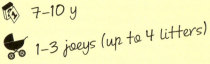

## interesting info
- While eating, the Bilby also eats the sandy soil, and its droppings contain 20–90% sand.
- Its eyesight isn't good, but it has excellent hearing and smell, which it uses to find food.
- **The large, almost hairless ears help to keep it cool.**
- The numbers of Bilbies dropped in the early 1900s, due to habitat loss, pests (like rabbits, cats and foxes), livestock grazing and fire. It has been successfully introduced into some reserves.
- **The Bilby is Australia's mascot for all endangered animals, and chocolate bilbies are sold at Easter.**

# Red Kangaroo
*Macropus rufus*

### What is it?
Australia's largest kangaroo and land mammal, the world's largest marsupial and one of the most athletic mammals. Its squarish face has white stripes from nostril to ear. Males are usually red, while females are blue-grey to reddish. Both have a white underbelly. One Indigenous name is *Marloo*, and the Red Kangaroo is an icon of arid, outback Australia.

### Where does it live?
On open grassy plains and woodlands of inland Australia, where scattered trees provide shade. It inhabits some regions with higher rainfall. It may also overlap with stock in the rangelands, although its diet differs.

### What's its life like?
Red Kangaroos are highly social, forming mobs from a few individuals to several hundreds. They shelter under trees during hot days, while in cooler weather they sunbake. Reds are crepuscular (active at dawn and dusk), feeding on short grass, herbs and shrubs. They're partly nomadic and may move up to 50 km to find new grass, especially after rain. Males establish dominance hierarchies and mating rights with spectacular boxing matches. Females have three young at different stages: a dormant embryo in the womb, a joey in the pouch, and a young at foot. The last two drink from different teats that have different kinds of milk, matched to their age.

- Cravens Peak Reserve
- Uluru-Kata Tjuta NP
- Witjira NP
- Diamantina NP
- Sturt NP
- Kinchega NP
- Wyperfeld NP

## interesting info

- Males are called 'boomers' and females 'blue flyers'.
- Reds can survive without water for long periods, but dams, bores and water troughs on farms provide water in dry seasons.
- Kangaroos and wallabies cool off by resting. They pant and lick their forearms. When their saliva evaporates, it absorbs body heat.
- Large Reds can hop at 50 km/hr in short bursts. When they move slowly, they use 5 limbs (including the tail!).
- The biggest recorded jump is 3.1 m high and 12.8 m long, but a jump this big would be very unusual.

## Fast Facts

M 164–240 cm (includes tail 71–100 cm)
F 138–200 cm (includes tail 64–90 cm)

2 m

M 22–92 kg, F 17–39 kg

av 1–9 y, max 22 y

1–3 (+ 1 dormant embryo)

460–3,700 ha (overlapping)

# Quokka
*Setonix brachyurus*

● Rottnest Island

### What is it?
A small wallaby-like marsupial with a broad head, compact body, small round ears, coarse fur and a short scaly tail.

### Where does it live?
In dense swampy heathlands and forest margins near waterways in high rainfall areas of mainland south-western WA. High numbers can occur in some years in the harsh and arid acacia and melaleuca scrub of Rottnest Island (off Perth). It also inhabits Bald Island off Albany.

### What's its life like?
The Quokka is mostly ground-dwelling, but it can climb 1–2 m to feed. It's gregarious, living in social groups dominated by males, according to a hierarchy based on age. Groups of 25–150 may defend a common territory. Individuals defend resting sites which provide shelter from the heat. In hot weather, they congregate at night around waterholes, travelling up to 2 km. Quokkas' herbivorous diet consists of grass, leaves and succulent plants and they use sturdy forearms to grip and strip small branches. They don't breed if conditions are too hot and dry. Most commonly, a single joey is reared in the pouch. Threats are foxes, fire and habitat clearing.

## Fast Facts
- 62–85 cm (includes tail 23–31 cm)
- 1.6–4.2 kg (M larger)
- up to 10 y, 14 y (captivity)
- 1–2 joeys (+ 1 dormant embryo)
- 4 ha (overlapping)

## Interesting info

- Quokkas were first spotted in 1658 on Rottnest Island by Dutch navigator Samuel Volckertzoon.
- Quokkas used to be common in south-western WA but, by the 1960s, they lived only on Rottnest Island and in a few small areas around Perth.
- **Because they were easy to catch on the island, scientists used them to find out more about macropods.**
- The environment on Rottnest Island is harsh, so Quokka numbers sometimes crash, through starvation and lack of water.
- Quokkas can get muscular dystrophy (like humans), so researchers use them to study the disease.

# Southern Marsupial Mole
*Notoryctes typhlops*

## Q&A

### What is it?
The most fossorial mammal in the world. The Southern Marsupial Mole, or the Itjaritjari, has no eyes, a cone-shaped head and creamy-golden fur. The Northern Marsupial Mole (*Notoryctes caurinus*), or the Kakarratul, looks the same as the Itjaritjari, but is slightly smaller.

### Where does it live?
Below the spiky spinifex (hummock) grass and burning sands of the vast sand-dune deserts of Central Australia. The Itjaritjari prefers the crests and slopes of sand dunes which may be more wind-sorted and so have more air space and be easier to dig. But it also occurs under sandplains.

### What's its life like?
The Itjaritjari digs rapidly with two spade-like claws on each front limb and pushes sand back with flattened hind limbs. While digging, it fills its burrow behind it—like it's swimming underground. It mostly burrows horizontally, 20–60 cm below the surface, breathing the air between sand grains. It saves energy by adjusting its body temperature to that of the surrounding sand. It rarely surfaces but, when it does, foxes, cats, Dingoes, goannas, snakes and birds are threats. It eats termites, ants and beetle larvae. The Itjaritjari is solitary and little is known about its breeding, but females have a backwards-opening pouch (to keep sand out) and 2 teats.

Itjaritjari

- Itjaritjari
- Kakarratul

- Uluru-Kata Tjuta NP
- Witjira NP

## interesting info

- On the sand surface, when the Itjaritjari drags its wedge-shaped tail, it forms a wavy track, but the Kakarratul does not.
- Australia's marsupial moles are like the Golden Moles of Africa, but they have come from different ancestors. Both are adapted to burrowing life in sandy deserts. Their size and shape are similar, their fur is fine, they have no eyes and no external ears, their snouts have a horny shield, their tails are a leathery stub.
- The Itjaritjari is probably quite common, because there are masses of its tunnels under the sand dunes.

## Fast Facts

- 8–16 cm
- 40–70 g
- unknown
- 2
- unknown

# Hopping-mouse: Spinifex & Mitchell's

*Notomys alexis* and *Notomys mitchellii*

■ Spinifex Hopping-mouse

## Q&A

### What are they?
Mice with large eyes and hind feet, and a very long tail with a white brush tip. The Spinifex Hopping-mouse (SHM), or Tarrkawarra, is chestnut above and grey-white below, and Mitchell's Hopping-mouse (MHM), or Pankot, is sandy grey with a white chest.

- Nambung NP
- Cravens Peak Reserve
- Uluru-Kata Tjuta NP
- Witjira NP
- Wyperfeld NP
- Little Desert NP

### Where do they live?
SHM: in the arid zone of Central Australia and WA in sandy flats and dunes covered with spinifex (hummock) grass, or mulga. MHM: in much of southern semi-arid SA and WA, in mallee woodland shrubs on sand dunes.

≡ Mitchell's Hopping-mouse

### What are their lives like?
These hopping-mice are nocturnal. By day, they shelter in deep burrows made up of a horizontal tunnel 1 m underground, with several vertical shafts to the surface. The shafts have hidden entrances and no heaps of excavated dirt. Each family group (of up to 12) shares a burrow. These mice regulate their body temperature to stay cool. Both mice species are omnivores, eating seeds, roots, shoots and insects, although the Mitchell's diet consists more of roots and green matter. Their main predators are owls, Dingoes, Mulgaras, cats and foxes. Breeding for both species depends on environmental conditions, and SHM population numbers explode after heavy rains in a 'boom-and-bust' pattern.

## Fast Facts
- 22.5–27.5 cm (includes tail 13–15 cm)
- SHM av 35 g, MHM av 52 g
- up to 5 y (captivity)
- 3–6 a litter (several litters)
- SHM & MHM: temporary when habitat is dry
- SHM: 500 m–2 km after rain

## Interesting info

- **Mitchell's Hopping-mouse was named in 1836 near Lake Boga, Victoria, by the explorer, Thomas Mitchell.**
- Hopping-mice travel on all fours when moving slowly, but hop on their long hind legs when moving fast, using the tail for balance.
- **They have a long lifespan for a mouse. This helps them survive periods of drought.**
- SHM may migrate up to 15 km to reach rainfall.
- **Both mice produce concentrated urine to save water.**
- More than half of the Mitchell's former range has been cleared for agriculture.

# MOUNTAINS

**Areas of higher elevation—alpine and subalpine regions, mountain ranges and hilly regions, including areas that receive snow and rocky escarpments**

Australia is a flat continent, with the lowest average elevation in the world—330 metres above sea level. Yet Australia has mountain ranges, rocky escarpments and hills in every state and territory. The highest mountain in Australia is Mount Kosciuszko (2,228 metres above sea level) in the Australian Alps. The top of the Alps is treeless but has herb fields, heath, grasses and bogs. The lower slopes have tall eucalypt forests with different trees becoming dominant with decreasing altitude.

Alpine NP (Victoria)

Cradle Mountain–Lake Saint Clair NP (Tasmania)

Blue Mountains NP (New South Wales)

Kosciuszko NP (New South Wales)

Flinders Ranges NP (South Australia)

Stirling Range NP (Western Australia)

The Australian Alps are the highest part of the Great Dividing Range. This is Australia's longest range of mountains, stretching for over 3,500 kilometres from Victoria to northern Queensland. It separates the eastern coastline from the drier inland plains and has a major influence on Australia's climate—and population.

Mountain ranges also occur further inland and in the west, such as the Flinders Ranges of South Australia, the Hamersley Range in central Western Australia, and the Stirling Ranges of south-western Australia. The ancient MacDonnell Ranges in central Australia have spectacular gorges and rare wildlife.

Mountain ranges and rocky escarpments are important habitats, especially in more extreme hot or cold landscapes, because they provide shelter, special climatic conditions and sources of water.

These national parks have examples of mountains where the animals in this section occur. The animals may also occur in other habitats and in other national parks.

# Blotched Blue-tongue Lizard
*Tiliqua nigrolutea*

- Blue Mountains NP
- Kosciuszko NP
- Alpine NP
- Cradle Mt–Lake St Clair NP

### Q&A

**What is it?**
A skink similar to the Common Blue-tongue, but with blotches on its body rather than stripes. It's the largest lizard in Tasmania. It's also called the Southern Blue-tongue Lizard.

**Where does it live?**
In a variety of habitats such as forests, woodlands, coastal heath and suburban gardens, in the south-eastern corner of Australia, including Tasmania, its islands and the Bass Strait islands. In NSW, the Blotched Blue-tongue occurs in montane woodlands of the Blue Mountains. Its distribution is much more restricted than the Common Blue-tongue's.

**What's its life like?**
Blotched Blue-tongues are omnivores, eating flowers, fruit and small, slow-moving animals like snails, slugs and some insects. Adults eat more plant matter than juveniles. The tongue 'tastes' the air and transfers chemical information to Jacobson's organ on the roof of the mouth, which helps the lizard find food. Predators include raptors, snakes, cats and dogs (similar to the Common Blue-tongue). In winter, the Blotched Blue-tongue enters a period of hibernation (called 'brumation' in reptiles) and emerges in the mating season in early spring. At this time, males often fight each other aggressively for females. Females give birth to live young that have developed internally in eggs with shells reduced to membranes.

## interesting info

- For defence, the Blotched Blue-tongue uses camouflage and bluff, such as sticking out its tongue and hissing.
- Several Australian skinks bear live young, instead of laying eggs. This can happen in cold climates where eggs wouldn't do well in the ground. In Tasmania, 14 of 17 species of skink bear live young.
- Reptile ticks are commonly found on blue-tongues but not on mammals (including people).
- Blotched Blue-tongues like to eat tinned cat and dog food!
- Snail bait, cars and lawn mowers can kill Blotched Blue-tongues.

## Fast Facts

- 35–55 cm
- av 300–500 g (max 800 g)
- up to 25 y (captivity)
- up to 17 live young

# Wedge-tailed Eagle
*Aquila audax*

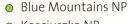

- Blue Mountains NP
- Kosciuszko NP
- Alpine NP
- Cradle Mt–Lake St Clair NP
- Flinders Ranges NP
- Stirling Range NP

 **Q&A**

### What is it?
Australia's largest eagle and largest raptor (bird of prey). The Wedge-tailed Eagle, or Wedgie, is the king and queen of the skies. It has a dark body, a whitish bill, long feathered legs and a diamond-shaped tail.

### Where does it live?
In forests (but not rainforests) and woodlands, from mountain tops to the coast.

### What's its life like?
These eagles are often seen soaring majestically in the sky on air currents (thermals). Males perform spectacular aerial courtship displays (pothooks)— diving and soaring at speed. Maturing at 6 years, they mate for life. The pair shares a home range of 30–100 km² and all nesting duties. The birds build a huge nest, or eyrie (2–5 m wide and 2–5 m deep), high in a tree, or among bushes inland, from sticks and gum leaves. An apex predator, the main prey is often rabbit, but the Wedgie also eats marsupials, other birds, reptiles and cats. A pair will hunt together for small kangaroos and several may eat carrion together.

## interesting info

- The strongest chick often kills the others in the nest to make sure it survives.
- When this eagle flies, each wing shows 6 'fingers' (separated flight-feather tips). It can soar up very high (up to 2 km or more).
- The Wedgie has excellent vision (including telephoto and infrared) so it can spot prey from far away.
- This bird has no natural enemies, but pesticides or poison in its food can kill it.
- Last century, people hunted thousands of eagles because they believed they took lambs. This wasn't so.

## Fast Facts

up to 1 m

85–110 cm

1.8–2.8 m

M up to 4 kg, F up to 5.3 kg

6–11 y
up to 40 y (captivity)

1–3 eggs
(1 surviving fledgling)

# Gang-gang Cockatoo
*Callocephalon fimbriatum*

- Blue Mountains NP
- Kosciuszko NP
- Alpine NP

## Q&A

### What is it?
A small, stocky, slate-grey cockatoo. The male has a fluffy scarlet head-crest.

### Where does it live?
In cooler and wetter forests and woodlands of the south-eastern coast and highlands, from sea level to 2,000 m. It's a rare visitor to Tasmania and the Bass Strait islands.

### What's its life like?
The Gang-gang is a gregarious cockatoo that only comes to the ground to drink. From autumn to winter, it moves from tall highland forests to coastal and sub-inland woodlands, farmlands and suburban areas. It feeds mainly on seeds, especially from eucalypts, wattles and introduced hawthorns. It also eats berries, nuts and insect larvae. During the breeding season, it feeds in pairs or small family groups, but at other times in flocks of about 60 birds. Most cockatoos nest in hollows of old trees, but Gang-gang females may also create nesting cavities in younger, solid trees. Males and females share nesting duties.

## interesting info

- The Gang-gang is a quiet cockatoo, but if it's in a tree you can hear it eating. You can also see leaves, twigs and bits of seeds falling as it feeds.
- Its call sounds like a creaky gate.
- Gang-gangs sometimes form 'creches', where pairs with nests close together leave their young roosting in the same tree while they are away foraging.

## Fast Facts

 32–37 cm

 62–76 cm

 260 g

 up to 75 y (captivity)

 2–3 eggs

# Crimson Rosella
*Platycercus elegans*

- Blue Mountains NP
- Kosciuszko NP
- Alpine NP

### What is it?
A medium-sized, crimson-red parrot with blue cheeks and tail, and black and blue wings. The juvenile has blue cheeks, but its body is olive-green to yellow until it's 15 months old. It's also called the Red Lowry.

### Where does it live?
In wetter and older forests with tall trees, but only on the edges of rainforest, and in coastal forests, woodlands and tree-lined waterways. It's often seen seasonally in gardens in south-eastern Australia.

### What's its life like?
The Crimson Rosella eats seed, fruit, nectar, berries and nuts from various plants. It also eats insects. Small feeding flocks chatter and whistle while foraging. This rosella is mostly sedentary but, during autumn and winter, some flocks move from upland forests to lowland and suburban areas. In spring, the female selects a nest site in a deep hollow inside a tall tree. She and her mate line it with wood strips and fiercely guard it so others can't nest nearby. Possums, currawongs or even other female Crimson Rosellas may take the eggs. Threats to adult birds include foxes and cats and the loss of nesting trees.

## Interesting info

- Rosellas crush seeds before eating them. This means the seeds can't germinate. So rosellas aren't very important in the spread of plants to other areas.
- Crimson Rosellas have been introduced to Norfolk Island. They compete with Norfolk Island Green Parakeets (*Cyanoramphus cookii*) for nest hollows.
- The Crimson Rosella's blue tail feathers are a favourite decoration used by Satin Bowerbirds.
- Its cousin, the Eastern Rosella (*Platycercus eximius*) has its picture on some Australian tomato sauce bottles.

## Fast Facts

- 30–38 cm
- 44–53 cm
- 115–170 g
- up to 27 y (captivity)
- 3–8 eggs

# Red Wattlebird
*Anthochaera carunculata*

- Blue Mountains NP
- Kosciuszko NP
- Alpine NP
- Flinders Ranges NP
- Stirling Range NP

### Q&A

**What is it?**
The largest honeyeater on mainland Australia. It's a noisy bird with red eyes and large fleshy red 'wattles' (lobes) on the cheeks, which grow larger and brighter with age. Its plumage is grey-brown with white streaks and a yellow belly patch.

**Where does it live?**
In the undergrowth and canopy of wet eucalypt forests and woodlands, or in rainforests. It often occurs near waterways and in suburban gardens. In spring and summer, it ranges to the highlands (up to 2,000 m altitude) and in autumn it migrates towards the lowlands.

**What's its life like?**
The Red Wattlebird is either solitary or lives in small groups. Usually in autumn and spring, it forms large nomadic flocks. It feeds on blossom and nectar, defending its food sources aggressively. Locally, it may range up to 2 km looking for food and often performs acrobatic manoeuvres when feeding on blossoms or catching flying insects on the wing (hawking). It hops when on the ground but is a strong flyer. When it flies, the white tips of the wings and tail show. Breeding is in winter and spring. The nest is an untidy saucer of twigs, leaves and bark, built high in a tree-fork. Both parents care for the young.

## interesting info

- The Red Wattlebird's call is like a hacking cough, *yak-yak*, with a deep ringing, *tew-tew-tew-tew*.
- Its bill is thin and curved and the tip of its tongue is like a brush. These are adaptations for feeding on nectar.
- Many Red Wattlebirds live permanently in people's gardens because food is available all year. So these birds don't always need to migrate.
- The Southern Cassowary also has red wattles, but on its neck.
- The Eastern Koel often leaves its eggs in the wattlebird's nest so that the wattlebird rears its young.

## Fast Facts

- 33–37 cm
- 40–49 cm
- 100–120 g
- up to 14 y
- 2–3 eggs (1–2 clutches)

# Short-beaked Echidna
*Tachyglossus aculeatus*

- Blue Mountains NP
- Kosciuszko NP
- Alpine NP
- Cradle Mt–Lake St Clair NP
- Flinders Ranges NP
- Stirling Range NP

## Q&A

### What is it?
Like the Platypus, the Short-beaked Echidna is a monotreme—an egg-laying mammal from the time of the dinosaurs. The echidna in Tasmania has thick fur that almost hides its spines.

### Where does it live?
In all habitats, including snow-covered mountains, deserts, forests, woodlands and the coast. With no fixed home, it takes shelter under rocks and bushes, and in caves and logs.

### What's its life like?
The Short-beaked Echidna has strong claws to dig up ant or termite nests, and a long sticky tongue to lick up the ants and termites. It has excellent smell and hearing, and its snout and feet have receptors to help detect prey. It has no teeth and grinds up food on horny pads in the mouth. When it eats, it takes in a lot of dirt, which forms the bulk of its droppings. It's solitary except in the breeding season when males jostle for a mate. Females may dig a nesting burrow. They lay one egg straight into the pouch. After 10 days, the puggle hatches and starts suckling.

## interesting info

- Monotremes are the longest surviving group of mammals in the world. Like reptiles, they lay eggs and, like mammals, they look after their young.
- A powerful muscle surrounds the echidna's body. It allows the echidna to change its body shape and to erect its long spines for defence or to regulate its temperature.
- For protection against predators, echidnas roll into a ball or dig themselves into the ground horizontally.
- They're great swimmers.
- They may hibernate in snow.
- The male echidna has ankle spurs but, unlike the Platypus, these spurs have no venom.

## Fast Facts
- 30–45 cm
- 2–7 kg
- up to 50 y
- 1 egg (every 3–5 y)

# Tasmanian Devil
*Sarcophilus harrisii*

○ Cradle Mt–
Lake St Clair NP

### Q&A

**What is it?**
The largest marsupial carnivore in the world. It's like a small black dog with white markings (10% are pure black) and long whiskers (for feeling in the dark).

**Where does it live?**
In Tasmania, from dry forests and coastal woodlands with open grasslands to alpine habitats.

**What's its life like?**
Tasmanian Devils are shy and easily killed by vicious dogs. But they can sound and look fierce, baring their teeth while delivering spine-chilling screeches. They're mainly scavengers rather than savage hunters, and eat mostly carrion. They also hunt prey, such as possums and pademelons. Devils can crush bone and eat whole carcasses using their massive jaws and strong teeth. They're active from dusk till dawn, travelling 10–20 km. A devil has several dens in vegetation, logs, caves or wombat burrows. It communicates by defecating in 'latrines' as noticeboards of its travels. It bears supernumerary young, but only 1–4 are reared as the female has only 4 teats in her backwards-opening pouch.

## Interesting info

- Devils are good swimmers and young devils can climb trees.
- Devils share large carrion. Once, a dead cow was seen with 22 feeding on it. A devil can eat 40% of its body weight in a night.
- It has the strongest bite of any land mammal in the world. Older devils are scarred from bites (mostly from fighting during the mating season).
- Facial tumour disease has killed over 80% of the devil population.
- A few thousand years ago, devils lived on mainland Australia, but Dingoes, human hunters and changing climate led to its extinction there.

## Fast Facts

- M 91 cm, F 81 cm (includes tail M 26 cm, F 24 cm)
- M 8–14 kg, F 5–9 kg
- 6–8 y
- 20–30 born (up to 4 raised)
- 4 to 27 km² (overlapping)

# Dusky Antechinus: Mainland & Tasmanian

*Antechinus mimetes* and *Antechinus swainsonii*

Mainland Dusky Antechinus

## Q&A

### What are they?
Small, stocky and inquisitive dark brown marsupial carnivores.

### Where do they live?
In alpine heath or tall open forests with dense understory on the south-eastern mainland and in Tasmania. The most numerous populations occur in mountainous areas, such as Kosciuszko National Park, where rainfall exceeds 1,000 mm per year.

- Mainland
- Tasmanian
- Blue Mountains NP
- Kosciuszko NP
- Alpine NP
- Cradle Mt–Lake St Clair NP

### What are their lives like?
Busy by night and sometimes by day, Dusky Antechinus spend most of their time foraging in rich topsoil. They have unusual, jerky movements. With powerful limbs and long curved claws on their forefeet, they dig out invertebrates like insects, spiders and worms. Dusky Antechinus find prey using smell, sight, hearing and their whiskers. They use their forefeet to hold food. Small lizards and small birds may also form part of the diet. Dusky Antechinus shelter in shallow burrows in creek banks or under logs or grass. The burrows end in grass-lined nesting chambers. Young are born one month after mating to coincide with spring and summer insect population explosions.

## interesting info

- During the short winter breeding season, males don't eat. They fight for females and, 3 weeks later, their immune systems collapse and they die. This is called semelparity (or 'big-bang') reproduction.
- Females don't have a true pouch. Before birth, ridges of skin form around the teats to make a shallow pouch. For about 6 weeks, the mother carries or drags the young around attached to her teats. She then leaves them in the nest until she weans them at 3 months.
- Threats include bushfire, habitat loss and predation by cats and foxes.

## Fast Facts

- 16.5–31 cm (includes tail 7.5–12 cm)
- M up to 540 g, F 35–180 g
- M 11.5 mo, F 3 y
- 6–10 (av 8)
- F 1–2 ha (M larger)

# Mountain Pygmy-possum
*Burramys parvus*

- Kosciuszko NP
- Alpine NP

## Q&A

### What is it?
A tiny hibernating possum and the only Australian mammal restricted to alpine habitats. The fine dense fur is grey on top and cream below, and the scaly prehensile tail is longer than its body. It's the largest of Australia's 5 pygmy possum species.

### Where does it live?
In alpine and subalpine regions above altitudes of 1,200 m where there's a period of snow cover and patches of boulders (called blockfields, blockstreams or screes) and shrubby alpine heath. Two small populations remain in the Victorian Alps and one in Kosciuszko National Park.

### What's its life like?
The Mountain Pygmy-possum is the only marsupial that hibernates for long periods, mostly under snow. It curls into a ball and hibernates for 5–7 months. Boulders shield it from extreme temperatures and are used as hibernation and nesting sites. It carries moss and grass in its curled tail for its nest, which it often shares with several others. Before hibernation, it eats a lot to double its body weight. This possum's omnivorous diet includes Bogong Moths, caterpillars, millipedes, beetles and spiders, as well as seeds and fruits from heath plants. It also caches seeds. Females give birth to supernumerary young after the snow melts, but carry only four in the pouch.

## Interesting info

- The first live Mountain Pygmy-possum was found in a ski hut in 1966 at Mount Hotham, Victoria. Before that, only fossils of this possum were known.
- Scientists have put radio trackers on some Mountain Pygmy-possums to see where they go. We now know that these tiny possums can travel 1–3 km a night.
- During hibernation, this possum's body temperature is 2°C for up to 3 weeks, with short periods of normal body temperature in between.
- When joeys leave the pouch, females expel the adult males, who must move away.

## Fast Facts

- 24–28 cm (includes tail 13–16 cm)
- 30–82 g
- M 2–5 y, F 5–12 y
- 4
- 0.06–5.3 ha

# Common Wallaroo
*Macropus robustus*

- Blue Mountains NP
- Kosciuszko NP
- Flinders Ranges NP

## Q&A

### What is it?
The Common Wallaroo, or Hill Kangaroo, is the most widespread macropod. It has an upright hopping style and stands with shoulders thrown back, elbows tucked in and wrists raised. It has a shaggy coat and large ears. The large black nose has no fur.

### Where does it live?
Over most of the mainland including in most arid regions and on grassy plains with dense scrub, from eastern NSW and Qld to the WA coast. Wallaroos prefer mountainous or rugged, hilly country with rocky habitat.

### What's its life like?
Common Wallaroos are nocturnal, mostly solitary and like to rest in caves, or under rock ledges or trees during the day. They're herbivores, eating grass, shrubs and succulent ground plants. With shelter and succulent plants, they can survive without water for 2–3 months. Breeding occurs all year round except during drought, although the timing of breeding differs between the east and the west. Joeys are in the pouch for 6 months, becoming independent at 9 months, when their mothers won't let them back into the pouch. Main predators are Dingoes and Wedge-tailed Eagles. The Common Wallaroo has to compete with domestic livestock for food in some regions.

## interesting info

- A wallaroo is bigger than a wallaby but smaller than a kangaroo.
- If alarmed, the Common Wallaroo emits a loud hiss by breathing out through its nose.
- During courtship, males rub scent from their chest gland over vegetation and fight over females. They have boxing matches that end when one of the two males surrenders.
- Common Wallaroos are hunted commercially in NSW, Qld and SA.
- There are two other wallaroo species, the Antilopine Wallaroo (*M. antilopinus*) and the Black Wallaroo (*M. bernardus*). Both live in the far north of Australia.

## Fast Facts

- M 114–199 cm, F 111–158 cm
- 1.2–1.6 m
- M 60 kg, F 28 kg
- up to 24 y
- 1 (+ 1 dormant embryo)
- 50–310 ha (overlapping)

# Yellow-footed Rock-wallaby
*Petrogale xanthopus*

● Flinders Ranges NP

### What is it?
Australia's largest and most colourful rock-wallaby. It has characteristic rings on the tail and a prominent white cheek stripe. Its forearms, hind legs and tail are coloured orange to yellow.

### Where does it live?
In rocky ranges and outcrops in open woodland in semi-arid zones, usually near water. Rocky outcrops create their own microclimate and often have more diverse plant species than surrounding plains, as well as water seepages. This wallaby is common in parts of the Flinders Ranges of SA.

### What's its life like?
The Yellow-footed Rock-wallaby is agile and social, forming colonies of 100 or more. It leaps over boulders and easily ascends steep rock faces, arching the tail over its back for balance. The pattern and colour of its fur provides camouflage in the rocky terrain. After rain, it feeds on herbs and grasses but, in dry times, it eats leaves, including dead leaves during drought. It's crepuscular but mainly active at night. On hot days, it shelters among deep shaded rocks, which can be up to 15° C cooler. In dry times, it may travel far in search of water, leaving its hidden juveniles behind. It generally breeds year round.

## interesting info

- Like other macropods (and cows), rock-wallabies have a special type of digestion so that they can digest the good nutrients from poor quality plant matter.
- Foot pads of the Yellow-footed Rock-wallaby are rough and granulated (with lots of small bumps) so it can grip onto rocks.
- **Rock-wallabies transfer water with their mouth to their young-at-foot.**
- More than half of juvenile rock-wallabies don't make it to adulthood.
- **Rabbits, goats and sheep may compete for food.**
- Predators include foxes, cats and raptors.

## Fast Facts

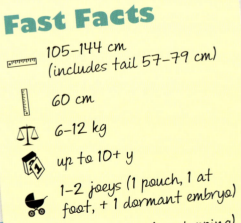

105–144 cm (includes tail 57–79 cm)

60 cm

6–12 kg

up to 10+ y

1–2 joeys (1 pouch, 1 at foot, + 1 dormant embryo)

24–200 ha (overlapping)

# Dingo
*Canis dingo*

- Blue Mountains NP
- Kosciuszko NP
- Alpine NP

## Q&A

### What is it?
Australia's largest land predator. Dingoes are often ginger with white points on the tail and feet, but colour can vary from almost white (in alpine areas) to black with tan markings. Dingoes and domestic dogs may have had a common wolf-like ancestor, but through isolation Dingoes evolved into a unique species. They yelp and howl rather than bark, their ears are always erect, the snout is slender and the tail bushy.

### Where does it live?
Across the continent, but not in Tasmania. It occurs in different habitats including mountain and alpine regions, arid deserts, coastal areas, woodlands and tropical forests, usually close to water. Fraser Island has one of the best pure-bred populations.

### What's its life like?
Dingoes are apex predators, typically active by night and sheltering by day. They're intelligent and secretive and can be solitary or live in family groups or packs of 3–12. They eats mammals (including feral animals like rabbits, foxes and cats), birds, reptiles, insects and carrion. Packs may hunt together cooperatively, taking down larger game like kangaroos. A pack marks its territory with scent to exclude competing Dingoes. Usually, only the dominant male and female breed. Young are reared in an underground den or cave and cared for by their parents and older juveniles. At 4 months old, pups can hunt independently.

## interesting info

- Asian visitors introduced Dingoes to Australia around 3,500–5,000 years ago.
- Particularly in the past, Dingoes were valued companions to Aboriginal people.
- Dingoes were blamed for the extinction of Tasmanian Tigers and Tasmanian Devils on mainland Australia, but scientists found that humans and changing climate were also responsible.
- The world's longest fence (5,614 km) was built in the 1880s to keep Dingoes out of south-eastern Australia because they killed sheep.
- Dingoes are protected in some places, but not in others.
- Pure Dingoes are declining because they are breeding with domestic dogs.

## Fast Facts

- 106–148 cm (includes tail 25–37 cm)
- 44–63 cm
- 11–22 kg (M larger)
- up to 10 y, 15+ y (captivity)
- 1–10, av 5 pups (1 litter)
- av 20–80 km²

# WETLANDS & WATERWAYS

**Freshwater lakes, ponds, billabongs, swamps and bogs, rivers and creeks, including their floodplains and riparian vegetation, and river mouths (estuaries) that are saltier**

Australia's wetlands and waterways can be still or flowing, fresh or salty. Some are permanently wet and others are wet for only part of the year, or in some years only. Some are seepages or springs from groundwater.

Rivers in the central arid zone rarely flow, but may after storms, when large areas can flood and form temporary wetlands. Tropical northern rivers usually flood each wet season, which fills up the billabongs and swamps on the floodplains. Many wetlands of south-eastern and south-western regions of Australia depend on winter rains and become dry in drought years.

Franklin–Gordon Wild Rivers NP (Tasmania)

Innamincka Regional Reserve (South Australia)

Bowling Green Bay NP (Queensland)

Kakadu NP (Northern Territory)

Snowy River NP (Victoria)

Oxley Wild Rivers NP (New South Wales)

Murray River NP (South Australia)

Inland in south-eastern Australia, the river system called the Murray–Darling Basin provides water for the landscape and fills many swamps, billabongs and lakes that are breeding grounds to huge flocks of birds. Bogs are common in the Snowy Mountains of NSW.

Riparian vegetation grows in the strip along the banks of rivers or at the edges of wetlands, and is a barrier between the water and the habitat next to it. Along with the water, riparian plants serve an important role in the health of aquatic ecosystems and their wildlife.

These national parks have examples of wetlands and waterways where the animals in this section occur. The animals may also occur in other habitats and in other national parks.

# Murray Cod
*Maccullochella peelii*

● Murray River NP

## Q&A

### What is it?
Australia's largest and longest living freshwater fish. It has a large mouth, a scooped head, mottled green patterning on the body and a creamy-white underside.

### Where does it live?
Within the Murray–Darling river system in south-eastern Australia, where it lives in lowland rivers and clear mountain streams. It likes the cover of submerged logs (snags) or rocks.

### What's its life like?
Apex predators, Murray Cod feed mainly on other fish, but also eat yabbies, mussels, turtles and frogs. They can take water dragons and birds at the surface. They can migrate upstream for 120 km to spawn before returning to their home snags. They breed in spring to early summer, when water temperatures are above 15° C. More than one spawning may occur in a season. Males invite females to lay their sticky eggs at nest sites on the surface of snags or rocks. Males guard the eggs and then the newly hatched larvae for about a week until they drift down river. This fish is bred in hatcheries and released into some rivers.

## interesting info

- Commercial fishing of Murray Cod is now banned but there are still many dangers to this fish, such as too much recreational fishing and the clearing of snags in rivers.
- Dams and weirs are also a problem because Murray Cod may not be able to migrate upstream to spawn. And when water is released from dams in the breeding season, Murray Cod larvae may be washed away by the fast-moving water.
- Non-native fish like European Carp and Redfin may eat and compete with Murray Cod juveniles and spread disease and parasites.

## Fast Facts
- 80–100 cm (max 180 cm)
- up to 100 kg (max 113 kg)
- up to 50 y or more
- 10,000–130,000 eggs (in each spawning)

# Freshwater Crocodile
*Crocodylus johnstoni*

• Kakadu NP

## Q&A

**What is it?**
A crocodile with a long and narrow snout with needle-sharp teeth. It's much smaller than its saltwater relative, the Saltie. It's also called a Freshie.

**Where does it live?**
In the tropical fresh waters of northern Australia, usually in areas where Saltwater Crocodiles don't live. However, the Freshie can tolerate salty water and the two species are occasionally neighbours in low-lying billabongs near the tidal parts of rivers.

**What's its life like?**
A nocturnal ambush predator, it feeds on fish, turtles, frogs, birds, bats, water rats and insects. Its sharp teeth help to grip slippery prey. Over a short few weeks in the dry season, females lay eggs in holes on sandbars above the floodline. Incubation temperature influences the gender of hatchlings, with around 32° C producing more males, and a couple of degrees above or below 32° C producing more females. Over 70% of eggs are destroyed, mainly by predators like goannas, pigs, snakes and Dingoes that raid the undefended nests. Hatching occurs at the start of the wet season and hatchlings often chirp to alert females to carry them to water.

## interesting info

- When a crocodile's mouth is shut, the large lower canine tooth can be seen on the outside. This doesn't happen with alligators, which do not occur in Australia.
- Freshies may bite in self-defence but don't attack humans.
- Digestion is aided by gastroliths—stones swallowed on purpose to help grind up food.
- Freshies live mainly in fresh water but they have salt glands in the tongue to excrete excess salt.
- Once hunted for its skin, the Freshie is now protected. But many die in some places when they eat poisonous Cane Toads.

## Fast Facts

av 1.5 m, M up to 3 m

M 50–100 kg
F up to 40 kg

20–50 y

4–21 eggs

# Water Dragon
*Intellagama lesueurii*

- Oxley Wild Rivers NP
- Snowy River NP
- Bowling Green Bay NP

## Q&A

### What is it?
A large, semi-aquatic dragon with a tail that's about two thirds of its body length. The keeled tail is like an oar to help it swim. A row of spines runs from the head down the body and tail, giving it a prehistoric look. There are 2 subspecies: the Eastern Water Dragon (*I. l. lesueurii*) and the Gippsland Water Dragon (*I. l. howittii*).

### Where does it live?
In the vegetation alongside creeks, rivers and lakes on the east coast of Australia, including in urban areas of Canberra, Sydney and Brisbane. It's also found in tropical rainforests in the north and beside alpine streams in the south.

### What's its life like?
In cooler climates, Water Dragons hibernate in winter by digging a small hole under a log or rock and sealing the entrance. They emerge in warmer weather and often bask in the sun. Juvenile Water Dragons are insectivorous. Older dragons are omnivorous, eating fruit and flowers, as well as animals like insects, molluscs, frogs, yabbies, mice and cicadas in the tree tops. Predators include snakes, cats, foxes and dogs, while birds eat young dragons. Females lay eggs in a nest away from the river and the gender of hatchlings depends on the incubation temperature. Water Dragons communicate using signals like head bobbing, arm waving and licking.

Eastern

Gippsland

## Interesting info

- Most lizards use their jaws to catch prey, but this dragon uses its tongue.
- Water Dragons are powerful climbers and swimmers. If disturbed, Water Dragons drop from a branch into the water and can stay underwater for up to an hour.
- A large dominant male lives in a group with several females and juveniles.
- Males fight for territory using posturing, chasing, lunging and biting.
- Water Dragons have excellent vision and often perch on elevated sites like rocks, fence posts or stumps to look out for predators, prey, rivals or mates.

## Fast Facts

- 80–100 cm (body 24.5 cm, max 30.4 cm)
- 500–700 g (max 1 kg)
- 20 y, 28 y (captivity)
- 6–18 eggs

# Red-bellied Black Snake
## Pseudechis porphyriacus

○ Oxley Wild Rivers NP
○ Snowy River NP
○ Bowling Green Bay NP

## Q&A

### What is it?
A glossy black snake with a red and cream belly and red sides. The small head is barely distinguishable from its body. It's usually shy and not aggressive.

### Where does it live?
On the eastern coast of Australia in a variety of habitats but mostly among vegetation in moist areas near water bodies like dams, swamps, streams and billabongs. It's often seen basking beside water.

### What's its life like?
The Red-bellied Black Snake specialises in eating frogs. In the north, where it eats the poisonous Cane Toads, its numbers have decreased. When hunting for food in water, either its whole body or just the head is submerged. It can even swallow food whole underwater. This snake also searches on land for prey, eating reptiles, small mammals and snakes, including other Red-bellied Black Snakes. During the breeding season, males travel up to 1.2 km a day searching for females. The Red-bellied Black Snake gives birth to live young rather than laying eggs. Pregnant females often gather in small groups for added protection.

## interesting info

- The Red-bellied Black Snake is dangerously venomous, but its bite doesn't generally kill people.
- A snakelet's bite is as venomous as an adult's.
- During the day, the Red-bellied Black Snake keeps its body at an even temperature by moving between sunny and shady spots.
- When avoiding a predator, it can stay under water for around 20 minutes.
- While searching for females, males often rear up, hook their necks around each other and wrap their bodies around each other. Sometimes they may bite each other, but they're immune to their own venom.

## Fast Facts

- 1.5–2 m (max 2.5 m)
- up to 3.3+ kg
- up to 25 y
- 5–40 live young

# Pig-nosed Turtle
*Carettochelys insculpta*

● Kakadu NP

### What is it?
A large freshwater turtle with a pig-like snout and nostrils. It's more closely related to Asian, African and North American turtles than to any other Australian turtle species.

### Where does it live?
In freshwater rivers and lagoons of the NT. The Pig-nosed Turtle prefers still waters with riparian vegetation, sandy riverbeds, overhanging banks and submerged fallen trees.

### What's its life like?
Pig-nosed Turtles feed mainly on aquatic plants, fallen fruit and flowers, but also take insects, snails, crustaceans and carrion. The snout has sensory receptors to help this turtle find food in murky water or sand. Females breed twice every second year and congregate with other females prior to nesting in sandy river banks, well above the waterline. When the young are fully developed inside the eggs, they wait until the nests are flooded by the river or by heavy rain. Then they explode out of the nest at the same time, offering them safety in numbers on their way to the water. Monitor lizards sometimes raid nests before the turtle eggs hatch.

## interesting info

- The Pig-nosed Turtle was only 'discovered' in Australia in 1970.
- It has broad flippers like a sea turtle, each with two claws.
- Its shell is covered by soft-pitted skin and has no hard plates like other turtles.
- It pulls its neck straight back into the shell, while other Australian freshwater turtles pull their necks in sideways.
- It's greatest threats are loss of vegetation alongside rivers and trampling of nests by water buffaloes, as well as young turtles being eaten by predators.

## Fast Facts
- 40–70 cm (carapace only)
- up to 20–30 kg
- 17–38 y (captivity)
- av 10 eggs (2 clutches every 2 y)

# Eastern Long-necked Turtle
*Chelodina longicollis*

- ● Oxley Wild Rivers NP
- ● Snowy River NP
- ● Bowling Green Bay NP

## Q&A

**What is it?**
A turtle with a neck that's more than half as long as the carapace (top part of the shell). The under part of the shell (plastron) is very wide and has yellow scutes with black edges. Its feet are webbed and the front feet have four claws. It's also called the Snake-necked Turtle.

**Where does it live?**
In eastern Australia in coastal and inland waterways. It prefers slow-moving rivers and creeks, lagoons and swamps. It can also be seen wandering overland in search of new water bodies.

**What's its life like?**
The Eastern Long-necked Turtle is carnivorous, feeding on anything small enough to seize and swallow, like tadpoles, frogs, fish, crustaceans, worms, insects (including mosquito larvae) and carrion. An ambush hunter, it uses its long neck to strike in a snake-like manner while opening its mouth to suck in prey. Females lay eggs in nesting holes in sand or soil along the banks of rivers or wetlands, and incubation takes 3–5 months. Hatchlings have a red-orange plastron. Water rats, lizards and foxes often raid the turtles' nests, and fish and birds may eat hatchlings. During drought, Eastern Long-necks can aestivate by digging under mud, logs or foliage.

## interesting info

- In Australia there are turtles but no tortoises. Turtles live in or near water and have flippers or webbed feet, while tortoises live on land and have stumpy legs and feet with no webbing.
- Eastern Long-necked Turtles can spray smelly fluid at predators.
- When crossing roads while in search of water, the turtles can be hit by cars. Other threats are habitat change and the introduced pest turtle—the Red-eared Slider.
- Cracked and broken carapaces can sometimes be repaired with artificial materials like fibreglass.

## Fast Facts

- 21–26 cm (carapace only, F larger)
- up to 1.5 kg
- up to 40 y
- 2–24 eggs (1–3 clutches)

# Banjo Frog: Eastern and Western
*Limnodynastes dumerilii* and *Limnodynastes dorsalis*

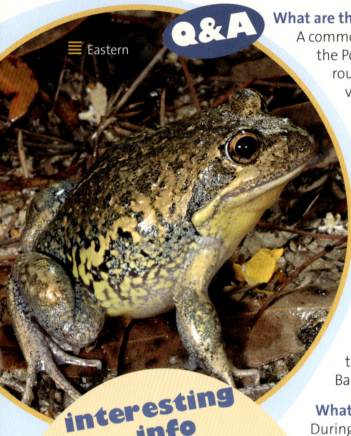
Eastern

## Q&A

### What are they?
A common burrowing frog, often called the Pobblebonk. Its back is often rough or warty and its colour varies from grey to green to black, with dark brown blotches. The underside is smooth and pale. It has a large tibial gland sticking out from the top of each hind leg and a broad black streak from the eye to the almost hidden tympanum (external ear). The Western Banjo has a red patch in the groin and a thin whitish-yellow stripe along the spine.

- Oxley Wild Rivers NP
- Snowy River NP
- Murray River NP

### Where do they live?
Usually near still, permanent water bodies like ponds, dams and lakes, in a variety of habitats, such as woodlands, grasslands and forests, but not in extremely arid areas. The Eastern may also breed in streams. Eastern Banjos occur throughout the south-eastern corner of Australia and Western Banjos throughout the south-western corner.

### What are their lives like?
During dry times and during the day, Banjo Frogs burrow underground. After rain, they congregate on the surface in large numbers and, in spring and summer, mass spawning occurs. Using their forefeet to mix air and water with the eggs, females make large frothy foam rafts (12–18 cm in diameter) that float on the water surface and help protect the eggs from predators. Tadpoles can be up to 9 cm long, longer than adult frogs. Depending on the temperature, the tadpole stage can last 4–11 months (the cooler the place, the longer the time). Banjo Frogs eat mainly small insects like flies, as well as worms and spiders.

## interesting info

- The male Banjo makes a musical, explosive note—*bonk*—that sounds a bit like a banjo string being plucked. It has a large voice sac under the lower jaw that puffs out like a balloon with each call.
- Like most frog species, females don't call.
- Males can travel 1–3 km to reach a breeding site.
- The Banjo's feet have no toe pads or webbing, just long, skinny toes.
- It digs with its hind feet, going backwards into its burrow.

## Fast Facts
- 5–8.5 cm (av 6–7 cm)
- 65 g
- 10 y
- up to 4,000 eggs

Western

# Black Swan
*Cygnus atratus*

Q&A

- Kakadu NP
- Bowling Green Bay NP
- Innamincka Regional Reserve
- Snowy River NP
- Franklin-Gordon Wild Rivers NP
- Murray River NP

### What is it?
A large powerful waterbird and the world's only black swan. It has a red bill. Its white flight feathers only show while flying. The long neck is curved like an 'S'.

### Where does it live?
On large open permanent wetlands with lots of aquatic plants. Black Swans can live on the fresh waters of lakes and swamps, as well as on the brackish waters of estuaries and bays.

### What's its life like?
Black Swans are often nomadic, moving in response to rainfall and food. They mostly fly at night. Males and females pair up for life but females may also mate with other males. The pair builds a large untidy nest (up to 1.5 m wide and 1 m high) from reeds and grasses on islands or floating on water. Both parents share in incubating the eggs and raising chicks, which takes 6–9 months. Chicks feed and swim as soon as they hatch. The Black Swan is herbivorous, eating plants in water or on land. It feeds standing or swimming, often up-ending and plunging its head and neck deep under the water.

- At night, flying swans can be heard making a musical, trumpet-like sound.
- This bird needs a stretch of 40 m of water to take off.
- After breeding, it moults, losing its flight feathers, so it can't fly for about a month and has to stay on open water for safety.
- A male swan is called a 'cob', the female a 'pen' and the young a 'cygnet'.
- It's very unusual to see cygnets travelling on the back of a Black Swan, but it's common among white swans.

## Fast Facts
- 100–142 cm
- 160–200 cm
- 4–9 kg
- up to 40 y
- 4–8 eggs

# Australian Wood Duck
*Chenonetta jubata*

- Bowling Green Bay NP
- Innamincka Regional Reserve
- Oxley Wild Rivers NP
- Snowy River NP
- Franklin-Gordon Wild Rivers NP

## Q&A

### What is it?
A brown-necked duck with two black stripes along the back. The male has a small black 'mane' and the female has a pale stripe above and below each eye. Its long neck and legs make it look like a small goose and it's also called the Maned Goose.

### Where does it live?
Near water in open grasslands and woodlands, wetlands, flooded pastures, farm dams and around ponds and lakes in urban parks.

### What's its life like?
Australian Wood Ducks occur in small flocks, and males and females mate for life. They make a nest from duck down in a tree hollow above or near water. The female incubates the eggs while the male stands guard. A few days after hatching, the ducklings leap to the ground, following their parents to water. Both parents look after the young for a month after they fledge. This duck is a grazer, eating grasses, herbs, grains and insects. Like other ducks, it can't digest bread. Better adapted to walking than swimming, it prefers to forage on land or dabble at the water's edge rather than being out on open water.

## Interesting info

- Male ducks are called 'drakes' and females are called 'hens'.
- The Australian Wood Duck is a 'dabbling duck', which means it feeds at the water surface rather than dives underwater for food.
- Australian Wood Ducks can fly well, but fly low and slowly.
- Like many ducks, it has a coloured patch on its wings that it uses in courtship to signal to other ducks.
- Hunters are allowed to kill Australian Wood Ducks in several states. In farming areas in WA, it is officially called a pest.

## Fast Facts
- 44–60 cm
- 78–80 cm
- 662–984 g
- unknown
- 8–18 eggs (av 10)

# Black-necked Stork
*Ephippiorhynchus asiaticus*

- Kakadu NP
- Bowling Green Bay NP

## Q&A

### What is it?
Australia's largest wading bird and only stork. It has extremely long red legs, a long glossy black bill and a huge wingspan. The male and female look alike, except the male's eyes are black and the female's eyes are yellow. It's often called the Jabiru.

### Where does it live?
In tropical and subtropical northern and eastern Australia in coastal habitats, such as mangroves and tidal mudflats, and subcoastal habitats like river floodplains and freshwater wetlands.

### What's its life like?
The Black-necked Stork strides through the water, probing and jabbing with its partly open bill to catch fish, frogs or invertebrates. It is strongly territorial when feeding and will fend off other waterbirds. The male and the female probably mate for life. They build a large platform-like nest of 1–2 m out of sticks and water plants, in secretive sites high up in isolated trees that are close to water. They often use the same nest year after year. The parents regurgitate food to feed the chicks in the nest. Usually only one chick survives. The survival of more chicks is closely linked to good rainfall and food supply.

## interesting info

- The Black-necked Stork has no voice box. It communicates by clapping its bills together.
- It has an interesting courtship dance in which the birds face each other, touch their fluttering wing tips and then clatter their bills together.
- The parents take turns at the nest and perform a greeting display when they change over.
- The Jabiru is seen mainly as single birds, pairs or small family groups.
- It's threatened in many places by habitat destruction, draining of wetlands and flying into power lines (which can cut off their large wings).

## Fast Facts

-  1.1–1.5 m
- 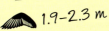 1.9–2.3 m
-  4.1 kg
- 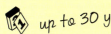 up to 30 y
-  2–4 eggs

# Purple Swamphen
*Porphyrio porphyrio*

- Kakadu NP
- Bowling Green Bay NP
- Innamincka Regional Reserve
- Snowy River NP
- Franklin-Gordon Wild Rivers NP
- Murray River NP

### What is it?
A large waterhen (or rail) with very long toes and a heavy red bill and forehead shield.

### Where does it live?
On the edges of freshwater lakes, marshes and streams in high rainfall areas. It also occurs in parks and gardens with ponds, where it particularly likes walking over waterlilies.

### What's its life like?
Purple Swamphens are noisy and, at times, aggressive birds that fly to escape danger. They're good swimmers, despite not having webbed feet, and roost on vegetation over water. In the west, they form mating pairs but, in the east, they form cooperative breeding groups. The group makes a nest from woven reeds and rushes, often on floating debris. Several females lay eggs in the nest, which may have up to 12 eggs, and the group shares incubation duties. The Purple Swamphen eats reed shoots, fish, frogs and insects. It also steals other birds' eggs and may eat ducklings. It serves an important ecological role as an apex predator of marsh invertebrates.

## Interesting info

- As the Purple Swamphen walks, it flicks its tail up and down, showing a bright white rump.
- It flies awkwardly with legs dangling and sometimes crash-lands into water or vegetation.
- It often takes food up to its bill, grasped in its long toes, rather than eating it on the ground.
- The male has an elaborate courtship display, holding reeds in his bill and bowing to the female with loud chuckles. A single female may mate with several males and lay more than one clutch per season.

## Fast Facts
- 44–50 cm
- 70–88 cm
- 725–1,050 g
- 6+ y
- 3–6 eggs (1–2 clutches)

# Platypus
## Ornithorhynchus anatinus

- Bowling Green Bay NP
- Oxley Wild Rivers NP
- Snowy River NP
- Franklin-Gordon Wild Rivers NP

### What is it?
One of the oddest and oldest living animals—an egg-laying mammal (a monotreme). The Platypus has a duck-like bill, clawed and webbed feet, and a flattened beaver-like body and tail. Its size varies greatly by location.

### Where does it live?
In and beside flowing and still fresh waters like streams, rivers, billabongs and lakes, from snowy mountain tops to the coast in eastern Australia, from the tropics to Tasmania.

### What's its life like?
Mainly nocturnal, the Platypus spends 6–18 hours a day in water. Its thick-layered fur keeps it warm, and dries quickly on land. Its soft rubbery bill has thousands of electroreceptors that detect tiny electromagnetic fields produced when aquatic invertebrates move. Underwater, with eyes and ears closed, the sensitive bill sifts the river bed to find prey. Platypuses store food in cheek pouches for chewing later while at the surface. Adults don't have teeth and chew with keratin grinding plates (babies have teeth). They're solitary and live in burrows in river banks. Females build nesting burrows (up to 30 m long), suckling their young there for 4 months.

## interesting info

- The female doesn't have a pouch. She curls up, holding the eggs between her belly and tail. The eggs hatch after 10 days.
- Females don't have teats, but milk oozes from patches of belly skin and 'platypups' suck it off the mothers' fur.
- A Platypus swims with webbed forefeet, with the hind feet and tail acting as rudders.
- Dives for food usually last up to 2 minutes.
- Males have a venomous spur on each ankle that's extremely painful to humans.
- Platypuses can drown in traps for fish and yabbies. Foxes may also kill them.

## Fast Facts

M 40–64 cm
F 37–55 cm

M 0.8–3.2 kg
F 0.6–1.8 kg

up to 21 y

av 2 eggs

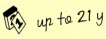
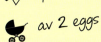

# Australian Water Rat
*Hydromys chrysogaster*

### Q&A

**What is it?**
A rabbit-sized, semi-aquatic native rodent, with a streamlined body for swimming. It has a flattened head and a blunt nose; broad, webbed hind feet; waterproof fur; a tail that acts as a rudder; and long whiskers that sense prey underwater. The last third of the tail has white fur. Its common (and Aboriginal) name is Rakali.

- Kakadu NP
- Bowling Green Bay NP
- Innamincka Regional Reserve
- Oxley Wild Rivers NP
- Snowy River NP
- Franklin-Gordon Wild Rivers NP
- Murray River NP

**Where does it live?**
In burrows (with a hidden entrance) on the banks of permanent bodies of fresh or brackish water, like rivers, lakes, harbours (including Sydney Harbour) and estuaries. It prefers slow flowing or still waters. It has also been found in the suburbs hundreds of metres from water and on smaller offshore islands.

**What's its life like?**
Unlike other native rodents, the Rakali's not entirely nocturnal. It's most active at sunset but may forage in the day. It's an opportunistic predator, foraging underwater for anything suitable it finds—aquatic insects, fish, crustaceans, molluscs, frogs, birds, reptiles and carrion. It dives among vegetation along shorelines and around sunken logs. It eats its catch on a favourite feeding platform, leaving tell-tale remains. Highly territorial, it fights to establish dominance. Nests are made at the end of tunnels in banks or in logs. Mothers suckle their young for 4 weeks. When the young rats' fur becomes waterproof at 8 weeks, they become independent. Predators include snakes, large fish, raptors, foxes and cats.

### interesting info

- The Rakali is one of only two Australian mammals living in fresh water—the other is the Platypus.
- One quarter of Australian native mammals are rodent species (rats and mice).
- The Rakali's waterproof fur is dark on top and gold on the belly. It moults its fur twice a year.
- It was hunted for its soft fur in the 1930s.
- In the NT, it can safely eat the poisonous Cane Toads.
- The Rakali helps to control the introduced pest, the Black Rat, near waterways.

### Fast Facts

- 46–70 cm (includes tail 23–33 cm)
- max 1.3 kg; M av 755 g  F av 606 g
- 3–4 y
- 3–5 (1–5 litters, av 2)
- 1–4 km of waterway

# COASTS, OCEANS & ISLANDS

**Coastal margins, estuaries, saltmarshes, mangroves, dunes, beaches, seagrasses, oceans and offshore islands, from tropical to polar regions**

Australia is an island continent and its combined coastline is over 60,000 km long, including the coastlines of the many nearby islands. There are 8,222 islands—the largest is Tasmania and one of the most famous is Lord Howe Island. Many islands are now sanctuaries that protect habitats for species that are threatened or extinct on the mainland.

The coastline of the mainland is about 37,000 km. The coastal zone includes 85% of Australia's population, 10,685 beaches and around 1,000 estuaries, which are important breeding areas for fish. The coast and estuaries form an important transition zone between the land and the sea. This zone has many other biodiverse habitats, like saltmarshes, mangroves, mud flats, seagrasses, rocky reefs and coral reefs.

Cape Le Grand NP (Western Australia)

Ningaloo Marine Park (Western Australia)

Cape Range NP (Western Australia)

Great Barrier Reef Marine Park (Queensland)

Flinders Chase NP (South Australia)

Port Campbell NP (Victoria)

Coorong NP (South Australia)

Royal NP (New South Wales)

Garig Gunak Barlu National Park (Northern Territory)

Australia's coast borders three great ocean systems: the Pacific Ocean in the east, the Indian Ocean in the west, and the Southern Ocean along the southern coast. Along the northern coast, the Timor Sea, Arafura Sea and the Torres Strait separate Australia from neighbouring countries.

Australia's marine environment has all five of the world's oceanic temperature zones, from tropical to polar; two world-famous coral reef systems (in the north-east and north-west); and high levels of biodiversity in the south, found nowhere else in the world.

These national parks have examples of coasts, oceans and islands where the animals in this section occur. The animals may also occur in other habitats and in other national parks.

# Whale Shark
*Rhincodon typus*

- Great Barrier Reef MP
- Ningaloo MP
- Cape Range NP

### What is it?
A large migratory oceanic fish (it's not a whale), and the largest shark and non-mammalian vertebrate animal in the world. It has a broad square head, a wide mouth (up to 1.5 m) and ridgelines down the back. Its blue-grey skin is patterned with bright white spots and lines on top, and its belly is white, providing camouflage.

### Where does it live?
In warm tropical waters worldwide, along coasts and out at sea. In Australian waters, teenage males (3–8 m) and some adults (12 m) visit the west coast around Ningaloo Marine Park from March to July. Sightings along the east coast are much rarer. They also appear off Christmas Island to feed on the annual red crab spawning.

### What's its life like?
Whale Sharks are solitary but feed in groups seasonally where plankton blooms occur. This shark swims slowly (5 km/hr) and acts like a filter-feeding whale, swimming open-mouthed, filtering plankton and krill through large gill slits. The female is larger than the male and lays eggs inside her body. The young hatch inside and feed off egg yolk. The pups are born fully formed at 40–60 cm long. It's still unknown where mating and pupping occurs. Whale Sharks can dive to great depths (down to 1,750 m). They are threatened by fisheries outside Australia, being hit by boats, habitat degradation and predatory sharks.

## Fast Facts
- 12–14 m (max 18 m)
- 15–20 tonnes (max 34 tonnes)
- up to 65–150 y (estimated)
- up to 300 eggs (many pups born over a long period)

## interesting info
- **The Whale Shark has one of the thickest skins of any animal— up to 14 cm.**
- Females can store sperm for long periods after mating. A female that was caught had 300 young inside, all at different stages of development, from eggs to ready-to-birth pups.
- **At Ningaloo Marine Park people can snorkel alongside Whale Sharks.**
- Whale Sharks are protected in only 13 of the 130 countries they visit.
- **Bits of plastic have been found in Whale Shark poo.**

# Saltwater Crocodile
*Crocodylus porosus*

- Great Barrier Reef MP
- Garig Gunak Barlu NP

## Q&A

### What is it?
A prehistoric species and the world's largest living reptile, with the strongest bite of any animal. It's also called a Saltie or Estuarine Crocodile. Its head and back have 'armour' made up of bony plates, bumps and ridges (called osteoderms) covered by thick skin. Juveniles are pale yellow with black stripes and spots.

### Where does it live?
In the less salty waters of tropical mangrove swamps, river estuaries and coastal lagoons. Salties can also live in freshwater. They can be found up to several hundred kilometres inland from the coast, and out to sea on occasion. They are strong swimmers and at sea they can travel long distances (up to 1,000 km), often aided by floating and riding on ocean currents.

### What's its life like?
An apex predator, the Saltie usually hunts at night. Its eyes, ears and nostrils sit on top of the head, with the rest of its body hidden below the water's surface. The powerful tail helps it leap from the water to attack and perform 'death rolls' on prey. A large adult can stay under water for up to 2 hours. Juveniles eat insects, crustaceans, fish and reptiles, while adults take fish, birds, sharks and mammals, including humans. Pairs defend their nesting territory and nest, a mound made from mud and vegetation. When newly hatched Salties cry out, the mother carries them to the water and stays with them for several months.

## Fast Facts
- 3–5 m (max 6.2 m)
- 400–1,000 kg (max 1,075 kg)
- 70+ y
- av 50 eggs (up to 90)

## Interesting info
- There are special glands on the Saltie's tongue that excrete salt. This is why these crocodiles can survive in saltwater.
- Only a few hatchlings (1%) grow to be adults.
- The Saltie can swim three times faster than the fastest human.
- It has 66 teeth. When a tooth falls out, another one grows. This can happen many times.
- Saltwater Crocodiles are protected in Australia, but there are farms that breed them for meat and leather.

# Green Turtle
*Chelonia mydas*

## Q&A

**What is it?**
The largest hard-shelled sea turtle, with large paddle-like flippers. The Green Turtle has green skin, but its shell is brown or olive.

**Where does it live?**
In shallow coastal waters and marine lagoons with lush seagrass beds. The male Green Turtle never leaves the sea, but the female lays her eggs on a tropical or subtropical beach, mainly along the Queensland coast. There are at least seven regional populations that nest in different locations of coastal northern Australia.

**What's its life like?**
Juveniles are carnivorous while adults eat mainly seagrass and seaweed, and occasionally jellyfish. Green Turtles mate in the sea near the nesting beach and lay eggs over late spring and summer. After hatchlings dig themselves out of the nest, they have to survive predators like crabs and seabirds on their journey to the sea. If they make it, and don't get eaten by a fish or shark, they get swept away by ocean currents and live in deeper waters of the open ocean for 5–10 years. Main threats to adult Green Turtles include hunting by people, sharks, pollution (chemical and plastic), beach habitat loss and getting tangled in fishing nets.

- Great Barrier Reef MP
- Cape Range NP
- Ningaloo MP
- Garig Gunak Barlu NP

## interesting info

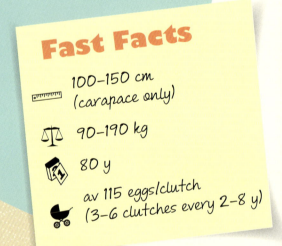

**Fast Facts**
- 100–150 cm (carapace only)
- 90–190 kg
- 80 y
- av 115 eggs/clutch (3–6 clutches every 2–8 y)

- Green Turtles get their water from seawater. The salt comes out of special glands next to their eyes—which makes them look like they're crying.
- The female scoops out a nest in the sand in which to lay her eggs. She lays them on the same beach where she was hatched many years before.
- Nest sites are often hundreds of kilometres from feeding grounds but all sea turtles have excellent navigation skills.
- Like all sea turtles, the gender of Green Turtle hatchlings depends on incubation temperature.
- In Australia, sea turtles are protected.

# Flatback Turtle
*Natator depressus*

## Q&A

**What is it?**
A sea turtle that has a flat carapace (upper shell) with turned up edges, covered by thick, olive-grey fleshy skin. Its plastron (lower shell or underside) is white.

**Where does it live?**
Over the continental shelf of Australia, in shallow bays and lagoons with seagrass beds, and around coral reefs. The Flatback Turtle nests only on beaches in northern Australia.

**What's its life like?**
Flatbacks feed on soft-bodied prey like sea cucumbers, soft corals and jellyfish. Every 1–3 years, females nest on the beach of their hatching. Nests are often raided by Dingoes, goannas, foxes and pigs. Hatchlings are 6 cm long, the largest of any sea turtle. On their way to the ocean, only safety in numbers saves them from predators like birds and crabs. Light reflected off the water guides females to the beach to lay their eggs, but artificial lights on land can confuse the turtles, causing them to go in the wrong direction. Other threats include predation, net entanglement, eating plastic rubbish, being struck by boats and global warming.

- Great Barrier Reef MP
- Garig Gunak Barlu NP

## Interesting info

- Sea turtles can't breathe underwater, but they can rest underwater for hours because they are good at holding their breath.
- Sea turtles can't pull their head into their shell.
- Unlike other sea turtles, Flatback juveniles don't spend years out in the open ocean. They stay in the shallower waters near the coast.
- In 1952, thousands of Flatback and Green Turtles died due to the first nuclear bomb test in Australia, which occurred off north-western WA.

## Fast Facts
- 88–96 cm (carapace only)
- up to 90 kg
- 50–80 y
- av 54 eggs/clutch (1–3 clutches every 1–3 y)

# Little Penguin
*Eudyptula minor*

## Q&A

**What is it?**
A seabird that can't fly and the smallest of all penguin species. It's also called the Little Blue Penguin or the Fairy Penguin.

**Where does it live?**
On the southern coast of Australia and its offshore islands. Bass Strait (between Victoria and Tasmania) has 60% of the Little Penguin breeding population.

**What's its life like?**
At sea, the Little Penguin forages for food up to 100 km from the coast, but stays within 30 km during the chick-rearing season. It breeds in colonies and its nesting burrow is made in sand or soil, or under rocks or vegetation. Both males and females rear the chicks. Parents come ashore at dusk in groups to feed the chicks. Favourite foods are small fish and squid. It can dive as deep as 70 m for food, but usually dives 2–30 m. Predators at sea include seals and sea-eagles. Other threats are habitat loss, feral animals (like cats, foxes and dogs), fire, getting tangled in plastic and oil spills.

- Royal NP
- Port Campbell NP
- Coorong NP
- Flinders Chase NP
- Cape Le Grand NP

## interesting info

- Little Penguins are the only penguins that nest on the Australian coast and islands.
- They swim faster than a human, using their flippers as propellers and the tail and webbed feet as rudders. On land, they waddle slowly on short legs.
- This penguin can dive 200–1,300 times a day.
- It waterproofs its feathers by rubbing in drops of oil from a gland above its tail and by preening.
- It uses many different calls to communicate.
- On Middle Island (near Warrnambool, Vic), maremma sheepdogs protect the penguin colony from foxes.

**Fast Facts**
- 40–45 cm
- 33 cm
- M 1.5 kg, F 1 kg
- up to 25 y
- 2 eggs

# Silver Gull
*Chroicocephalus novaehollandiae*

## Q&A

**What is it?**
A seabird with a white head, tail and underparts, a silver-grey back and black-tipped wings. The red bill of the adult Silver Gull, or Seagull, gets brighter with age. Juveniles have a dark bill and a mottled brown pattern on the wings.

**Where does it live?**
Along the entire coast, on offshore islands, and far inland near wetlands and waterways. Seagulls especially occur where people live. They may flock around fishing boats in high numbers as they leave or return to the coast but they don't often go far out to sea.

**What's its life like?**
Silver Gulls are successful scavengers that pester people for food and feed at rubbish dumps. They also eat fish, worms, crustaceans and insects, turtle hatchlings and the eggs and young of other seabirds. They form flocks, especially where there's food, on land or on water. Since the 1950s, their numbers have exploded, causing overcrowding on some breeding islands. As a result, other seabirds, like terns, are suffering. Predators of the Silver Gull include birds-of-prey and snakes. It nests in large colonies on offshore islands or headlands. The nest is a saucer made out of seaweed and grass. Both parents share in nest building, egg incubation and feeding the chicks.

- Great Barrier Reef MP
- Royal NP
- Port Campbell NP
- Coorong NP
- Flinders Chase NP
- Cape Le Grand NP
- Cape Range NP
- Ningaloo MP
- Garig Gunak Barlu NP

## interesting info

- The Silver Gull has a sharp voice and makes a rumbly *korr* sound or a more screeching *karr-karr-karr* sound.
- It's easy to tell the Silver Gull apart from the two other Australian gulls—the Pacific Gull and the Kelp Gull. The Silver Gull is smaller and a different colour.
- All gulls, including the Silver Gull, are protected under Australia's national environment law, the Environment Protection and Biodiversity Conservation Act (EPBC Act).
- Silver Gulls seem to really like cricket grounds.

## Fast Facts

- 36-45 cm
- 91-96 cm
- 265-315 g
- 10-28 y
- 1-3 eggs (2 clutches)

# Australian Pelican
*Pelecanus conspicillatus*

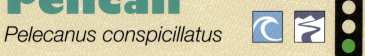

## Q&A

**What is it?**
A huge, mostly white bird with black wings and a large pink bill and bill-pouch.

**Where does it live?**
From the coast to far inland waters on large expanses of shallow water (fresh or salty), such as lakes, billabongs, rivers, estuaries and coastal lagoons.

**What's its life like?**
The Australian Pelican migrates to where there's food. It feeds by plunge-diving while on the water's surface, eating fish, shrimp or yabbies. It also preys on smaller birds and bird eggs. Pelicans often forage in groups, working cooperatively to herd fish. The sensitive bill helps find food in murky water and the bill-pouch acts like a fishing net. It breeds in colonies, with up to 40,000 individuals grouping on islands, near lakes or on secluded beaches. These places often have little shade, but pelicans can cool themselves by stretching open and rippling the bill-pouch. During courtship displays, the bill and pouch change colour to red-orange, yellow and blue.

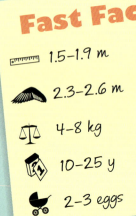

### Fast Facts
- 1.5–1.9 m
- 2.3–2.6 m
- 4–8 kg
- 10–25 y
- 2–3 eggs

- ○ Royal NP
- ○ Port Campbell NP
- ○ Coorong NP
- ○ Flinders Chase NP
- ○ Cape Le Grand NP
- ○ Cape Range NP
- ○ Ningaloo MP
- ○ Garig Gunak Barlu NP
- ○ Great Barrier Reef MP

## interesting info

- The Australian Pelican has the largest bill (50 cm) of any bird in the world.
- It sometimes steals food (this is called kleptoparasitism) from other seabirds, like cormorants.
- Australian Pelicans can be in the air for 24 hours, covering thousands of kilometres, often flying in a single line or in a 'V' shape.
- They soar high (to 3,000 m or more), using thermal currents so they can travel long distances without using too much energy. This can help them find water in a large, dry landscape.

# White-bellied Sea-Eagle
*Haliaeetus leucogaster*

### What is it?
The second largest Australian raptor. The White-bellied Sea-Eagle is white and grey, with unfeathered legs and a white tail.

### Where does it live?
Mainly in or near coastal regions, although it can occur inland. It also inhabits some offshore islands, such as Kangaroo Island and the Bass Strait islands. It's often seen perched on a tall tree or soaring over waterways like estuaries, rivers and lakes.

### What's its life like?
This species is mostly sedentary and territorial, but inland it moves around as water bodies fill and dry up. Fish form half of its diet, which also includes turtles, sea snakes, water dragons, birds, mammals and carrion. It power-dives to seize a fish or waterbird from the water's surface. It can live in the same place as Wedge-tailed Eagles, but they don't compete for food as they have different diets. The White-bellied Sea-Eagle mates for life but finds a new mate if one dies. Amazing aerial acrobatics are part of its courtship display. The large bowl-shaped nest is made of twigs and grass or seaweed. Usually only one chick survives.

- Great Barrier Reef MP
- Royal NP
- Port Campbell NP
- Coorong NP
- Flinders Chase NP
- Cape Le Grand NP
- Cape Range NP
- Ningaloo MP
- Garig Gunak Barlu NP

## Fast Facts
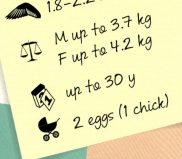

- 70–90 cm
- 1.8–2.2 m
- M up to 3.7 kg / F up to 4.2 kg
- up to 30 y
- 2 eggs (1 chick)

## interesting info
- The White-bellied Sea-Eagle nests in tall trees or on coastal cliffs, or on the ground on islands, at least 2 km from other pairs.
- On sunny days, it flies over water in such a clever way as to avoid casting a shadow and alerting its prey.
- A skilled hunter, it attacks prey up to the size of a swan and can eat while it's flying. It uses only one foot to seize prey.
- White-bellied Sea-Eagle numbers are declining due to the removal of large trees needed for nesting.

# Hooded Plover
*Thinornis rubricollis*

- Port Campbell NP
- Coorong NP
- Flinders Chase NP
- Cape Le Grand NP

### What is it?
A small ground-dwelling shore bird with a black hood and throat and a white rear collar. The Hooded Plover is endangered in the east, but not in the west. It's also called the Hooded Dotterel or Hoodie.

### Where does it live?
On broad, sandy ocean beaches on the southern mainland and in Tasmania, and around the mouths of rivers (estuaries) that have wide sandy areas. Hooded Plovers also inhabit inland salt lakes in southern WA.

### What's its life like?
Highly sedentary, it occurs in pairs or in small groups near the water's edge. It eats bivalve shells, worms and sandhoppers, which it digs out of the sand or seaweed. Females lay speckled eggs from August to March—the period when people use beaches the most. Pairs defend their nests in the sand above the high water mark, often in dunes. Eggs don't have much protection as the nest is just a shallow scrape in the sand, lined with pebbles and seaweed. Eggs incubate for 30 days, but chicks can't fly for several weeks, making them vulnerable to many threats for at least 2 months.

**Fast Facts**
- 19–23 cm
- 23–44 cm
- 90–100 g
- 10–15 y
- 1–4 eggs (av 2)

## interesting info

- The Hooded Plover was voted the third favourite Australian bird in a national survey, after the Superb Fairy-wren and the Australian Magpie.
- Populations of Hooded Plovers are declining because not many chicks survive. This is because high seas can wash away eggs and chicks, predators can take eggs and chicks, and people, dogs and vehicles can trample nests on beaches.
- Signs are put up on beaches to warn people not to disturb the Hooded Plovers.

# Dugong
*Dugong dugon*

## Q&A

### What is it?
A round-bodied, herbivorous marine mammal that's also called a Sea Cow. It has no dorsal fin or hind fins and adult males have small tusks.

### Where does it live?
Australia has the largest populations of Dugongs in the world. Here it occurs in shallow warm tropical and subtropical waters around the northern coast from Shark Bay, WA, to Moreton Bay, Qld. It prefers calm waters that have seagrass meadows (usually less than 15 m deep). It spends most of its time in depths of 1.5–3 m.

### What's its life like?
The Dugong feeds on seagrass and invertebrates, moving large distances to find new meadows. Its body is adapted for eating on the seabed, with a heavy skeleton to weigh it down, a downwards-turned snout and mouth, a flexible upper lip for grabbing the seagrass and horny pads on the jaws to grind it up. Digestion of the plant fibre occurs in the long large intestine (up to 25 m long). Dugongs may live alone or in large herds. After a pregnancy of 12–14 months, females give birth in very shallow water to avoid sharks. The young suckle for up to 18 months but can eat seagrass within weeks of birth.

- Great Barrier Reef MP
- Cape Range NP
- Ningaloo MP
- Garig Gunak Barlu NP

## Fast Facts
- 2.2–3.3 m
- 250–570 kg
- up to 73 y
- 1 calf every 2.5–7 y

## interesting info
- **Dugongs evolved from four-legged land mammals over 60 million years ago.**
- Dugongs can move at speeds of up to 22 km/hr because of their large triangular tail flukes. Their paddle-like forelimbs help them to 'walk' on the seabed.
- **The nostrils take in air above the water and close when the Dugong goes under the water.**
- Dugongs dive about 12 times/hr and the average dive time is 2.7 minutes.
- **Dugongs are a favourite food for Indigenous Australians in northern Australia.**
- Seeing Dugongs might have led sailors to believe in mermaids.

# Whale: Humpback & Southern Right
*Megaptera novaeangliae* and *Eubalaena australis*

Southern Right | Humpback

■ Humpback

- Great Barrier Reef MP
- Royal NP
- Port Campbell NP
- Flinders Chase NP
- Cape Le Grand NP
- Cape Range NP
- Ningaloo MP
- Coorong NP

≡ Southern Right

## Q&A

**What are they?**
The two most commonly seen baleen whales off the Australian coast. Humpback Whales (HWs) are dark above and white below, with extremely long knobbly flippers, throat grooves, a small dorsal fin and serrated tail flukes. Southern Right Whales (SRWs) are black, often with white belly patches, no dorsal fin, white lumpy callosities (due to whale lice) on the head and no throat grooves. They have a V-shaped spray from their 'blow'.

**Where do they live?**
During summer, SRWs feed in the productive waters of the Southern Ocean and HWs in the seas around Antarctica. In winter, they migrate north to mate, give birth, rest and socialise. SRWs occur and breed in southern temperate waters of Australia, while HWs occur along the eastern and western coast, and breed in tropical and subtropical waters.

**What are their lives like?**
Their hundreds of baleen plates sieve tiny crustaceans from seawater—mainly krill for HWs and copepods for SRWs. HWs also round up schools of small fish by surrounding them with 'bubble nets'. Both whales consume up to 1.5 tonnes of food a day and accumulate blubber (fat) to sustain them on their annual migrations. They must breed in warmer seas and don't feed for up to 8 months. They travel individually or in small groups. Male HWs announce their arrival north by repeatedly singing a sophisticated song. HWs often leap from the water, rolling in mid-air (breaching) and tail slapping. SRWs may breach or float belly-up, and come closest to shore to calve.

## interesting info

- Whales evolved from a common ancestor 55 million years ago into two main types—baleen whales that filter-feed plankton, and toothed whales that feed on larger prey.
- HWs and SRWs can swim 15–20 km/hr and dive for 10–30 minutes underwater without breathing.
- Their 'blow' can be seen several km away.
- HWs have the longest migration of any mammal—up to 25,000 km.
- Both species have been hunted nearly to extinction but are now protected.
- Their close relative, the Blue Whale, is the largest species ever to appear on Earth.

**Fast Facts**

HW 13–18 m
SRW 13–18 m
(F larger for both)

HW 45 tonnes
SRW 40–80 tonnes

HW 50 y
SRW up to 80 y

1 calf (HW every 2 y, SRW 3–4 y)

# Bottlenose Dolphin: Common & Indo-Pacific
*Tursiops truncatus* and *Tursiops aduncus*

## Q&A

**What are they?**
Similar looking dolphins from a distance. The thick tail stock and tail fluke is the most muscular part of the body. The Indo-Pacific Bottlenose (IPB) is smaller, with a longer rostrum and, in warmer waters, it develops speckling on its body when an adult.

**Where do they live?**
Common Bottlenose (CB): worldwide, mainly in deeper offshore waters of the continental shelf and open ocean. IPB: in the Indian and western Pacific Oceans, particularly in shallower coastal waters. Both species occur in the temperate and tropical waters of Australia, with their distribution overlapping in some places.

**What are their lives like?**
CBs can form large transitory groups offshore of up to hundreds, while IPBs tend to form smaller, more stationary inshore groups of 1–30. All dolphins have excellent senses of sight, hearing, taste and touch. They use echolocation to navigate and catch prey (like fish), and use different sounds and body language to communicate with each other. Bottlenoses are very social and playful. They show cooperative behaviour when feeding, defending themselves and caring for young. The calf stays with its mother for about 5 years. Females and calves tend to group together while males form bonds and travel farther away as they get older.

*Common Bottlenose*

- Great Barrier Reef MP
- Royal NP
- Port Campbell NP
- Coorong NP
- Flinders Chase NP
- Cape Le Grand NP
- Cape Range NP
- Ningaloo MP
- Garig Gunak Barlu NP

■ Common Bottlenose
■ Indo-Pacific Bottlenose

## interesting info

- These dolphins can ride the wave off a ship's bow and can swim for short bursts at up to 40 km/hr.
- Dolphins need to be awake to breath (through the blowhole). So they don't drown, they rest with one half of the brain at a time.
- CBs can dive about 450 m underwater and hold their breath for up to 15 mins.
- Calves are born tail first. Mothers nudge them quickly to the surface to breathe.
- Bottlenose dolphins have large brains. Research shows they're self-aware, very intelligent and can understand language.

## Fast Facts

CB 2–4 m
IPB 2–2.8 m

CB M 500 kg, F 250 kg
IPB 230 kg

M up to 40–50 y
F up to 50–60 y

1 calf (every 3–6 y)

# Orca
*Orcinus orca*

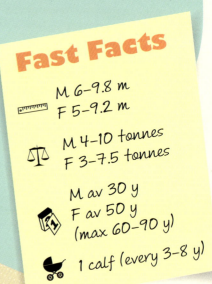

## Q&A

**What is it?**
The largest dolphin. It's black with a white patch behind the eye, and other white and grey patches on the body. The dorsal fin is up to 2 m tall in males. Individuals can be identified by the dorsal fin and patch patterns behind the dorsal fin. It's also called a Killer Whale (it's a toothed whale).

**Where does it live?**
In all oceans from the polar seas to the tropics. Orcas prefer colder and coastal waters.

**What's its life like?**
Orcas are apex predators in the world's oceans, with strong teeth and jaws and no natural predators. They're skilful pack hunters, organising attacks to round up schools of fish or to take down larger animals, like sharks or other whales. In Australian waters, prey includes Humpback Whales, Dugongs, dolphins, seals and fish. Orcas have complex social structures, such as pods, clans and communities that often include their mother. Orcas have excellent vision and hearing, and use echolocation to navigate and detect prey. Males usually breed with females from other pods to avoid interbreeding. Up to half of new-born calves die in their first 6 months.

- Great Barrier Reef MP
- Royal NP
- Port Campbell NP
- Flinders Chase NP
- Cape Le Grand NP
- Ningaloo MP

### Fast Facts
- M 6–9.8 m
- F 5–9.2 m
- M 4–10 tonnes
- F 3–7.5 tonnes
- M av 30 y
- F av 50 y (max 60–90 y)
- 1 calf (every 3–8 y)

## interesting info

- **Some believe that the Orca is the most intelligent of all whale and dolphin species.**
- Hunting techniques are often passed down generations of Orcas, like a form of 'culture'. Their 'language' (clicks, whistles, pulsed calls) is also passed down.
- **The Orca is one of the fastest marine mammals, reaching speeds of 56 km/hr.**
- In Eden, NSW, in the 1840s, Killer Whales worked cooperatively with human whale hunters to hunt other whales.
- **Dolphins first appeared 11 million years ago; there are now about 35 species around the world.**

# Australian Sea-lion
*Neophoca cinerea*

## Q&A

### What is it?
The only Australian sea-lion species. It has a bulky but streamlined body and torpedos through the water with large flippers. Its dog-like head has very long whiskers and small external ears. Females and juveniles are silver-grey. The much larger males are dark brown with a mane of whitish hair.

### Where does it live?
In cool temperate coastal waters off SA and WA where there are sandy and rocky coastlines. There are about 80 breeding sites on near-shore islands and several mainland sites. Most stay within 300 km of their breeding ground.

### What's its life like?
Australian Sea-lions rest and breed on sandy beaches and rocky shores. On land, they have a quadrupedal walk or a fast gallop. They're strong swimmers, using fore-flippers to swim, dive and leap out of the water onto the beach. At breeding time, dominant males have one or two females who they aggressively defend against other males. Females give birth on rocky platforms, sandy beaches, or saltbush-covered sand dunes. Pups have thick soft fur, begin to moult at 2 months, swim at 3 months and suckle for 15–18 months. Sea-lions feed on the ocean floor on squid, octopus, lobster and fish, and mothers return every couple of days to feed their pup.

- Flinders Chase NP
- Cape Le Grand NP
- Coorong NP

## Interesting info

- Australian Sea-lions dive 10–11 times/hr while feeding.
- The deepest recorded dive for a male is 250 m. The longest recorded time that a male has stayed underwater is 12 minutes.
- Sea-lion poo is rich in nutrients, which are important for rich coastal marine life.
- Males may kill pups. Females may adopt pups.
- After European settlement, sea-lions were heavily hunted, but hunting was stopped 40 years ago.
- Australian Sea-lions drown when they get tangled in fishing nets. Other dangers are rubbish in the seas, water pollution and predators like the Great White Shark.

## Fast Facts

- M 1.8–2.5 m
- F 1.3–1.85 m
- M 180–250 kg
- F 65–105 kg
- up to M 21 y, F 24 y
- 1 pup every 18 mo

# Australian Fur Seal

*Arctocephalus pusillus doriferus*

### What is it?
The largest and most common seal in Australia. It has a streamlined body, a rolled external ear and long whiskers. Adult males are much bigger than females and have massive necks and shoulders, large canine teeth and a mane of coarse hair.

### Where does it live?
In cool temperate coastal waters and on rocky coastlines and islands of south-eastern Australia. It spends most of the year at sea but is never far from land. There are about 10 breeding colonies of 500–1,500 on offshore rocky islands and isolated peninsulas, mostly in Bass Strait.

### What's its life like?
Australian Fur Seals forage on the floor of the continental shelf for squid, fish, octopus and lobster, vomiting up indigestible bits. They swim with up and down strokes of the webbed hind limbs, using large fore-flippers for propulsion. When breeding, bulls don't eat and they defend their territories of 60 m² with barking, roaring and posturing. Males only breed when they become territorial at 8–13 years, and stop when they're defeated 3–6 years later. Huge numbers of females and juveniles occur at pupping sites. Females return weekly from foraging to suckle their pups (mothers recognise calls and smells) for 6–8 months. Predators include Great White Sharks and Orcas.

- Royal NP
- Port Campbell NP
- Flinders Chase NP
- Coorong NP

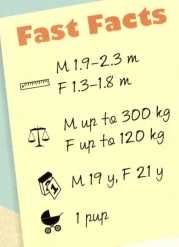

**Fast Facts**

M 1.9–2.3 m
F 1.3–1.8 m

M up to 300 kg
F up to 120 kg

M 19 y, F 21 y

1 pup

## interesting info

- **Australian Fur Seals can dive down 300 m and hold their breath underwater for up to 7 minutes.**
- On land, they use their flippers to walk or gallop, or to climb rocks.
- **Their vision is excellent underwater but poor on land.**
- They can detect underwater vibrations from prey with their whiskers.
- **Females mate 5–7 days after giving birth; the embryo is dormant for 4 months and takes another 8 months to develop.**
- Pups are born black, but within 3–5 months become grey with a pale throat.

# LITTLE CRITTERS

**Insects are invertebrates that have three main body parts— the head, thorax (with 3 pairs of legs) and abdomen. Spiders and scorpions are invertebrates called arachnids. Spiders are different from insects as they have 2 main body parts and 4 pairs of legs. Scorpions have 4 pairs of legs as well. They also have lobster-like pincers and a poisonous sting at the end of the tail that is often held curved over the back.**

About half of the world's animal species are insects and they're the most successful group of animals that ever lived. Insects, together with spiders and scorpions, add up to around 70,000 known species in Australia, although scientists estimate there may be over 150,000 more species of 'little critter'. If you look hard, you will find our national parks are filled with little critters of all shapes, sizes and colours. They can be found in every type of habitat, from below the ground to the tops of trees, and they have many important ecological roles. It may help to have a magnifying glass to be able to see the smallest species.

Greengrocer Cicada

Caterpillar of Double-Headed Hawk Moth

Monarch Butterfly

Redback Spider

## Termites

Termites are the greatest architects in the insect world. Australia has around 300 species, living in wood, underground or in soil mounds. In the northern grasslands and woodlands, termites build mounds up to 6 m tall, shaped like cathedrals. Termite mounds can survive a long time—some are over 100 years old. Mounds act like air conditioners, keeping termites at comfortable temperatures and humidity.

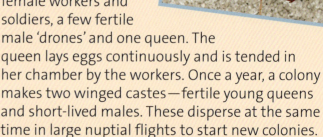
Giant Northern Termite

A termite colony has different members called castes. The queen lays the eggs, the 'king' fertilises them, and up to millions of sterile workers and soldiers look after the nest. The workers build and repair the nest, gather food and care for young. The soldiers have hard heads and often produce a toxic sticky spray that they can use to defend the nest, often against ants. Once a year, new winged queens and males leave the colony to mate and start new nests.

Termites are sensitive to hot sun so are mostly nocturnal. They eat grass, wood and fungi, and are a favourite food of many insectivorous animals, like the Short-beaked Echidna.

## Ants

There are about 1,300 native ant species in Australia. The highest number of species is in rainforests and the lowest in deserts. Ants are important habitat engineers whose activities improve soil richness. Their tunnels mean that water can better soak into the soil and they also play a role in dispersing seeds.

Bull Ant

Ants nest in colonies, mainly underground, but sometimes in logs or clumps of leaves. A colony often has thousands of ants, mostly sterile wingless female workers and soldiers, a few fertile male 'drones' and one queen. The queen lays eggs continuously and is tended in her chamber by the workers. Once a year, a colony makes two winged castes—fertile young queens and short-lived males. These disperse at the same time in large nuptial flights to start new colonies.

Adult ants eat only liquid food, mainly nectar, dew, or the blood of insect prey. One of the best-known ants is the Bull Ant, a fierce ant with a painful bite. Another is the Honeypot Ant, which has special workers with huge bellies so stuffed with food that they can't move. They are living food containers that vomit up their stored food for other ants.

## Native Bees

Native bees feed on nectar and collect pollen with their hairy legs to feed their young. Australia has over 1,500 species of native bee, and more than half occur in WA. Native bees are usually solitary, not aggressive, and live in all habitats, including the humid tropics, snowy mountain tops and hot dry deserts. They forage among shrubs and in tree tops and are important pollinators of flowering plants. Native bees often make complex nests and have a variety of nesting sites in the ground, among trees or plants, and even on buildings.

Halictine Bee

About 10 species are stingless, social and make a small amount of honey, which they need to survive winter. All have a queen and worker bees, and occur in warmer climates of eastern and northern Australia. The honey we eat mostly comes from the European Honey Bee, introduced in the 1820s, which has become feral. It's a problem in some national parks, competing with native bees for food and taking over tree hollows that might have provided nesting sites for birds or possums.

## Beetles

Nearly half of the world's insects are beetles, with about 350,000 known species. Australia has around 30,000 known species, with possibly thousands more. Their forewings have become hard cases, called 'elytra', which are held vertically while the beetle flies with its delicate hind wings.

Golden Stag Beetle

Beetles live in all habitats, including on plants, inside wood, under water (like the water beetle and whirligigs) and underground. Many beetles are nocturnal, so they are not often noticed. Common types include weevils, and scarab, jewel, rove and longicorn beetles.

Beetles have chewing mouthparts and may be herbivores, scavengers or predators. They are often important decomposers of rotting matter. Males and females usually work together to provide food for their larvae, which eat plants, fungi, dung, wood, or carrion. Life cycles vary from a few weeks to several years.

Some well-known beetles are the luminescent firefly, the spotted ladybird, the horned rhinoceros, the metallic Christmas beetle and the Golden-green Stag Beetle. Another is the dung beetle, which gathers large balls of dung to feed its young.

## Bugs and Flies

Bugs and flies are not closely related insects but both groups come in many colours, shapes and sizes, and have compound eyes and special mouthparts (beak or proboscis) for piercing and sucking out food.

Most bugs suck plant juices but some hunt insects (these are called assassin bugs) and some feed on blood (like bed bugs). While feeding on plants, bugs create a lot of sugary liquid waste, called honey dew, which ants like to feed on—so they often protect the bugs.

Hibiscus Harlequin Bug

Australia has over 6,000 species of true bugs, found in all habitats, including water. Common types are shield bugs, harlequin bugs, jewel bugs, leaf hoppers, water boatmen and cicadas. Many species can reproduce quickly when there is plentiful food and some can become pests.

Australia has over 7,500 fly species from all habitats. Other insects have two pairs of wings, but flies have only forewings—their hind wings have become small club-shapes called halteres, which are used for balance.

Fly larvae are important decomposers and eggs are laid close to the food source, often decaying animal and plant matter. This matter is eaten by the legless maggots that hatch from the eggs. Some species can grow to an adult in a week. Mosquitoes have aquatic larvae and adults feed on blood. March flies also feed on blood and can give a stinging prick. Some flies hover over flowers like bees.

## Cicadas

Bladder Cicada

Cicadas are often heard in summertime, the male song echoing through the bush. It's the loudest sound made by any insect, up to 100 decibels. Males are calling to females, and make their sound with two drum-like membranes (tympanums) on either side of the abdomen. The sound is made louder by an air-filled cavity in the abdomen.

There are 250 Australian species of cicada. Cicadas are a type of true bug, and have a straw-shaped mouth to feed on liquids. They feed on tree sap and must drink a lot of it to get enough nutrients. They regularly squirt out leftover fluid.

Females lay eggs in slits in tree bark and the hatching young (called nymphs) fall and dig themselves underground. Nymphs feed on tree-root sap and emerge after several years. They shed their skins, which are left on the nearest tree trunk before they fly away to mate and live for only a few weeks in tree tops. They are well camouflaged to protect them from birds that eat them.

# Dragonflies and Damselflies

Dragonflies and damselflies are colourful insects of freshwater habitats. Adults have an elongated abdomen, a large head and eyes, and two pairs of large membranous wings with networks of veins. Dragonflies tend to be stockier and hold their wings horizontally while resting, while the more slender damselflies usually hold their wings vertically together over their back.

There are about 330 Australian species of dragonflies and damselflies and about 80 species are threatened. They are usually from 3–9 cm long, but one species from tropical Queensland (the Giant Petaltail, *Petalura ingentissima*) has a wingspan of up to 17.5 cm.

Australian Emperor Dragonfly

Dragonflies and damselflies fly at incredible speeds of up to 50 km/hr, making them amazing aerial insect predators. While on the wing, they can catch and eat large prey like butterflies. Dragonfly and damselfly larvae are also predatory, but live underwater, breathing through gills.

Adult females dip their abdomens into the water surface to lay their eggs. These insects are good environmental indicators, and a healthy stream or wetland usually has a diverse range of dragonflies and damselflies. Polluted sites may have only a couple of species.

# Moths and Butterflies

Emperor Gum Moth

Moths and butterflies have wings and bodies covered in delicate, overlapping scales. Butterflies are active by day, while most moths are active at night. Butterflies and some day-flying moths are generally brightly coloured. This can signal to would-be predators that these insects might not taste good. The unpleasant taste is caused by plant toxins stored during the caterpillar stage.

Australia has over 20,000 species of moth and 400 species of butterfly. Both have good vision—butterfly eyes have a wide range of colour perception and moth eyes are adapted for low light. Most moths and butterflies have tubular mouthparts (proboscis) that suck up nectar but are coiled when not in use.

Eggs are laid on a food source, usually a plant, and hatch into caterpillars, which are often brightly coloured and furry. When fed and grown, the caterpillar pupates in a cocoon of silk that it makes, or while hanging freely from a support. After metamorphosis, it emerges as an adult, which can reproduce and colonise new areas.

# Grasshoppers, Crickets and Katydids

Mountain Grasshopper

Grasshoppers and crickets are large, winged insects with hind legs developed for jumping. They can only fly short distances (except for migrating locusts, which are strong flyers and can form plagues that damage crops).

They have chewing mouthparts. Grasshoppers are active during the day, feeding mainly on ground plants. Crickets are more nocturnal and are omnivores, occurring in vegetation of all heights and in ground burrows.

Australia is 'grasshopper country', and there are close to 3,000 native species of grasshoppers, crickets and katydids. Crickets and katydids have long antennae (half or more than the body length), and females have an ovipositor for egg laying. Grasshoppers (and locusts) have shorter antennae (less than half the body length) and no ovipositor.

Grasshoppers, crickets and katydids make sounds by rubbing together their legs or wings. The nocturnal songs of the male cricket are complex and loud. Grasshoppers tend to have simple clicks and chirps.

## Stick and Leaf Insects

Stick Insect

Stick and leaf insects eat plants and have slender bodies resembling stems or leaves. This camouflage protects them from predators. Their other defences include swaying, startling predators with bursts of brightly coloured wings, hissing or spraying irritating chemicals.

There are around 150 species in Australia. They often don't fly, or fly only short distances. The females of some species are parthenogenetic, which means that they can produce fertile eggs on their own if they don't find a mate. Females drop eggs to the ground. The eggs of the Spiny Leaf Insect resemble wattle seeds and, like those seeds, have a knob that ants like to feed their young. Eggs are carried back to the ant nest, where they hatch into small ant-like nymphs, so they're protected by the ants.

The Titan Stick Insect can grow to 25 cm. The Lord Howe Island stick insect is also large, resembling a sausage with legs. It was thought to be extinct but was rediscovered on a cliff in 2001. It's being bred in captivity to conserve the species.

## Spiders

Golden Orb Weaver

Spiders are arachnids. They have two body parts and eight legs, while insects have three body parts and six legs. There are about 3,300 spider species known in Australia, but many new species keep being discovered. Spiders are found in most habitats, from deserts to rainforests— and in our homes.

Spiders can build remarkable webs. They have spinnerets at their rear, where silk is made and drawn out in threads. They produce several types of silk, including sticky silk on which to catch prey, and non-sticky silk that they use to walk around the web on. Orb weavers build beautiful huge webs, often overnight, where they wait to trap prey. Redbacks and daddy long-legs build smaller tangled webs. Most spiders, like huntsmen and jumping spiders, don't actually build webs, but ambush their prey instead.

Spiders are predators that kill by injecting prey with venom. Most spiders have a painful bite but are harmless to people. Australia has two deadly species—the Redback and the Sydney Funnel Web. Luckily, there is antivenom for both.

## Scorpions

Like spiders, scorpions are arachnids. They have pincer-like claws (called pedipalps) that are used for catching prey. Their abdomen ends in a thin, curved tail with a venomous sting. Australia has about 100 scorpion species, found across all habitats, although they are most abundant in the arid zone. Scorpions are nocturnal, and 'glow' in the dark when exposed to ultraviolet light, which makes them easy to find at night. They live in burrows that can be quite deep. A female gives birth to live young that are cared for by riding on their mother's back.

Urodacus Scorpion

Scorpions play an important ecological role as ground-dwelling predators, eating mainly insects. They only feed on live prey and do this by sucking out the body fluids, instead of chewing. Scorpions only sting if their prey can't be captured with their pincers.

Their sting is very painful to humans. While scorpions overseas can have deadly venom, there have been no reported deaths from scorpions in Australia.

# GLOSSARY

**Note:** These words appear in this book on the listed pages. The words underlined in red are also in this glossary.

**abdomen** belly (contains digestive and reproductive organs) 135, 137, 138, 139

**alpine** high mountain areas, usually 1,100 m above sea level, where snow occurs in winter and not many trees grow. Australia's alpine habitat occurs on the highest parts of the Great Dividing Range; the highest peak is Mt Kosciuszko at 2,228 m above sea level 16, 17, 88, 96, 97, 98, 101, 106

**altitude** height or elevation above sea level 15, 65, 66, 67, 88, 94, 98

**Australian Bat Lyssavirus (ABL)** ABL is a virus that can be carried by several bat species. People can catch it from bats, so it's best not to touch any bat. There is a vaccine 52

**acacias** various kinds of wattle trees and shrubs. *Acacia* is the scientific name 10, 82, 84

**aestivate/aestivating** become dormant; animal dormancy is characterised by a period of inactivity and reduced metabolism; often triggered by high temperatures or drought 75, 109

**akimbo** elbows or knee joints turned outward 13

**ambush predator (or wait-and-pounce hunter)** predator (a carnivore that hunts and kills other animals—the prey—for food) that hides and launches a surprise attack. Prey is caught by stealth or strategy, rather than by mainly speed or strength 15, 56, 57, 105

**anal gland** gland that discharges a secretion or scent near the final opening of the digestive canal; often used for marking territory or authority 48

**antiphonal** a two-part bird call, or 'duet', between two birds (usually mates). Although the notes alternate between the birds, they often sound like a song from one individual 62

**apex predator (or hunter)** At the top of the food chain, nothing else eats them; e.g. Dingoes, eagles, sharks 91, 101, 104, 114, 121, 132

**appendix** a small blind-ended tube in mammals that comes off the cecum (a pouch coming off the large intestine in many mammals; the cecum is best developed in some herbivores). The appendix contains bacteria that help digest food (especially cellulose from plants) 46

**aquatic** living in water 59, 75, 103, 106, 108, 111, 115, 116, 137

**arboreal** living in trees 12, 13, 43, 49, 56, 57, 58, 59, 65, 67

**autotomy** when an animal sheds a limb or tail in self-defence; often the limb or tail regrows 16, 57

**baleen (plates)** fibrous plates attached to the upper jaw of baleen whales that filter krill and plankton from seawater for food. Humpback Whales have 270–400 baleen plates on each side of the jaw; Southern Right Whales have 205–270 130

**banksias** various kinds of banksia trees and bushes; *Banksia* is the scientific name 18, 29, 41

**bill (or beak)** The term 'bill' and 'beak' are often used interchangeably, although beak is actually a type of bill. Raptors are referred to as having a beak, while wading birds and small birds have a bill. Bill is the better term, as it only applies to birds (and the Platypus), while beak can be applied to other animals, like turtles and some insects 20, 21, 25, 27, 39, 40, 41, 76, 78, 79, 91, 94, 95, 111, 113, 115, 125, 126, 136, 137

**billabong** a dead-end branch of a river that is cut off after a flood and forms a separate pool; also called an 'oxbow lake' 23, 102, 103, 105, 107, 115, 126

**biodiversity/biodiverse** biological diversity—the number and abundance of different living things in an area 55, 118, 119, 125

**bipedal** walking on or using two limbs; e.g. Frill-necked Lizards run on their back legs; macropods use a bipedal hop with their power-packed hind legs (hopping saves energy at high speeds, the tail provides balance) 13

**bivalve** an aquatic mollusc that has a compressed body inside two shells connected by a hinged ligament; e.g. oysters, mussels, pipis 128

**blow/blowhole** a jet of cloudy mist from a whale's blowhole (like a 'nostril' on top of its head) when it breathes; baleen whales have two blowholes, and toothed whales have one 130, 131

**bog** an area of wet muddy ground that is too soft to support a heavy body 88, 102, 103

**bolus** a mass of food that has been chewed 30

**boom-and-bust (cycle)** when the number of animals in a population repeatedly increases and decreases significantly, usually as a result of an increase and then decrease in food supplies 24, 79, 86

**brackish (water)** Saltwater and fresh water mixed together (it's less salty than sea water) 111, 116

**breach/breaching** When a whale energetically leaps out of the water; a whale breaches to communicate with others, to remove parasites or just as part of playing 130

**browse/browser** to feed on leaves and twigs of trees and shrubs 30, 32, 50, 51

**brumation** reptile hibernation—a period of inactivity and not eating, when the animal retreats to a burrow, slows down its metabolism and enters a state of torpor 90

**buttress (roots)** large roots on all sides of a shallowly rooted tree that show above ground 54

**cache/caching** to hide food away for later 27, 66, 98

**callosities** growths of keratinised skin ('rock gardens') on the rostrum and jaw of Southern Right Whales; they're white due to parasitic whale lice and can be used to identify individual whales 130

**camouflage/camouflaged** to blend in with the natural background environment so an animal is difficult to see 12, 13, 15, 20, 22, 56, 57, 59, 70, 76, 90, 100, 120, 137, 139

**camp** site where many bats or flying-foxes gather to establish territory, roost, breed, raise young and exchange information 52

**canopy/canopies** uppermost branches of trees in a forest, forming a spreading layer of foliage 10, 11, 13, 34, 53, 54, 56, 64, 65, 94

**carapace** the hard upper shell covering the back of a turtle, tortoise, crustacean or arachnid 108, 109, 122, 123

**carnivore/carnivorous** An animal (the predator) that eats other animals (the prey) 25, 37, 63, 65, 80, 81, 96, 97, 109, 122

**carolling** A magpie call used to let other birds know about its territory; one bird starts the song, and another (usually the mate) joins in so they are singing together 27

**carrion** bodies of dead animals 14, 37, 73, 91, 96, 101, 108, 109, 116, 127, 137

**casque** a helmet-like structure 60

**casuarina** a tree called a she-oak; its scientific name is *Casuarina* 10

**cathemeral** irregularly active at any time of the day or night 67

**caudal luring** wiggling the tail to attract prey 15

**cere** the bare, wax-like or fleshy structure at the base of a bird's upper bill; the cere contains the nostrils 79

**clan** a close-knit group of interrelated families 132

**claypan** a shallow, normally dry depression in the ground, with a dense layer of clay that holds water after rain 75

**climate change** a long-term change in Earth's climate caused mainly by increased atmospheric carbon dioxide (from using fossil fuels), resulting in increased temperatures and reduced rainfall in many areas, sea level rise and ocean acidification 67

**cold-blooded (animal)** an animal whose body temperature varies according to the temperature of its environment 38

**clutch** a group of eggs before they hatch 36, 71, 79, 94, 108, 109, 114, 122, 123, 125

**colony/colonies** a group of animals (or plants) of the same species that live closely together, usually for mutual benefit like protection from predators 18, 53, 100, 124, 125, 126, 134, 136

**communal nesting** when two or more animals of the same species care for their young in a shared nest 43

**communal roosting** when two or more birds of the same species share a resting place 40

**conservation** the act of protecting, preserving or restoring something to prevent its loss 9, 125

**constriction** making something narrower by pressure or tightening 17, 38, 58

**continental shelf** the area of seabed around a land mass where the sea is shallow compared with the open ocean 123, 131, 134

**copepod** a microscopic crustacean in the plankton of marine and fresh waters 130

**coprophagia** feeding on dung (poo) 48

**courtship** behaviour to attract a mate, resulting in mating and producing young 18, 22, 91, 99, 113, 114, 126, 127

**cracked clay soils (cracking clays)** clay-rich soils that form deep cracks when they dry out 81, 82

**crepuscular** active mostly around dawn and dusk 83, 100

**crustacean** mostly aquatic animals that have a hard shell, segmented body and jointed limbs; e.g. crabs, prawns, copepods 25, 108, 109, 116, 121, 125, 130

**culling** reducing an animal population by killing some of the animals 32

**dabbling duck** a duck that feeds at the water's surface rather than diving under the water 112

**defecating** pooing 96

**dimorphic** when the male and female bird of a species have different plumage (colour and/or pattern) 78

**dispersal/dispersing** movement or spreading out from one area to other areas 60, 136

**distribution range** the overall area in which a species is known to occur (it may not occur in all parts of the area) 8

**diurnal** active during the day 44, 56, 72, 74

**dominance (hierarchies)** when members of a social group interact, often aggressively, to create a ranking system, and may compete for resources or mating rights 32, 83, 116

**dominant** having power or influence over others (includes plants) 25, 32, 47, 54, 60, 79, 88, 101, 106, 133

**dormant** when normal physical function and activity is suspended or slowed down for a time (as if in a deep sleep) 75

**dormant embryo** in some macropod species, when the birth of a joey is closely followed by mating, a new embryo can be the result but it stops developing; if the first young dies, and conditions are good, the dormant embryo starts developing again and is born a month later 29, 30, 31, 32, 50, 66, 83, 84, 99, 100, 134

**dorsal fin** an unpaired fin on the back of a fish or whale 129, 130, 132

**drey** a mammal's nest that is constructed in tree branches and is usually spherical 48

**dry season** a yearly period of low rainfall, especially in the tropics 13, 83, 105

**duck down** fine duck feathers (found under the tougher outside feathers), which are good thermal insulators 112

**duetting** when one bird calls and another bird answers; useful when visual contact is lost between individuals; occurs in many birds, including magpies 27

**echolocation** used by dolphins to detect prey and to navigate; they create a 'sound picture' of their environment by producing ultrasonic sounds (clicks) that bounce off objects and then listen for the returning echo 53, 131, 132

**'eclipse' (plumage)** the dull-coloured plumage of male birds (e.g. ducks, fairy-wrens) after moulting their colourful breeding plumage; it lasts for a few weeks or months and then their bright colouring returns 26

**ecological role** the role an organism plays in its community or ecosystem—how it interacts with and fits into its environment, including how it finds food and shelter and how it reproduces; e.g. predator, pollinator, decomposer, habitat engineer 29, 32, 41, 60, 63, 114, 135, 139

**ecosystem** a community of living organisms interacting with each other and with the environment (e.g. air, water, soil) as a system 38, 103

**electromagnetic** related to the behaviour and interaction of electric charges, and electric and magnetic fields 115

**electroreceptor** the ability of the body to receive an electric or electromagnetic stimulus 115

**embryo** an animal before birth or hatching from an egg 29, 30, 31, 32, 50, 51, 66, 83, 84, 99, 100, 134

**EPBC Act** *Environment Protection and Biodiversity Conservation Act 1999* is Australia's national environment law; it protects threatened species and ecological communities, marine species in Commonwealth waters, and migratory species; under this law, an animal is considered a 'native species' to Australia if it were present before the year 1400 125

**epiphyte** a plant that grows on another plant (but it is not parasitic) 54, 64

**estuaries** the tidal sections of rivers, where seawater mixes with fresh river water 102, 111, 116, 118, 121, 126, 127, 128

**eucalypt/eucalyptus** a gum tree; its scientific name is *Eucalyptus* 10, 11, 23, 29, 34, 39, 41, 43, 44, 46, 47, 48, 51, 52, 62, 63, 76, 77, 88, 92, 94

**evaporate** turn from liquid to vapour 83

**evolved** developed gradually over a long time 7, 67, 101, 129, 130

**extinct/extinction** when a species is believed to have died out entirely or in a particular area 9, 19, 30, 46, 50, 80, 96, 101, 118, 130, 139

**eyrie** the nest of an eagle or other bird-of-prey built in a high, inaccessible place 91

**feral** non-native animals living in the wild that are descended from introduced or domesticated animals (e.g. foxes, cats, pigs, deer) 13, 14, 16, 17, 43, 45, 53, 60, 63, 73, 77, 80, 81, 101, 124, 136

**fertilise** when a female's egg joins with the male's reproductive material (sperm) to develop a new individual 136

**filter-feeding** used by some aquatic animals to filter small particles or organisms out of the water for food; e.g. whales use filter-feeding to catch plankton 120, 130

**fledgling** a young bird that has developed, but is not yet fully independent of its parents 27, 39, 91

**fledge** when a young bird's wing feathers are developed enough to fly 112

**flock** a group of birds of the same species feeding, resting or travelling together 21, 27, 39, 40, 41, 42, 77, 78, 79, 92, 93, 94, 103, 112, 125

**floodline** the line next to a river marked by the previous or highest flood 105

**floodplain** an area of low-lying ground next to a river that sometimes floods 14, 39, 81, 102, 113

**foliage** plant leaves 48, 54, 58, 59, 109

**folivore** an animal that feeds on leaves 48, 49, 67

**forage/foraging** to search for food 12, 16, 27, 28, 29, 36, 37, 48, 52, 53, 60, 61, 63, 66, 92, 93, 97, 112, 116, 124, 126, 134, 136

**fossorial** living underground most of the time and adapted to digging or burrowing 18, 85

**froglet** a small frog 18, 59

**frugivore** an animal that feeds on fruit 60

**fungi** a diverse group of organisms, such as mushrooms, moulds, yeasts, that live by decomposing and absorbing the organic material in which they grow; they live above or below the ground 30, 51, 60, 66, 82, 136, 137

**gastrolith** a stone swallowed by a bird, reptile or fish to help digestion in the gizzard/gut 19, 105

**gender** the state of being male or female 13, 105, 106, 122

**gestation (period)** the time it takes for an animal to develop from conception (fertilisation of the egg) to birth 32, 45, 66, 67

**gibber (plain)** a flat area covered in loose rocks and stones of various sizes in arid and semi-arid parts of Australia; 'gibber' is Aboriginal for stone 68

**gizzard** the front end of a bird's digestive tract, where muscular walls grind up food 19

**gland** an organ in an animal that secretes chemical substances for use in the body or for discharge into the surroundings 46, 48, 49, 99, 105, 110, 121, 122, 124

**global warming** a gradual increase in the average temperature of Earth's atmosphere, climate and oceans caused by humans 123

**Great Dividing Range** a chain of mountains curving along the eastern Australian coast; Australia's longest mountain range, and the third longest land-based range in the world 22, 61, 72, 89

**grazer** an animal that eats mainly grass and herbs 32, 50, 51, 80, 112

**gregarious** lives in flocks or loosely organised communities 84, 92

**groin** the place on the body where the thigh joins the abdomen 110

**groundwater** water held underground in the soil or in the pores and crevices in rocks; a source of drinking water for animals when it seeps to the surface 102

**habitat fragmentation** when the loss of habitat (the natural home or environment of an animal) results in the division of large areas of habitat into smaller, more isolated patches 45, 46, 63

**hatchling** a young animal recently emerged from its egg 13, 17, 36, 37, 70, 105, 106, 109, 121, 122, 123, 125

**hawking** when birds hunt and catch flying insects while flying ('on the wing') 94

**heathland** land covered with low-lying shrubs, bushes and herbs, often on sandy soils 62, 84

**herbivore/herbivorous** an animal that eats only plants 84, 99, 111, 129, 137

**hibernate/hibernation** slowing down the metabolic rate and entering a deep sleep as a strategy to survive winter; the animal survives on fat it has stored during the summer 12, 73, 90, 95, 98, 106

**(a) hide** a hidden home or nest 31

**highland** land that is at higher altitudes (above sea level), like mountains and alpine areas 50, 55, 66, 92, 94

**hind (hindquarters, hind legs, hind limbs, hind feet, hind fins, hind wings)** back area of an animal; back legs, feet, fins or wings 13, 14, 15, 44, 45, 47, 48, 49, 66, 67, 75, 85, 86, 100, 110, 115, 116, 129, 134, 137, 138

**home range** area that an animal covers when searching for food or mates; it is not generally defended (as is the territory) 43, 46, 48, 63, 82, 91

**hummock (grass)** a mound of spinifex grass 68, 69, 82, 85, 86

**humid/humidity** a relatively high level of water vapour in the air 13, 14, 57, 59, 136

**immature** not fully developed or grown 26, 42

**incubate/incubation** to keep eggs at a suitable temperature while they develop and hatch 12, 14, 19, 21, 22, 23, 25, 39, 41, 60, 62, 76, 79, 105, 106, 109, 111, 112, 114, 122, 125, 128

**infrared (vision)** vision that can detect infrared radiation (or heat); infrared is electromagnetic radiation with wavelengths longer than visible light 91

**insectivore/insectivorous** an animal that feeds on insects 44, 106, 136

**inshore** close to the coast or shoreline 131

**invertebrate** an animal without a backbone, such as insects, worms, slugs, snails 14, 30, 57, 60, 62, 66, 71, 81, 97, 113, 114, 115, 129, 135

**IUCN Red List** the International Union for the Conservation of Nature's (IUCN) Red List has the most comprehensive information on the conservation status of the world's animals, plants and fungi; the IUCN uses internationally agreed criteria to assess a species' risk of extinction 9

**Jacobson's organ** an organ in the roof of the mouth in many vertebrates, especially snakes and lizards, that senses chemical information from the environment 37, 72, 90

**keratin** a fibrous protein forming the main structural component of hair, feathers, hoofs, claws, horns, etc. 115

**kleptoparasitism** when an animal takes food from another animal that has caught or collected it 126

**krill** a shrimp-like crustacean that forms large schools; 'krill' is a Norwegian word meaning whale food 120, 130

**lagoon** a stretch of saltwater separated from the sea by a low sandbank or coral reef, or a small freshwater lake near a larger lake or river 108, 109, 121, 122, 123, 126

**larvae** the immature stage of insects or other animals that undergoes metamorphosis and usually looks different from the adult 61, 77, 82, 85, 92, 104, 109, 137, 138

**latrine** toilet 96

**lichen** an organism that is a combination of algae and fungus; lichens often grow on rocks and trees 54, 57

**lowland** land that is close to sea level, like the coast or flat inland areas 39, 67, 93, 94, 104

**luminescent** glows or emits light (usually caused by a chemical) 137

**macropods** group of marsupials that includes kangaroos and wallabies 51, 66, 84, 99, 100

**mallee (woodlands, scrub)** semi-arid woody scrub dominated by low-growing eucalypts (gum trees) that have several stems 11, 28, 32, 53, 68, 70, 73, 76, 77, 79, 86,

**mammal/mammalian** a warm-blooded vertebrate that has hairy skin and produces milk to feed its young 7, 14, 20, 29, 37, 43, 45, 46, 52, 53, 58, 83, 85, 95, 96, 98, 115, 116, 129, 130, 132

**mange** a skin disease of mammals caused by parasitic mites; mange causes itching, scabs and hair loss 28

**mangrove** a tree or shrub of tidal, coastal swamps; it can grow in salty conditions and many of its roots grow above the ground 52, 113, 118, 121

**marsh** an area of vegetation that often floods or is permanently flooded; marshes are generally nutrient-rich wetlands that support mainly reeds and grasses rather than trees. In Australia, 'marsh', 'swamp' and 'wetland' mean the same thing 114

**marsupial** a type of mammal whose young are very undeveloped when born and are typically carried and suckled in a pouch on the mother's belly. They are mostly found in Australia 7, 28, 29, 30, 43, 44, 45, 46, 49, 51, 63, 65, 67, 80, 81, 83, 84, 85, 96, 97, 98

**mature** when an animal reaches the age when it can reproduce and have young 21, 40

**membrane/membranous** a flexible sheet-like structure acting as a boundary or lining in an organism 47, 52, 53, 90, 137, 138

**megabat** fruit-eating bats such as flying-foxes; they are usually larger than microbats 52, 53

**melaleuca** a paperbark tree. *Melaleuca* is the scientific name 10, 23, 59, 84

**metabolic rate** the rate at which metabolism occurs in a living organism (metabolism is the chemical processes in the body that sustain life, such as respiration, heart rate, digestion, excreting waste products) 67

**metamorphose/metamorphosis** transforming from an immature form to an adult (e.g. a maggot to a fly, a caterpillar to a butterfly, a tadpole to a frog) 59, 138

**microbat** bats with large ears that feed mainly on insects; usually smaller than flying-foxes 53

**microclimate** the climate of a very local area 100

**microorganism** microscopic single-celled creatures such as bacteria and protozoa 46

**migrate/migration/migrating/migratory** to move from one region or habitat to another, usually according to the seasons 86, 94, 104, 120, 126, 130, 138

**mimic** to look like (or sound like) another animal 27, 42, 57, 61, 78, 79

**mollusc** aquatic invertebrate that includes snails, slugs, mussels and octopuses 106, 116

**monotreme** a primitive mammal that lays eggs; it is found only in Australia and Papua New Guinea, e.g. the platypus and echidna 95, 115

**montane** of or inhabiting mountainous country 90

**mortality** death, rate of death 45

**moult/moulted** when an animal or bird sheds its outer layer of skin, hair or feathers, to make way for new growth 61, 111, 116, 133

**mulga** open and arid scrubland formed by certain acacia (wattle) trees; a widespread and important habitat in inland Australia 26, 68, 77, 79, 86

**Murray–Darling Basin** a large area in south-eastern Australia, named after the Murray River and the Darling River; the basin drains one-seventh of the Australian land mass and is an important agricultural area 103

**native (species)** species that are from a particular place; Australia's native species are recognised by the EPBC Act as those that were here before the year 1400 7, 19, 20, 25, 39, 41, 60, 63, 64, 71, 77, 79, 116, 136, 138

**nectar** a sugary fluid secreted within flowers to encourage pollination by insects and other animals, and collected by bees to make into honey 29, 41, 47, 52, 93, 94, 136, 138

**nectivorous** feeding on the nectar of flowers 29, 52

**nestling** a baby bird that is too young to leave the nest 40, 41, 61, 62, 77

**nocturnal** active during the night 22, 31, 45, 47, 48, 49, 50, 59, 65, 71, 74, 80, 86, 99, 105, 115, 116, 136, 137, 138, 139

**nomadic** having no permanent home or territory; moving from place to place, usually following food 21, 77, 78, 79, 83, 94, 111

**non-native** not native to a particular place or country 39, 104

**offshore** out at sea, some distance from the shore 24, 116, 118, 124, 125, 127, 131, 134

**omnivore/omnivorous** an animal that eats both animals and plants 19, 82, 86, 90, 98, 106, 138

**on the wing** while flying 23, 53, 94, 138

**opposable/opposing** a thumb is opposable when it is opposite the fingers on the same hand, enabling the animal to grasp and handle objects 46, 48, 49, 66

**opportunistic predator** a predator that eats anything suitable it comes across (opportunistic breeding is breeding whenever environmental conditions are good) 116

**osteoderm** a bony plate or bump beneath the skin of crocodiles and turtles 121

**palate** the roof of the mouth; in vertebrates, the palate separates the cavities of the mouth and nose 44

**parasite** an organism that lives in or on another organism (its host) and benefits by getting nutrients at the other's expense 59, 104

**patagium** a membrane between the fore and hind limbs that assists an animal to glide or to fly. It occurs in bats, birds and gliding mammals, such as the Sugar Glider 47, 53

**placental mammal** a mammal that has a placenta, a structure connecting the circulatory system of an unborn young to that of its mother 7, 53

**plankton** small and microscopic organisms drifting in the sea or in fresh water, consisting mainly of diatoms, protozoans, small crustaceans, and the eggs and larval stages of larger animals 120, 130

**plastron** the flat lower shell on the underside of turtles and tortoises 109, 123

**platypup** a baby Platypus 115

**plumage** the covering of feathers on a bird; the condition and colour of plumage may vary with age, sex and sometimes time of year 20, 22, 26, 27, 42, 60, 62, 94

**pod** group of whales, often a family group 132

**pollen** the fine powder-like material whose individual grains contain the male reproductive cells of flowering plants; it is often yellow and is transported by water, wind, or insects and other animals 29, 41, 47, 52, 136

**pollinate/pollinator/pollinating** to carry the pollen grains (the male sex cells in plants) to the female sex cells in plants for fertilisation 29, 41, 47, 52, 136

**pop-hole** one of a number of entrances to a complex burrow system 80

**posturing** positioning the body and behaving in a way that is intended to impress or mislead 106, 134

**'pothook'** a courtship display of Wedge-tailed Eagles, either by the male alone or together with the female. The eagle folds his or her wings together and takes a dive, then soars upwards with wings half open, then dives again, then soars upwards again. It is an acrobatic display of great speed, strength and agility 91

**preening** when a bird or animal tidies and cleans the feathers or fur with its bill or tongue 21, 124

**prehensile (tail)** able to grip; some animals have tails that can grasp or hold objects like tree branches or nest-building material 29, 30, 48, 49, 58, 64, 65, 66, 67, 98

**puggle** a baby Echidna 95

**pulsed call** bursts of calls that have patterns that can be recognised ('heard'); they are important for communication or echolocation for dolphins and whales, and bats 132

**quadrupedal (gait, walk, movement)** pattern of movement or walking using four limbs 66, 133

**rail** a type of bird that has short wings, a narrow body and long toes; many can't fly 114

**raptor** bird of prey, such as eagles, hawks and owls 16, 17, 20, 22, 38, 41, 44, 52, 79, 90, 91, 100, 116, 127

**recurved (teeth)** teeth that curve backwards in the mouth, making it very hard for prey to escape 15

**riparian (habitat)** the vegetation alongside the banks of a river or around the edge of wetlands 14, 102, 103, 108

**rodent** a type of mammal (mice and rats) that has a single pair of continuously growing incisor teeth in each of the upper and lower jaws that must be kept short by gnawing 17, 20, 24, 58, 80, 116

**roost/roosting** a place where birds regularly settle at night, or where bats congregate to rest in the day 23, 24, 27, 40, 41, 52, 53, 61, 76, 92, 114

**rostrum** a beak-like projection from the snout or head of an insect, crustacean, or whale or dolphin 131

**saltmarsh** a coastal ecosystem that is regularly flooded by tides; it is dominated by low-lying, shrubby salt-tolerant plants 118

**savanna** a grassy plain with few, scattered trees in tropical and subtropical regions 11

**scats** animal excrement (poo) 63

**scavenger** an animal that feeds on carrion, dead plant material, or rubbish 72, 96, 125, 137

**scent** a distinctive odour (smell) often left as a trail by an animal to mark its territory or authority 28, 44, 46, 47, 49, 72, 99, 101

**scrape** the simplest form of bird nest construction—a shallow depression in the ground or vegetation, with a rim just high enough to stop the eggs from rolling out 22, 128

**scute** scutes are made of keratin; they cover the bony plates of a turtle shell 109

**seagrass** a grass-like plant that lives in the sea close to the coast 118, 122, 123, 129

**sedentary** not moving around much, or fixed to one spot (like a barnacle) 21, 41, 62, 76, 77, 80, 93, 127, 128

**seepage (water)** a moist place where groundwater reaches the surface 100, 102

**semelparity** also known as 'big bang' reproduction, usually a large and fatal event, in which the males die soon after breeding; several dasyurid marsupials show semelparity 97

**shrubland** a plant community dominated by shrubs and often includes grasses and herbs 31, 36, 53, 68, 73

**snag** trees, branches, roots or wood underwater in rivers and streams 104

**snakelet** a baby snake 107

**solitary** living alone 28, 29, 31, 32, 37, 42, 44-46, 50, 51, 65, 66, 85, 94, 95, 99, 101, 115, 120, 136

**spawn/spawning** eggs and sperm of aquatic animals such as fish, frog, crabs; spawning is when the eggs and sperm are released into water 104, 110, 120

**species** a group of living organisms consisting of similar individuals that can breed with each other (most pages)

**sperm** male reproductive cells 29, 120

**spinifex** a tough, spiky tussock grass that dominates much of the red sand desert and rocky ranges of Central Australia (not to be confused with coastal grasses, *Spinifex*) 15, 26, 68, 70, 71, 80, 82, 85, 86

**strangler** a vine or tree whose aerial roots extend down the trunk of a supporting tree and wrap around it, eventually strangling it 54

**subspecies** a category below the species level; a subspecies population can interbreed and is usually geographically isolated from the species 9, 28, 106

**succulent** a plant with thick, fleshy leaves and stems adapted to storing water (or, if food is 'succulent', it means it is tender and tasty) 31, 84, 99

**suckle/suckling** feed a young animal milk from the breast or teat 46, 50, 51, 95, 115, 116, 129, 133, 134

**supernumerary (young)** more young than there are teats; those newborns that can't attach to a teat do not survive 43, 96, 98

**swamp/swampy/swampland** *see* marsh 23, 25, 59, 84, 102, 103, 107, 109, 111, 121

**syndactylous** having the second and third toes of the hind foot joined, as far as to the start of the nails; macropods, bandicoots and some possums use their syndactylous toes for grooming 45, 48

**tail flukes** the lobes of a whale's tail used to propel it 129, 130, 131

**tail stock** the area to which the tail flukes are joined on a dolphin, whale or seal 131

**teat** the nipple of a female mammal, from which the young sucks milk 29, 43, 44, 45, 53, 63, 64, 80, 81, 82, 83, 85, 96, 97, 115

**telephoto (vision)** giving a larger (magnified) image of a distant object 91

**temperate** the climatic zone occurring between the tropics and the polar zone; moderate in heat 10, 34, 40, 43, 51, 52, 54, 55, 61, 130, 131, 133, 134

**termites** ant-like social insects that build elaborate mounds (nests) above ground that are linked underground by galleries through the soil to their feeding sites (usually wood) 18, 25, 37, 38, 44, 49, 64, 82, 85, 95, 136

**territory/territorial** an area occupied by one or more individuals and defended against other members of the species; it is usually centred around a nest or burrow 12, 13, 24, 25, 26, 27, 28, 44, 46, 47, 48, 49, 52, 56, 61, 62, 65, 67, 76, 77, 84, 101, 106, 113, 116, 121, 127, 134

**thermals** columns of rising air caused by local unequal heating of the land surface, and used by gliders and birds to fly high 91, 126

**thermoconform** not able to regulate its body temperature internally, which means the animal's body temperature fluctuates with changing environmental temperatures 56

**thermoregulator/thermoregulate/thermoregulation** the ability of an animal to keep its body temperature fairly constant, even when the surrounding environmental temperature is very different 12, 15, 56

**tibial gland** a gland at the top of the hind leg on Banjo frogs that produces toxic or distasteful chemicals 110

**torpor** a sleep-like state in which the body processes slow down (lowered temperature and metabolic rate); torpor helps animals to survive tough times when food and water are scarce, or when there are extreme cold temperatures; torpor lasts a few hours a day, or a few days or weeks, whereas hibernation can last for months 12, 20, 29, 47, 53, 81

**transitory** lasting for a short time; not permanent 131

**triangulate** divide (an area) into triangles for surveying purposes 24

**tridactyl** having three toes—an adaptation for running, e.g. the Emu 19

**tripod/tripoding** when an animal stands on its hind legs and tail to search for prey or to make itself look bigger when it's threatened 14, 72

**tropics/tropical** between the Equator and the Tropic of Cancer or the Tropic of Capricorn; temperatures and humidity are higher than in the temperate zone 6, 10, 11, 13, 14, 22, 25, 34, 38, 40, 41, 43, 51, 52, 54, 55, 59, 64, 101, 102, 105, 106, 113, 115, 118, 119, 120, 121, 122, 129, 130, 131, 132, 136, 138

**tuber** a thickened underground stem or shoot 30

**tussock** dense clump of grass 31, 73, 82

**tympanum** external 'ear' in frogs, toads and insects; it does not actually process sound but transmits it to the inner 'ear' 59, 110, 137

**ultraviolet** electromagnetic radiation of a higher frequency than light visible to the human eye 139

**understorey** an underlying layer of vegetation (shrubs, low trees) between the forest canopy and the ground cover; it receives less light than the canopy 11, 30, 32, 34, 35, 47, 51, 97

**undergrowth** the plants growing beneath the canopy of a woodland or forest 10, 11, 26, 30, 34, 48, 51, 54, 56, 62, 81, 94

**urine** wee 31, 75, 80, 86

**vegetation** the plants (trees, flowers, grasses etc.) in an area 15, 29, 36, 42, 48, 50, 61, 62, 69, 81, 96, 99, 102, 103, 106, 107, 108, 114, 116, 121, 124, 138

**venom/venomous** poison made by an animal (e.g. snakes, scorpions, spiders, bees) and injected into prey or aggressors by biting or stinging 17, 38, 58, 74, 95, 107, 115, 139

**vertebrate** an animal with a backbone, such as mammals, birds, reptiles, fish 14, 43, 64, 80, 120

**warm-blooded (animal)** an animal (mammals and birds) that maintains a constant body temperature, typically above that of the surroundings 58

**warren** a network of interconnecting burrows 14, 28

**watercourse** a natural or artificial channel through which water flows 25, 67, 75, 77

**wattle (part of an animal)** a fleshy, wrinkled and often brightly coloured fold of skin hanging from the neck or throat of certain birds and reptiles 60, 94

**wattle (plant)** acacia trees and shrubs 10, 68, 92, 139

**wean/weaned** to start getting a young animal used to food other than its mother's milk 43, 45, 64, 97

**wetlands** an area that is saturated with water, either permanently or seasonally 6, 23, 102, 103, 109, 111, 112, 113, 125, 138

**wet season** 1–3 months of a year when most of a region's average annual rainfall occurs 13, 14, 102, 105

**Wet Tropics** an area of tropical rainforests in the north of Queensland that is on the World Heritage List 55, 56, 57, 59, 60, 66, 67

**World Heritage Area** a site of special cultural or environmental significance with listing by the United Nations Educational, Scientific and Cultural Organisation (UNESCO), which gives it international recognition and some protection 55, 66

**yabbies** small freshwater crayfish 104, 106, 115, 126

**zygodactylous** where the foot has two forward facing toes and two backward facing toes; this occurs in parrots, including cockatoos, and enables them to hold and manipulate objects in one foot while standing on the other 40

# Table of Featured Parks and Animals

| State | # | Park | Murray Cod | Whale Shark | Black-headed Python | Blotched Blue-tongue Lizard | Boyd's Forest Dragon | Burton's Legless Lizard | Common Bearded Dragon | Common Blue-tongue Lizard | Common Thick-tailed Gecko | Eastern Brown Snake | Eastern Long-necked Turtle | Flatback Turtle | Freshwater Crocodile | Frill-necked Lizard | Green Python | Green Turtle | Lace Monitor | Mulga Snake | Northern Leaf-tailed Gecko | Perentie | Pig-nosed Turtle | Red-bellied Black Snake | Saltwater Crocodile | Shingleback Lizard | Smooth Knob-tailed Gecko |
|---|---|---|---|---|---|---|---|---|---|---|---|---|---|---|---|---|---|---|---|---|---|---|---|---|---|---|---|
| QLD | 1 | Kutini–Payamu | | | ● | | | ● | | ● | | | | | | ● | ● | ● | | ● | | | | | ● | | |
| | 2 | Daintree | | | | | ● | ● | | | | | | | | | | | | | ● | | | ● | ● | | |
| | 3 | Crater Lakes | | | | | ● | ● | | | | | | | | | | | | | ● | ● | | ● | | | |
| | 4 | Great Barrier Reef | | ● | | | | | | | | | | ● | | | | ● | | | | | | | ● | | |
| | 5 | Bowling Green Bay | | | | | | ● | ● | ● | ● | ● | | ● | | ● | | ● | ● | | | | | | ● | | |
| | 6 | Cravens Peak | | | | | | ● | | | | | | | | | | | | | | ● | | | | | |
| | 7 | Diamantina | | | | | | ● | | | | | | | | | | | | ● | | | | | | | ● |
| | 8 | Carnarvon | | | ● | | | ● | ● | ● | | ● | | | ● | | | | ● | | | | | ● | | | |
| | 9 | Lamington | | | | | | ● | | ● | | | | | | | | | ● | | | | | ● | | | |
| | 10 | Main Range | | | | | | ● | ● | ● | | ● | | | | | | | ● | | | | | ● | | | |
| NSW | 11 | Oxley Wild Rivers | | | | | | ● | ● | ● | | ● | ● | | | | | | ● | | | | | ● | | | |
| | 12 | Dorrigo | | | | | | ● | ● | ● | | ● | | | | | | | ● | | | | | ● | | | |
| | 13 | Sturt | | | | | | ● | ● | | ● | | | | | | | | | ● | | | | | | ● | ● |
| | 14 | Warrumbungle | | | | | | ● | ● | ● | | ● | | | | | | | ● | | | | | ● | | ● | |
| | 15 | Kinchega | | | | | | ● | ● | ● | | | | | | | | | | ● | | | | | | ● | ● |
| | 16 | Wollemi | | | | ● | | ● | ● | ● | | ● | | | | | | | ● | | | | | ● | | | |
| | 17 | Blue Mountains | | | | ● | | | ● | ● | | | | | | | | | ● | | | | | ● | | | |
| | 18 | Royal | | | | | | ● | | ● | | ● | | | | | | | ● | | | | | ● | | | |
| | 19 | Kosciuszko | | | | ● | | | | ● | | ● | | | | | | | ● | | | | | ● | | | |
| ACT | 20 | Namadgi | | | | ● | | | | ● | | ● | | | | | | | ● | | | | | ● | | | |
| VIC | 21 | Wyperfeld | | | | | | ● | ● | ● | | ● | | | | | | | ● | | | | | | | ● | |
| | 22 | Little Desert | | | | | | | ● | ● | | ● | | | | | | | ● | | | | | | | ● | |
| | 23 | Grampians | | | | ● | | | ● | ● | | ● | | | | | | | ● | | | | | ● | | ● | |
| | 24 | Snowy River | | | | | | | | ● | | ● | | | | | | | ● | | | | | ● | | | |
| | 25 | Alpine | | | | ● | | | | | | ● | | | | | | | | | | | | | | | |
| | 26 | Dandenong Ranges | | | | ● | | | | ● | | | | | | | | | ● | | | | | ● | | | |
| | 27 | Great Otway | | | | ● | | | | ● | | ● | | | | | | | | | | | | | | | |
| | 28 | Port Campbell | | | | ● | | | | ● | | | | | | | | ● | | | | | | | | | |
| | 29 | Wilsons Promontory | | | | ● | | | | ● | | ● | | | | | | ● | ● | | | | | | | | |
| TAS | 30 | Freycinet | | | | ● | | | | | | | | | | | | | | | | | | | | | |
| | 31 | Cradle Mountain–Lake Saint Clair | | | | ● | | | | | | | | | | | | | | | | | | | | | |
| | 32 | Franklin–Gordon Wild Rivers | | | | | | | | | | | | | | | | | | | | | | | | | |
| | 33 | Mount Field | | | | ● | | | | | | | | | | | | | | | | | | | | | |
| | 34 | Southwest | | | | | | | | | | | | | | | | | | | | | | | | | |
| SA | 35 | Flinders Chase | | | | | | | ● | ● | ● | | | | | | | ● | | | | | | | | | |
| | 36 | Coorong | | | | | | | | | | | | | | | | ● | | | | | | | | | |
| | 37 | Murray River | ● | | | | | ● | | | | ● | | | | | | | ● | | | | | | | ● | |
| | 38 | Flinders Ranges | | | | | | ● | | ● | | | | | | | | | | | | | | | | ● | |
| | 39 | Innamincka | | | | | | ● | | | ● | | | | | | | | | ● | | | | | | ● | ● |
| | 40 | Witjira | | | | | | ● | | | | | | | | | | | | ● | | ● | | | | | ● |
| WA | 41 | Cape Le Grand | | | | | | | ● | | | | | | | | | | | | | | | | | | |
| | 42 | Stirling Range | | | | | | | | | | | | | | | | | | | | | | | | | |
| | 43 | Walpole–Nornalup | | | | | | | | | | | | | | | | | | | | | | | | ● | |
| | 44 | Tone–Perup | | | | | | | ● | | | | | | | | | | | | | | | | | ● | |
| | 45 | Rottnest Island | | | | | | ● | | | | | | | | | | ● | | | | | | | | ● | |
| | 46 | Yanchep | | | | | | ● | | | | | | | | | | | | | | | | | | ● | |
| | 47 | Nambung | | | | | | ● | | | | | | | | | | | | ● | | | | | | ● | |
| | 48 | Ningaloo | | ● | | | | | | | | | | | | | | ● | | | | | | | | | |
| | 49 | Cape Range | | ● | | | | ● | | | | | | | | | | ● | | ● | | ● | | | | | |
| | 50 | Karijini | | | | | | ● | | | | | | | | | | | | ● | | | | | | | |
| NT | 51 | Judbarra/Gregory | | | ● | | | ● | | ● | | | | | ● | ● | | | | ● | | | | | ● | | |
| | 52 | Litchfield | | | | | | ● | | | | | | | ● | ● | | | | ● | | | | | | | |
| | 53 | Kakadu | | | ● | | | ● | | ● | | | | | ● | ● | | ● | | ● | | | ● | | ● | | |
| | 54 | Garig Gunak Barlu | | | | | | ● | | | | | | | | ● | | ● | | ● | | | | | ● | | |
| | 55 | Uluru–Kata Tjuta | | | | | | ● | | | | | | | | | | | | ● | | ● | | | | | ● |

**Note:** NLA Publishing has prepared this table using numerous sources. The information here is indicative only. Ask for a species list when you visit a national park.

# Table of Featured Parks and Animals

| State | # | Park | Satin Bowerbird | Silver Gull | Southern Cassowary | Splendid Fairy-wren | Sulphur-crested Cockatoo | Superb Fairy-wren | Superb Lyrebird | Tawny Frogmouth | Wedge-tailed Eagle | White-bellied Sea-Eagle | Yellow-tailed Black-Cockatoo | Short-beaked Echidna | Platypus | Bilby | Brush-tailed Phascogale | Common Brushtail Possum | Common Ringtail Possum | Common Spotted Cuscus | Common Wallaroo | Common Wombat | Crest-tailed Mulgara | Dusky Antechinus | Eastern Grey Kangaroo | Giles' Planigale | Honey Possum |
|---|---|---|---|---|---|---|---|---|---|---|---|---|---|---|---|---|---|---|---|---|---|---|---|---|---|---|---|
| QLD | 1 | Kutini–Payamu |  | • | • |  | • |  |  | • | • | • |  | • |  |  | • |  |  | • |  |  |  |  |  |  |  |
|  | 2 | Daintree |  | • | • |  | • |  |  | • | • | • |  |  |  |  |  | • | • |  |  |  |  |  |  |  |  |
|  | 3 | Crater Lakes | • | • | • |  | • |  |  | • | • | • |  | • | • |  |  | • |  |  |  |  |  |  |  |  |  |
|  | 4 | Great Barrier Reef |  | • |  |  |  |  |  |  |  | • |  |  |  |  |  |  |  |  |  |  |  |  |  |  |  |
|  | 5 | Bowling Green Bay |  | • |  |  | • |  |  | • | • | • |  | • | • |  |  | • |  |  | • |  |  |  |  |  |  |
|  | 6 | Cravens Peak |  |  |  |  |  |  |  | • | • |  |  | • |  |  |  |  |  |  | • |  |  |  |  |  |  |
|  | 7 | Diamantina |  | • |  | • | • |  |  | • | • |  |  | • |  | • |  |  |  |  | • |  |  |  | • | • |  |
|  | 8 | Carnarvon |  |  |  |  | • | • |  | • | • |  | • | • | • |  |  | • | • |  | • |  |  |  | • |  |  |
|  | 9 | Lamington | • | • |  |  | • | • |  | • | • | • | • | • | • |  | • | • | • |  |  |  |  |  |  |  |  |
|  | 10 | Main Range | • |  |  |  | • | • |  | • | • | • | • | • | • |  |  | • | • |  | • |  |  |  | • |  |  |
| NSW | 11 | Oxley Wild Rivers | • |  |  |  | • | • | • | • | • | • | • | • | • |  |  | • | • |  | • | • |  |  | • |  |  |
|  | 12 | Dorrigo | • |  |  |  | • | • | • | • | • |  | • | • | • |  | • | • | • |  |  |  |  |  |  |  |  |
|  | 13 | Sturt |  | • |  | • | • |  |  | • | • |  |  | • |  |  |  |  |  |  | • |  |  |  | • | • |  |
|  | 14 | Warrumbungle |  |  |  |  | • |  |  | • | • |  |  |  |  |  |  | • | • |  |  |  |  |  | • |  |  |
|  | 15 | Kinchega |  | • |  |  | • |  |  | • | • | • |  | • |  |  |  | • |  |  | • |  |  |  | • | • |  |
|  | 16 | Wollemi | • |  |  |  | • | • | • | • | • | • | • | • | • |  |  | • | • |  | • | • |  | • | • |  |  |
|  | 17 | Blue Mountains | • |  |  |  | • | • | • | • | • | • | • | • | • |  |  | • | • |  |  | • |  | • | • |  |  |
|  | 18 | Royal | • | • |  |  | • | • | • | • | • | • | • | • |  |  |  |  |  |  | • | • |  | • |  |  |  |
|  | 19 | Kosciuszko | • | • |  |  | • | • | • | • | • | • | • | • | • |  |  | • | • |  | • | • |  | • | • |  |  |
| ACT | 20 | Namadgi | • | • |  |  | • | • | • | • | • | • | • | • | • |  |  | • | • |  | • | • |  | • | • |  |  |
| VIC | 21 | Wyperfeld |  | • |  | • | • | • |  | • | • |  | • | • |  |  |  | • |  |  |  |  |  |  | • |  |  |
|  | 22 | Little Desert |  | • |  |  | • | • |  | • | • |  | • | • |  |  |  | • |  |  |  |  |  |  |  |  |  |
|  | 23 | Grampians |  | • |  |  | • | • | • | • | • |  | • | • | • |  |  | • | • |  |  | • |  |  | • |  |  |
|  | 24 | Snowy River |  |  |  |  | • | • | • | • | • |  | • |  | • |  |  | • | • |  |  | • |  | • | • |  |  |
|  | 25 | Alpine | • | • |  |  | • | • | • | • | • | • | • | • | • |  |  | • | • |  |  | • |  | • | • |  |  |
|  | 26 | Dandenong Ranges | • | • |  |  | • | • | • | • | • |  | • | • | • |  | • | • | • |  |  | • |  |  |  |  |  |
|  | 27 | Great Otway | • | • |  |  | • | • | • | • | • | • | • | • | • |  |  | • | • |  |  |  |  |  | • |  |  |
|  | 28 | Port Campbell |  | • |  |  | • | • |  |  | • | • | • | • |  |  |  | • |  |  |  |  |  |  |  |  |  |
|  | 29 | Wilsons Promontory |  | • |  |  | • | • | • | • | • | • | • | • |  |  |  | • | • |  |  | • |  |  | • |  |  |
| TAS | 30 | Freycinet |  | • |  |  | • |  |  | • | • | • | • | • |  |  |  | • |  |  |  | • |  |  |  |  |  |
|  | 31 | Cradle Mountain–Lake Saint Clair |  | • |  |  | • | • |  | • | • | • | • | • | • |  |  | • | • |  |  | • |  |  | • |  |  |
|  | 32 | Franklin–Gordon Wild Rivers |  | • |  |  | • |  |  | • | • | • | • | • | • |  |  | • | • |  |  | • |  |  |  |  |  |
|  | 33 | Mount Field |  | • |  |  | • | • | • | • | • | • | • | • | • |  |  | • | • |  |  | • |  |  |  |  |  |
|  | 34 | Southwest |  |  |  |  | • | • |  | • | • | • | • |  |  |  |  | • | • |  |  | • |  | • |  |  |  |
| SA | 35 | Flinders Chase |  | • |  |  | • | • |  | • | • | • | • | • | • |  |  | • | • |  |  |  |  |  |  |  |  |
|  | 36 | Coorong |  | • |  |  |  | • |  | • | • | • | • | • |  |  |  |  |  |  |  |  |  |  |  |  |  |
|  | 37 | Murray River |  | • |  |  | • | • |  | • | • | • |  | • |  |  |  | • |  |  |  |  |  |  |  |  |  |
|  | 38 | Flinders Ranges |  | • |  | • | • |  |  | • | • |  |  | • |  |  |  | • | • |  | • |  |  |  |  |  |  |
|  | 39 | Innamincka |  |  |  |  |  |  |  | • | • |  |  |  |  |  |  |  |  |  |  |  |  |  |  |  |  |
|  | 40 | Witjira |  |  |  |  |  |  |  |  | • |  |  |  |  |  |  |  |  |  |  |  | • |  |  | • |  |
| WA | 41 | Cape Le Grand |  | • |  |  |  |  |  | • | • | • |  |  |  |  |  |  |  |  |  |  |  |  |  |  | • |
|  | 42 | Stirling Range |  |  |  | • |  |  |  | • | • |  |  | • |  |  |  | • |  |  |  |  |  |  |  |  | • |
|  | 43 | Walpole–Nornalup |  | • | • |  | • |  |  | • | • | • | • |  |  |  |  | • | • |  |  |  |  |  |  |  | • |
|  | 44 | Tone–Perup |  | • |  |  | • |  |  | • | • |  | • |  |  |  |  | • | • |  |  |  |  |  |  |  |  |
|  | 45 | Rottnest Island |  | • |  |  |  |  |  | • | • | • |  |  |  |  |  |  |  |  |  |  |  |  |  |  | • |
|  | 46 | Yanchep |  | • |  |  | • | • |  | • | • | • | • | • |  |  |  |  |  |  |  |  |  |  |  |  | • |
|  | 47 | Nambung |  | • |  |  | • | • |  | • | • |  |  | • |  |  |  |  |  |  |  |  |  |  |  |  | • |
|  | 48 | Ningaloo |  | • |  |  |  |  |  |  | • | • |  |  |  |  |  |  |  |  |  |  |  |  |  |  |  |
|  | 49 | Cape Range |  | • |  |  |  |  |  | • | • | • |  | • |  |  |  |  |  |  |  |  |  |  |  |  |  |
|  | 50 | Karijini |  |  |  |  |  |  |  | • | • |  |  |  |  |  |  |  |  |  |  |  |  |  |  |  |  |
| NT | 51 | Judbarra/Gregory |  |  |  |  | • |  |  | • | • | • |  | • |  |  |  | • |  |  | • |  |  |  |  |  |  |
|  | 52 | Litchfield |  | • |  |  | • |  |  | • | • | • |  | • |  |  |  | • |  |  | • |  |  |  |  |  |  |
|  | 53 | Kakadu |  |  |  |  | • |  |  | • | • | • |  | • |  |  |  | • |  |  | • |  |  |  |  |  |  |
|  | 54 | Garig Gunak Barlu |  | • |  | • |  |  |  | • | • | • |  |  |  |  |  |  |  |  |  |  |  |  |  |  |  |
|  | 55 | Uluru–Kata Tjuta |  | • |  | • |  |  |  | • | • |  |  | • |  |  |  |  |  |  | • |  |  |  |  |  |  |

**Note**: NLA Publishing has prepared this table using numerous sources. The information here is indicative only. Ask for a species list when you visit a national park.

| | Koala | Long-nosed Bandicoot | Lumholtz's Tree-kangaroo | Mountain Pygmy-possum | Musky Rat-kangaroo | Numbat | Quokka | Red Kangaroo | Rufous Bettong | Southern Marsupial Mole | Spectacled Hare-wallaby | Spotted-tailed Quoll | Striped Possum | Sugar Glider | Swamp Wallaby | Tasmanian Devil | Tasmanian Pademelon | Western Grey Kangaroo | Yellow-footed Rock-wallaby | Australian Fur-seal | Australian Sea-lion | Australian Water Rat | Bottlenose Dolphin | Dingo | Dugong | Gould's Wattled bat | Humpback Whale | Little Red Flying-fox | Mitchell's Hopping-mouse | Orca | Southern Right Whale | Spinifex Hopping-mouse |
|---|---|---|---|---|---|---|---|---|---|---|---|---|---|---|---|---|---|---|---|---|---|---|---|---|---|---|---|---|---|---|---|---|
| | | ● | | | | | | | | | | | ● | ● | ● | | | | | | | ● | | ● | | | | | | | | |
| | | ● | | | ● | | | | | | | | ● | ● | ● | | | | | | | ● | | ● | | | | | | | | |
| | | ● | ● | | ● | | | | ● | | | | ● | ● | | | | | | | | ● | | ● | | | | ● | | | | |
| | | | | | | | | | | | | | | | | | | | | | | ● | | ● | | ● | | | ● | | |
| | | | | | | | | | ● | | | | | ● | ● | | | | | | | ● | | ● | | | | | | | | |
| | | | | | | | | ● | | | | | | | | | | | | | | | | | | | | | | | ● |
| | ● | ● | | | | | | ● | ● | | | | | ● | ● | | | | | | | ● | | ● | | | | | | | | |
| | ● | ● | | | | | | | ● | | | | ● | ● | ● | | | | | | | ● | | ● | | | | ● | | | | |
| | ● | ● | | | | | | | ● | | | | ● | ● | ● | | | | | | | ● | | ● | | | | ● | | | | |
| | ● | ● | | | | | | | | | | | ● | ● | ● | | | | | | | ● | | ● | | | | | | | | |
| | | ● | | | | | | | | | | | ● | ● | ● | | | | | | | ● | | ● | | | | | | | | |
| | ● | | | | | | | ● | | | | | | | | | | | | | | ● | | ● | | | | ● | | | | |
| | | | | | | | | ● | | | | | | | | | | ● | | | | | | | | | | | | | | |
| | ● | ● | | | | | | | | | | | ● | ● | ● | | | | | | | ● | | ● | | ● | | | | | | |
| | ● | ● | | | | | | | | | | ● | ● | ● | ● | | | | | | | ● | | ● | | ● | | | | | | |
| | ● | ● | | | | | | | | | | | | ● | ● | | | | | ● | | ● | ● | ● | | | | ● | | ● | ● | |
| | ● | ● | | ● | | | | | | | | | | ● | ● | | | | | | | ● | | ● | | | | | | | | |
| | | | | | | | | | | | | | | ● | ● | | | | | | | ● | | ● | | | | | | | | |
| | | | | | | | | ● | | | | | | ● | ● | | | ● | | | | | | ● | | ● | | | ● | | | |
| | | | | | | | | | | | | | | ● | ● | | | ● | | | | | | ● | | ● | | | ● | | | |
| | ● | | | | | | | | | | | | | ● | ● | | | | | | | ● | | ● | | | | | | | | |
| | | ● | | | | | | | | | | | | ● | ● | | | | | | | ● | | ● | | | | | | | | |
| | | ● | ● | | | | | | | | | | | ● | ● | | | | | | | ● | | ● | ● | | | | | | | |
| | | | | | | | | | | | | | | ● | ● | | | | | | | ● | | ● | | | | | | | | |
| | | ● | | | | | | | | | | | | ● | ● | | | | | ● | | ● | | ● | | | | | | ● | ● | |
| | | ● | | | | | | | | | | | | ● | ● | | | | | ● | | ● | ● | ● | | | | | | ● | ● | |
| | | | | | | | | | | | | | | ● | ● | | ● | ● | | ● | | ● | | ● | | | ● | | | ● | |
| | | | | | | | | | | | | | | ● | ● | ● | ● | | | ● | | ● | | ● | | | | | | | | |
| | | | | | | | | | | | | | | ● | | ● | ● | | | | | | | | | | | | | | | |
| | | | | | | | | | | | | | | ● | | ● | ● | | | | | | | | | | | | | | | |
| | ● | | | | | | | | | | | | | | | | | ● | | ● | ● | | ● | | ● | | | | | ● | ● | |
| | | | | | | | | | | | | | | | | | | ● | | ● | ● | | ● | | | | | | | | ● | |
| | | | | | | | | ● | | | | | | | | | | ● | | | | | ● | | ● | | | | | | | |
| | | | | | | | | ● | | | | | | | | | | ● | ● | | | | ● | | | | | | | | | |
| | | | | | | | | ● | | ● | | | | | | | | | | | | | ● | | | | | | | | | ● |
| | | | | | | | | | | | | ● | | | | | | | | | | | ● | | ● | | | | | ● | ● | |
| | | | | | | | | | | | | | | | | | | ● | | | | | | ● | | ● | ● | | | ● | |
| | | | | ● | ● | | | | | | | | | | | | | ● | | | | | | ● | | | | | | | | |
| | | | | ● | ● | | | | | | | | | | | | | | | | | | ● | | ● | | | | | | | |
| | | | | | | | | | | | | | | | | | | ● | | ● | | | ● | | | ● | | | | | | |
| | | | | | | | | | | | | | | | | | | ● | | | | | | | | | | | ● | | | |
| | | | | | | | | | | | | | | | | | | | | | | ● | ● | | ● | | | | | ● | | |
| | | | | | | | | ● | | | | | | | | | | | | | | | ● | ● | ● | | | | | | | |
| | | | | | | | | ● | | | ● | | | | | | | | | | | | | ● | | | | | | | | |
| | | | | | | | | | | | | | | ● | | | | | | | ● | | ● | | ● | | | ● | | | | |
| | | | | | | | | | | | | | | ● | | | | | | | ● | | ● | ● | | | | ● | | | | |
| | | | | | | | | | | | | | | ● | | | | | | | ● | | ● | ● | | | | | | | | |
| | | | | | | | | ● | | | | | | | | | | | | | | | ● | | | | | | | | | ● |

# MAMMALS: AGE AT MATURITY

'Age at maturity' is the age when mammals can breed and have young. Sometimes it's the same for males and females, and sometimes it's not. The age at maturity affects how well a species can survive. It also influences a species' conservation status.

| Monotremes | M & F | M | F |
|---|---|---|---|
| Echidna, Short-beaked | 4–12 y | | |
| Platypus | 2–4 y | | |
| **Marsupials** | | | |
| Antechinus, Dusky | 8 mo | | |
| Bandicoot, Long-nosed | | 1 y | 5 mo |
| Bettong, Rufous | | 12–13 mo | 11 mo |
| Bilby | 6 mo | | |
| Cuscus, Common Spotted | 1 y | | |
| Glider, Sugar | | 1 y | 8–15 mo |
| Hare-wallaby, Spectacled | 1 y | | |
| Kangaroo, Eastern Grey | | 2–4 y | 1.5 y |
| Kangaroo, Red | | 2–3 y | 1.5–2 y |
| Kangaroo, Western Grey | | 2–4 y | 1.5 y |
| Koala | | 3–4 y | 2–3 y |
| Marsupial Mole, Southern | ? | | |
| Mulgara, Crest-tailed | 10–11 mo | | |
| Numbat | | 2 y | 1 y |
| Pademelon, Tasmanian | 11–18 mo | | |
| Phascogale, Brush-tailed | 10–12 mo | | |
| Planigale, Giles' | 8–11 mo | | |
| Possum, Common Brushtail | | 2 y | 1 y |
| Possum, Honey | 6–8 mo | | |
| Possum, Ringtail | 13 mo | | |
| Possum, Striped | ? | | |
| Pygmy-possum, Mountain | | 1 y | 1–2 y |
| Quokka | 1–2 y | | |
| Quoll, Spotted-tailed | 1 y | | |
| Rat-kangaroo, Musky | 1–1.5 y | | |
| Rock-wallaby, Yellow-footed | 1.5 y | | |
| Tasmanian Devil | 2 y | | |
| Tree-kangaroo, Lumholtz's | | 4.5 y | 2 y |
| Wallaby, Swamp | 15–18 mo | | |
| Wallaroo, Common | 1.5–2 y | | |
| Wombat, Common | 2 y | | |
| Wombat, Southern Hairy Nosed | 3 y | | |

| Placental Mammals | M & F | M | F |
|---|---|---|---|
| Bat, Gould's Wattled | 1 y | | |
| Dingo | 1–2 y | | |
| Dolphin, Bottlenose | | 10–13 y | 9–10 y |
| Dugong | 6–17 y | | |
| Flying-fox, Little Red | 2.5 y | | |
| Fur Seal, Australian | | 4–5 y | 3–6 y |
| Hopping-mouse, Mitchell's | 2.5 mo | | |
| Hopping-mouse, Spinifex | 2.5 mo | | |
| Orca | 15 y | | |
| Rat, Australian Water | | | 4–8 mo |
| Sea-lion, Australian | | 6–9 y | 4–6 y |
| Whale, Humpback | 4–5 y | | |
| Whale, Southern Right | 9–10 y | | |

# ACKNOWLEDGEMENTS

The author and the National Library of Australia would like to thank the close to 100 scientists and organisations whose expertise has helped to make the information in this book as up-to-date as possible.

Australian Museum; Australian Herpetological Society; Australian Mammal Society; Australian Marine Sciences Association; Australian National Insect Collection, CSIRO; Australian Koala Foundation; Australian Platypus Conservancy; Australian Wildlife Secrets (Sean and Simon Watharow); Birdlife Australia; Canberra Ornithologists Group; Commonwealth Department of the Environment; Eubalaeuna Pty Ltd/Curtin University; Foundation for National Parks and Wildlife; Bruce Gall; Great Barrier Reef Marine Park Authority; Museum Victoria; Mark Norman; Parks Australia; Queensland Museum; South Australian Primary Industries and Regions; and the Western Australian Department of Parks and Wildlife.

**Reptiles and Frogs:** Marion Anstis; Mike Bamford; Bill Bateman; Melissa Bruton; Mark Cowen; Scott Eipper; Ryan Ellis; Arthur Georges; Tony Griffiths; Gordon Grigg; Scott Keogh; Stephen Mahony; Nicki Mitchell; Joanne Ocock; Lynette Plenderleith; and Ashleigh Wolfe.

**Birds:** Allan Briggs; Peter Dann; Helen Fallow; Frank Harrison; Gisela Kaplan; Keith Lightbody; Dale Mengel; Raoul Mulder; Jerry Olsen; Rob Parker; Dejan Stojanovic; Mike Weston; and Dez Wells.

**Monotremes:** Tom Grant; Mike McKelvey; Ramon Newmann; Peggy Rismiller; Melody Serena; and Geoff Williams.

**Marsupials:** Jerry Alexander; Andrew Baker; Juliey Beckman; Joe Benshemesh; Peter Bird; Felicity Bradshaw; Delma Clifton; Sebastien Comte; Peter Copley; Graeme Maxwell Coulson; Simon de Salis; Mark Elridge; Jai Green-Barber; Sean FitzGibbon; Tony Friend; Aaron Greenville; Ian Gynther; Emily Hynes; Christopher Johnson; Matthew Marrison; John McIlroy; Clementine Menz; Stewart Nicol; Liberty Olds; Steve Phillips; William Poole; Randy Rose; Michael Swinbourne; Peter Temple-Smith; Lisa Warnecke; and Rod Wells.

**Placental Mammals:** Peter Banks; Michelle Blewitt; Linda Broome; Patrina Birt; Claire Charlton; Christopher Dickman; Julie Fencher; Simon Goldsworthy; Kim Kliska; Lindy Lumsden; Helene Marsh; Rebecca McIntosh; and Thomas Newsome.

**Fish:** Simon Kaminskas; and Mark Meekan.

**Insects and Arachnids:** John Vranjic.

Finally, the author wishes to thank Oskar and Jazmin Newton-McKay for their help and support.

**Image Donations**

The National Library greatly appreciates the generosity of all the photographers who donated their photographs, not only to this book but also to the National Library collection.

Tony Ashton; John Barkla; Peter Bird; Linda Broome; Matt Clancy; Commonwealth Department of the Environment; Lindsay Cooke; John Cooper; Aliesha Dodson; Bill Doyle; Scott Eipper; Helen Fallow; Ray Fox; Sharon Gillam; Paul Hagon; Aaron Greenville; Lorraine Harris; Ross Heywood; Sandy Ingleby; Paul Jensen; Peter Johnston; Russell Jones; Tim Kaminskas; Gary King; Alan Kwok; Markus Low; Dixie Makro; Jessica Masson; Angus McNab; Dale Mengel; David Newell; Ramon Sierra Newmann; Pam Osborn; Wayne Osborn; Lois Padgham; Jaime Plaza; Glenn Pure; Ken Rainsbury; Bryon Samuels; Marcus Salton; John Sexton; David Seymour; Callum Shakespeare; John Stirling; Bobby Tamayo; Tom Tarrant; Jenny Thynne; Mark Tindale; Andrew Turner; Lisa Warnecke; Grant Webster; Roger Williams; Warren Wilson; Dan Wood; and Sharon Wormleaton.

# LIST OF ILLUSTRATIONS

Page numbers are in **bold**.
Those images from Flickr have been reproduced under Creative Commons Attribution 2.0 and Creative Commons Attribution 3.0.
Any image caption that includes 'NLA' is held in the National Library of Australia's collections.

**10** *Carnarvon National Park*, © The State of Queensland (Department of Environment and Heritage Protection; Markus Low, *In the Grampians* 2011, NLA, Courtesy Markus Low; Dan Wood, *Karijini NP: Fortescue* 2013, NLA, Courtesy Dan Wood; **11** Sue Brookhouse, *Mt Exmouth Walking Track, Warrumbungle National Park* 2013, Courtesy Sue Brookhouse/NSW National Parks & Wildlife Service, Office of Environment and Heritage; Andrew Turner, *Refuge Cove, Wilsons Promontory National Park* 2009, NLA, Courtesy Andrew Turner; Kimble Young, *Darwin, Litchfield, Katherine* 2008, Flickr, flickr.com/photos/kbcool/2455433667; Oor Wolle, *Yanchep NP* 2014, Flickr, flickr.com/photos/kaskaandjim/16412529826; **12** Stephen Mahony, *Common Bearded Dragon, Coonabarabran Area, New South Wales* 2014, Courtesy Stephen Mahony; **13** Stephen Mahony, *Frilled Dragon, Southern Kimberley, Western Australia* (detail) 2014, Courtesy Stephen Mahony; **14** Stephen Mahony, *Yellow-spotted Monitor, Goldfields Highway, West of Mt Magnet, Western Australia* (detail) 2009, Courtesy Stephen Mahony; **15** Matt Clancy, *Burton's Legless Lizard, Lialis burtonis, Big Desert Wilderness Park, Victoria* 2013, NLA, Courtesy Matt Clancy; **16** Scott Eipper, *Common Blue-tongue Lizard*, NLA, Courtesy Scott Eipper; **17** Matt Clancy *Eastern Brown Snake, Pseudonaja textilis, Melbourne, Victoria* 2013, NLA, Courtesy Matt Clancy; **18** Stephen Mahony, *Turtle Frog, Perth, Western Australia* 2011, Courtesy Stephen Mahony; **19** Warren Wilson, *Emu and Chicks, Woollamia, New South Wales* 2014, Courtesy Warren Wilson; Richard Fisher, *Emu at Australia Zoo* 2008, Flickr, flickr.com/photos/richardfisher/3139753253/; **20** John Sexton, *Tawny Owls at 'Yacka Yacka', Adelaide Hills, S.A.* (detail) 2010, NLA, Courtesy John Sexton; **21** Glenn Pure, *Galahs, Kambah, ACT* 2015, NLA, Courtesy Glenn Pure; **22** Gary King, *Bush Stone-curlew, Wonga Beach, Queensland* 2013, NLA, Courtesy Gary King; **23** John Barkla, *Barking Owl, Townsville Palmetum, Queensland* 2009, NLA, Courtesy John Barkla; **24** Dale Mengel, *Eastern Barn Owl, Tyto javanica delicatula, Goorganga Wetlands, Proserpine* 2012, NLA, Courtesy Dale Mengel; **25** Helen Fallow, *Laughing Kookaburra, Murrumbateman, NSW* between 2012 and 2013, NLA, Courtesy Helen Fallow; Tony Ashton, *Blue-winged Kookaburra with prey, Tyto Wetlands, Ingham, Queensland* (detail) 2012, NLA, Courtesy Tony Ashton; **26** Bryon Samuels, *Superb Fairy-wren, Bendalong, New South Wales* (detail) 2013, NLA, Courtesy Bryon Samuels; Ken Rainsbury, *Splendid Fairy-wrens, WA* (detail) 2014, NLA, Courtesy Ken Rainsbury; **27** Paul Jensen, *Australian Magpie Feeding Young, Bli Bli, Queensland* 2013, NLA, Courtesy Paul Jensen; John Cooper, *Australian Magpie Feeding Young in Nest, Quandialla NSW* 2001, NLA, Courtesy John Cooper; **28** Sharon Wormleaton, *Common Wombat, Cleland Wildlife Park, South Australia* 2014, NLA, Courtesy Sharon Wormleaton; Lorraine Harris, *Southern Hairy-nosed Wombat, Whiteman Park, Perth, Western Australia* (detail) 2006, NLA, Courtesy Lorraine Harris; **29** Jessica Masson, *Honey Possum on Banksia Grandis, Torndirrup National Park* (detail) 2015, NLA, Courtesy Jessica Masson; **30** Angus McNab, *Rufous Bettong (Aepyprymnus rufescens), Moranbah, Central Queensland* 2014, NLA, Courtesy Angus McNab; **31** Ryan Francis, *Spectacled Hare-wallaby*, Courtesy Ryan Francis; **32** Aliesha Dodson, *Mother Eastern Grey Kangaroo with Pouch* (detail), NLA, Courtesy Aliesha Dodson; Sandy Ingleby, *Western Grey Kangaroos taken at Dryandra National Park in Western Australia* 2007, NLA, Courtesy Sandy Ingleby; **33** Lois Padgham, *Wildflowers and Snow Gum Woodland on Stockyard Spur, Namadgi National Park, Australian Capital Territory* (detail) 2014, NLA, Courtesy Lois Padgham; **34** Mark Tindale, *Mountain Ash, Sherbrooke Forest, Dandenong Ranges National Park, Victoria* 2013, NLA, Courtesy Mark Tindale; Tatiana Gerus, *Hike in Mount Mathieson Trail, Spicers Gap in Main Range National Park, Australia* 2015, Flickr, flickr.com/photos/tgerus/19535976593/; John Cooper, *Wineglass Bay, Freycinet National Park, Tasmania* 2006, NLA, Courtesy John Cooper; **35** Bron Anderson, *Tone-Perup Nature Reserve* 2012, Courtesy Western Australian Department of Parks and Wildlife; Denisbin; *Walpole, Valley of Giants the Tree Top Walk* 2014, Flickr, flickr.com/photos/82134796@N03/15441273066; Sarah Burgess, *Escarpment—Judbarra/Gregory National Parks (NT)* 2015, Courtesy Parks and Wildlife Commission of the Northern Territory; **35** Barry Armstead, *Orroral Ridge Aerial View* 2015, PCL Collection; Jaime Plaza, *Wollemi Pines* 2014, NLA, Courtesy Jaime Plaza; **36** Stephen Mahony, *Common Thick-tailed Gecko, Hunter Valley, New South Wales* 2013, Courtesy Stephen Mahony; **37** Stephen Mahony, *Lace Monitor, Newcastle, New South Wales* 2013, Courtesy Stephen Mahony; **38** Matt Clancy , *Black-headed Python, Aspedites melanocephalus, Adelaide River region, Northern Territory* 2015, NLA, Courtesy Matt Clancy; **39** Gary King, *Yellow-tailed Black-Cockatoo, Risdon Dam, Tasmania* (detail) 2014, NLA, Courtesy Gary King; Keith Lightbody, *Red-tail Landing* (detail), Courtesy Keith Lightbody; **40** Paul Jensen, *Sulphur-crested Cockatoos, Bli Bli, Queensland* (detail) 2013, NLA, Courtesy Paul Jensen; **41** Lindsay Cooke, *Rainbow Lorikeet feeding in Pussy Willow, Lake Wendouree, Ballarat, Victoria* 2014, NLA, Courtesy Lindsay Cooke; Richard Fisher, *Rainbow Lorikeet at Cairns Esplanade* (detail) 2008, Flickr, flickr.com/photos/richardfisher/3012436508/; **42** Peter Johnston, *Satin Bowerbird, Audley, Royal National Park, New South Wales* (detail) 2014, NLA, Courtesy Peter Johnston; **43** Russell Jones, *Brush-tailed Phascogale (Tuan)* (detail), NLA, Courtesy Russell Jones; **44** Sharon Wormleaton, *Numbat, Dryandra Woodland, Western Australia* 2008, NLA, Courtesy Sharon Wormleaton; **45** Lorraine Harris, *Long-nosed Bandicoot, Crater Lakes National Park, Queensland* 2013, NLA, Courtesy Lorraine Harris; **46** Sharon Wormleaton, *Koala, Cape Otway, Victoria* 2012, NLA, Courtesy Sharon Wormleaton; **47** Lorraine Harris, *Sugar Glider, near Lake Eacham, Crater Lakes National Park, Queensland* 2013, NLA, Courtesy Lorraine Harris; **48** Jenny Thynne, *Jessica and Her Joeys* 2013, NLA, Courtesy Jenny Thynne; Jenny Thynne, *Common Ringtail Possum (Pseudocherius peregrinus)* 2012, NLA, Courtesy Jenny Thynne; **49** Lorraine Harris, *Common Brushtail Possum Mother and Juvenile, Atherton, Queensland* 2009, NLA, Courtesy Lorraine Harris; Aaron Greenville, *Brush-tail Possum* 2011, NLA, Courtesy Aaron Greenville; **50** Sharon Wormleaton, *Tasmanian Pademelon, Narawntapu National Park, Tasmania* 2014, NLA, Courtesy Sharon Wormleaton; **51** Lorraine Harris, *Swamp Wallaby and Joey, Atherton, Queensland* 2008, NLA, Courtesy Lorraine Harris; **52** Todd Burrows, *Little-red Flying Fox, Paradise Point, Queensland* (detail) 2014, Courtesy Todd Burrows; **53** Angus McNab, *Gould's Wattled Bat (Chalinolobus gouldii), Central Queensland* 2014, NLA, Courtesy Angus McNab; **54** Andrew Turner, *Daintree Ricer, Daintree National Park, Queensland* 2009, NLA, Courtesy Andrew Turner; Ross Heywood, *Triplet Falls, Great Otway National Park, Victoria, Australia* 2014, NLA, Courtesy Ross Heywood; R. Cleary, *Syndicate Ridge Track Area, of Great Importance to the Gumbaynggirr People,*

*Gondwana Rainforests of Australia World Heritage Area, Dorrigo National Park* 2013, Courtesy R. Cleary Seen Australia/ NSW National Parks & Wildlife Service, Office of Environment and Heritage; **55** Owen Allen, *Vines_LakeEacham_0001* 2014, Flickr, flickr.com/photos/owen59/15606790173; Doug Beckers, *Littoral Rainforest, Chilli Beach, Kutini-Payamu (Iron Range) National Park, Cape York, Queensland, Australia* 2014, Flickr, flickr.com/photos/dougbeckers/14752350792; *Lamington National Park,* © The State of Queensland (Department of Environment and Heritage Protection; Sharon Wormleaton, *Horseshoe Falls, Mt Field National Park, Tasmania,* NLA, Courtesy Sharon Wormleaton; Joe Shemesh, *Pandani, Southwest National Park, Tasmania* 2005, Courtesy Tasmania Parks and Wildlife Service; **56** Ray Lloyd, *Boyd's Forest Dragon, Mossman, Queensland* 2006, Courtesy Ray Lloyd; **57** Ray Lloyd, *Northern Leaf-tailed Gecko, Mount Lewis, Queensland* 2007, Courtesy Ray Lloyd; **58** Ray Lloyd, *Green Python, Cape York Peninsula, Queensland* 2011, Courtesy Ray Lloyd; **59** Grant Webster, *Litoria infrafrenata (White-lipped Tree Frog), Port Douglas, Queensland* 2009, NLA, Courtesy Grant Webster; **60** Tony Ashton, *Southern Cassowary stopping for Quandongs, Wallaman Falls Road, Queensland* 2013, NLA, Courtesy Tony Ashton; **61** Ray Fox, *Superb Lyrebird, Healesville Sanctuary, Victoria* 2013, NLA, Courtesy Ray Fox; Sharon Wormleaton, *Superb Lyrebird, Southwest National Park* 2015, NLA, Courtesy Sharon Wormleaton; **62** Peter Johnston, *Eastern Whipbird, Mardi near Gosford, New South Wales* 2014, NLA, Courtesy Peter Johnston; **63** Sharon Wormleaton, *Spotted-tailed Quoll, Southwest National Park, Tasmania* 2015, NLA, Courtesy Sharon Wormleaton; **64** Lorraine Harris, *Striped Possum, Lake Eacham, Queensland* 2013, NLA, Courtesy Lorraine Harris; **65** Tom Tarrant, *Common Spotted Cuscus (Spilocuscus maculatus) Iron Range NP, N. Queensland, Australia* 2008 Courtesy Tom Tarrant, www.aviceda.org; **66** Lorraine Harris, *Musky Rat-kangaroo, near Kuranda, Queensland* 2013, NLA, Courtesy Lorraine Harris; **67** Lorraine Harris, *Lumholtz's Tree-kangaroo, Malanda, Queensland* 2013, NLA, Courtesy Lorraine Harris; **68** Aaron Greenville, *Dune, Cravens Peak Reserve, Queensland* 2008, NLA, Courtesy Aaron Greenville; John Spencer, *Mount Wood Summit Walking Track, Sturt National Park, North-western NSW, Semi-desert Country* 2013, Courtesy John Spencer/NSW National Parks & Wildlife Service, Office of Environment and Heritage; Bill Doyle, *Little Desert National Park, Western Australia* 2011, NLA, Courtesy Bill Doyle; John Cooper, *Wineglass Bay, Freycinet National Park, Tasmania* 2006, NLA, Courtesy John Cooper; **69** Parks Australia, *Uluru-Kata Tjuta*, NLA, Courtesy Commonwealth Department of the Environment; Dan Wood, *Simpson Desert* 2014, NLA, Courtesy Dan Wood; S_porter0, *Rottnest Island, Western Australia,* Shutterstock 247667224; Brett Lewis, *Wyperfeld National Park* 2015, Courtesy Brett Lewis; John Tann, *Black Box, Eucalyptus largiflorens habitat, Kinchega National Park, NSW, Australia, November 2014,* Flickr, flickr.com/photos/31031835@N08/15299466244; David Elliott, *Gibber, Diamantina National Park* 2015, Flickr, flickr.com/photos/drelliott0net/19702676114; **70** Stephen Mahony, *Thorny Devil, Western Queensland* 2013, Courtesy Stephen Mahony; **71** Stephen Mahony, *Smooth Knob-tailed Gecko, Central Australia* 2014, Courtesy Stephen Mahony; **72** Stephen Mahony, *Perentie, near Longreach, Queensland* 2012, Courtesy Stephen Mahony; **73** John Cooper, *Shingleback Lizard, Conimbla National Park, NSW* 1998, NLA, Courtesy John Cooper; **74** Matt Clancy, *Mulga Snake, Pseudechis australis, Brigalow Belt, Queensland* 2014, NLA, Courtesy Matt Clancy; **75** Grant Webster, *Cyclorana platycephala (Water-holding Frog), Moree, New South Wales* 2008, NLA, Courtesy Grant Webster; **76** Sharon Gillam, *Malleefowl Working Its Mound, Gum Lagoon Conservation Park, SA, January 2010,* NLA, Courtesy Sharon Gillam; **77** Helen Fallow, *Major Mitchell's Cockatoo, NSW* between 1997 and 1998, NLA, Courtesy Helen Fallow; **78** David Newell, *Gum Waterhole, Diamantina National Park, Queensland* (detail) 2014, NLA, Courtesy David Newell; **79** John Barkla, *Budgerigars, Strzelecki Crossing, South Australia* 2010, NLA, Courtesy John Barkla; **80** Aaron Greenville, *Mulgara* 2010, NLA, Courtesy Aaron Greenville; **81** Lisa Warnecke, *Giles' Planigale* (detail), NLA, Courtesy Lisa Warnecke; **82** Sharon Wormleaton, *Bilby, Cleland Wildlife Park, Adelaide, South Australia* 2014, NLA, Courtesy Sharon Wormleaton; **83** Sharon Wormleaton, *Red Kangaroo, Cleland Wildlife Park, Adelaide, South Australia* 2014, NLA, Courtesy Sharon Wormleaton; **84** Angus McNab, *Quokka (Setonix brachyurus), Rottnest Island, Western Australia* (detail) 2012, NLA, Courtesy Angus McNab; **85** Joe Benshemesh, *Southern Marsupial Mole,* Courtesy Joe Benshemesh; **86** Sharon Wormleaton, *Spinifex Hopping Mouse, Cleland Wildlife Park, South Australia* 2014, NLA, Courtesy Sharon Wormleaton; Peter Bird, *Mitchell's Hopping Mouse* (detail), NLA, Courtesy Peter Bird; **87** David Elliot, *Rattlepod on Sunset Dune* (detail) 2015, Flickr, flickr.com/photos/drelliott0net/20135625528/; **88** *Snow on Mt Bogong, Alpine National Park* 2012, Australian Alps collection, Parks Australia; Dixie Makro, *Dove Lake, Cradle Mountain National Park, Tasmania* 2014, NLA, Courtesy Dixie Makro; John Cooper, *The Three Sisters, Blue Mountains National Park, New South Wales* 2015, NLA, Courtesy John Cooper; **89** John Spencer, *Kosciuszko National Park Winter Snowfield Wilderness* 2013, Courtesy John Spencer/NSW National Parks & Wildlife Service, Office of Environment and Heritage; Callum Shakespeare, *Bluff Knoll from Stirling Range Ridge Walk* 2015, NLA, Courtesy Callum Shakespeare; Glenn Pure, *Wilpena Pound Rim, Flinders Ranges National Park, South Australia* 1988, NLA, Courtesy Glenn Pure; **90** J.J. Harrison, *Blotched Blue-tongue Lizard (Tiliqua nigrolutea), Austin's Ferry, Tasmania, Australia* (detail) 2009, Wikipedia Commons, commons.wikimedia.org/wiki/File:Tiliqua_scincoides_scincoides.jpg; **91** Aaron Greenville, *Wedge-tailed Eagle* 2012, NLA, Courtesy Aaron Greenville; Roger Williams, *A Wedge-tailed Eagle on the Road from Balranald to Oxley, New South Wales* (detail) 2013, NLA, Courtesy Roger Williams; **92** Helen Fallow, *Gang-gang Cockatoo, Male, Canberra* 2009, NLA, Courtesy Helen Fallow; Helen Fallow, *Gang-gang Cockatoo, Female, Canberra* 2009, NLA, Courtesy Helen Fallow; **93** Helen Fallow, *Crimson rosella, Canberra* between 2011 and 2012, NLA, Courtesy Helen Fallow; **94** Helen Fallow, *Red Wattlebird, Murrumbateman, NSW* 2008, NLA, Courtesy Helen Fallow; **95** Andrew Turner, *Echidna, Sealers Cover, Wilsons Promontory National Park, Victoria* 2009, NLA, Courtesy Andrew Turner; Ramon Newmann, *A Digital Photograph of a Tasmanian Echidna,* NLA, Courtesy Ramon Newmann; **96** Sharon Wormleaton, *Tasmanian Devil, Bonorong Wildlife Sanctuary, Tasmania* 2014, NLA, Courtesy Sharon Wormleaton; **97** Angus McNab, *Dusky Antechinus (Antechinus mimetes), New England National Park, New South Wales* 2013, NLA, Courtesy Angus McNab; **98** Linda Broome, *Mountain Pygmy Possum, Kosciuszko National Park, New South Wales* 1988, NLA, Courtesy Linda Broome; **99** Angus McNab, *Common Wallaroo (Macropus robustus), Blackwater, Central Queensland* 2014, NLA, Courtesy Angus McNab; **100** Sharon Wormleaton, *Yellow-footed Rock Wallaby, Monarto Zoo, South Australia* 2014, NLA, Courtesy Sharon Wormleaton; **101** Bobby Tamayo, *Dingo on Ethabuka Reserve,* NLA, Courtesy Bobby Tamayo; **102** Peter Dombrovskis, *Serenity Sound from the top of Coruscades, Great Ravine, Franklin River, Franklin–Gordon Wild Rivers National Park, Tasmania, 1979,* nla.gov.au/nla.cat-vn4978418; Courtesy Liz Dombrovskis; Ric Raftis, *Around Innamincka* 2011, Flickr, flickr.com/photos/bushie/5959433599; *Bowling Green Bay National Park,* © The State of Queensland (Department of Environment and Heritage Protection); **103** Parks Australia, *Kakadu National Park,* NLA, Courtesy Commonwealth Department of the Environment; Andrew Turner, *Snowy River, Snowy River National Park, Victoria* 2011, NLA, Courtesy Andrew Turner; R. Cleary, *Oxley Wild Rivers National Park* 2013, Courtesy R. Cleary Seen Australia/NSW National Parks & Wildlife Service, Office of Environment and Heritage; Bill Doyle, *Murray River*

*National Park, Lyrup Flats Section, South Australia* 2010, NLA, Courtesy Bill Doyle; **104** Tim Kaminskas, *'Agro' the Murray Cod, Narrandera Fisheries Centre* (detail) 2010, NLA, Courtesy Tim Kaminskas; **105** Lorraine Harris, *Freshwater Crocodile, Kununurra, Western Australia* 2009, NLA, Courtesy Lorraine Harris; **106** Lorraine Harris, *Eastern Water Dragon, Brisbane, Queensland* (detail) 2015, NLA, Courtesy Lorraine Harris; Lorraine Harris, *Eastern Water Dragon, Atherton, Queensland* (detail) 2007, NLA, Courtesy Lorraine Harris; **107** Matt Clancy, *Red-bellied Black Snake, Pseudechis porphyriacus, Pambula, New South Wales* 2013, NLA, Courtesy Matt Clancy; Stephen Mahony, *A Red-bellied Black Snake in a Swampy Area of Newcastle in NSW* 2014, Courtesy Stephen Mahony; **108** Paul Hagon, *Pig-nosed Turtle (Carettochelys insculpta), National Zoo & Aquarium, Canberra* (detail) 2011, NLA, Courtesy Paul Hagon; **109** John Cooper, *Eastern Long-necked Turtle, Cowra NSW* 1995, NLA, Courtesy John Cooper; **110** Stephen Mahony, *Eastern Banjo Frog, Yengo National Park, New South Wales* 2010, Courtesy Stephen Mahony; Grant Webster, *Limnodynastes dorsalis (Western Banjo Frog), near Karlgarin, Western Australia* 2013, NLA, Courtesy Grant Webster; **111** Bryon Samuels, *Black Swan and Cygnets, Bool Lagoon, South Australia* 2012, NLA, Courtesy Bryon Samuels; Keith Lightbody, *Cygnet Ride* (detail), Courtesy Keith Lightbody; **112** Paul Jensen, *Australian Wood Duck Pair, Parklakes Wetland, Bli Bli, Queensland* 2015, NLA, Courtesy Paul Jensen; **113** Helen Fallow, *Black-necked Stork, Tyto Wetlands, Queensland* (detail) 2013, NLA, Courtesy Helen Fallow; Djambalawa, *Female Black-neck Stork in flight, Ephippiorhynchus* asiaticus 2008, Wikimedia Commons, commons.wikimedia.org/wiki/File:JabiruMcArthurRiver.jpg; **114** Helen Fallow, *Purple Swamphen, Sale, Victoria* (detail) 2015, NLA, Courtesy Helen Fallow; David Seymour, *Purple Swamphen, Goulds Lagoon, Granton, Tasmania* (detail) 2015, NLA, Courtesy David Seymour; **115** Sharon Wormleaton, *Platypus, Mersey River, Latrobe, Tasmania* 2015, NLA, Courtesy Sharon Wormleaton; **116** Alan Kwok, *Rakali* (detail), NLA, Courtesy Alan Kwok; **117** Michael Maconachie, *Orroral River, Namadgi National Park* 1999, Courtesy Michael Maconachie; **118** *Cape Le Grand*, Western Australian Department of Parks and Wildlife; John Turnbull, *Chromis atripectoralis—Blue-green Chromis* 2015, Courtesy John Turnbull, marineexplorer.org; Dan Wood, *Yardie Creek Gorge* 2014, NLA, Courtesy Dan Wood; **119** David Wachenfeld, *Purple Rain* 2013, Triggerfish images; Paul Asman and Jill Lenoble, *Remarkable Rocks* 2012, Flickr, flickr.com/photos/pauljill/8273421080/; Sharon Wormleaton, *Coorong National Park, South Australia*, NLA, Courtesy Sharon Wormleaton; Mark Tindale, *Twelve Apostles, Port Campbell, Victoria* 2014, NLA, Courtesy Mark Tindale; D. Finnegan, *Native Vegetation and Waterfall near Eagle Rock, Royal National Park* 2012, Courtesy D. Finnegan/NSW National Parks & Wildlife Service, Office of Environment and Heritage; Vanda Stewart, *Caiman Creek/Wnarn—Garig Gunak Barlu National Park (NT)* 2005, Parks and Wildlife Commission of the Northern Territory; **120** Wayne Osborn, *Whale Shark, Ningaloo Reef, WA* (detail) 2010, NLA, Courtesy Wayne Osborn; **121** Andrew Turner, *Saltwater Crocodile, Daintree River, Daintree National Park, Queensland* 2009, NLA, Courtesy Andrew Turner; Lorraine Harris, *Saltwater Crocodile, Daintree River, Queensland* 2014, NLA, Courtesy Lorraine Harris; **122** David Wachenfeld, *Chilling* 2013, Courtesy David Wachenfeld, Triggerfish images; **123** S. Whiting, *Tagged Flatback Turtle Nesting at Bare Sand* (detail) 2002, © Commonwealth of Australia (Great Barrier Reef Marine Park Authority); **124** Sharon Wormleaton, *Little Penguin, Penguin Centre Granite Island, Victor Harbor, South Australia* 2014, NLA, Courtesy Sharon Wormleaton; **125** Gary King, *Silver Gulls, Bridport, Tasmania* 2015, NLA, Courtesy Gary King; **126** Helen Fallow, *Australian Pelican, Burrill Lake, NSW* 2011, NLA, Courtesy Helen Fallow; Keith Lightbody, *Pelicans*, Courtesy Keith Lightbody; **127** Sharon Wormleaton, *White-bellied Sea-Eagle, Tamar River, Launceston, Tasmania* (detail) 2015, NLA, Courtesy Sharon Wormleaton; Richard Fisher, *White-Bellied Sea Eagle at Lone Pine Koala Sanctuary* 2008, Flickr, flickr.com/photos/richardfisher/3115005955; **128** John Stirling, *Hooded Plover, Killarney Beach, Victoria* (detail) 2012, NLA, Courtesy John Stirling; **129** B. Cropp, *Dugong Swimming Over Seagrass Beds at Shark Bay, Western Australia* (detail) 1978, © Commonwealth of Australia (Great Barrier Reef Marine Park Authority); B. Cropp, *Dugong Calf Rides Upon Mother's Back at Shark Bay, Western Australia* (detail) 1978, © Commonwealth of Australia (Great Barrier Reef Marine Park Authority); **130** Pam Osborn, *Humpback Whale Calf Breach, Exmouth Gulf, WA* 2012, NLA, Courtesy Pam Osborn; Claire Charlton, *Southern Right Whales*, Courtesy Claire Charlton; **131** Lorraine Harris, *Common Bottlenose Dolphins, between Queenscliff and Sorrento, Victoria* (detail) 2013, NLA, Courtesy Lorraine Harris; **132** Keith Lightbody, *Orca* (detail), Courtesy Keith Lightbody; **133** Simon Goldsworthy, *Australian Sea-lions*, Courtesy Simon Goldsworthy; **134** Marcus Salton, *Australian Fur-seal, Seal Rocks, Victoria* 2015, NLA, Courtesy Marcus Salton; **135** Entomology, *Cyclohila Austraal Cicada*, CSIRO Science Image; Entomology, *Caterpillar of Double-Headed Hawk Moth*, CSIRO Science Image; David McClenaghan, *A Redback Spider, Latrodectus hasseltii, of the Family Threidiidae*, CSIRO Science Image; *Danaus Plexippus (Nymphalidae)*, CSIRO Science Image; **136** Forestry and Forest Products, *Giant Termite Mound, Kakadu, November 1986* (detail), CSIRO Science Image; *Mastotermes Darwiniensis, Giant Northern Termite*, CSIRO Science Image; David Paul, *Formicidae, Myrmecia nigriscapa, Bull Ant*, Museum Victoria; David Paul, *Lasioglossum (Chilalictus) lanarium, Halictine Bee, Male* (detail), Museum Victoria; **137** David Paul, *Lamprima aurata, Golden Stag Beetle, Female*, Museum Victoria; Alan Kwok, *Bladder Cicada, Cytosoma saundersii*, NLA, Courtesy Alan Kwok; Jeff Wright, *Hibiscus Harlequin Bug* © Queensland Museum, Jeff Wright; **138** David Paul, *Percassa rugifrons, Mountain Grasshopper*, Museum Victoria; Jeff Wright, *Australian Emperor* © Queensland Museum, Jeff Wright; David Paul, *Opodiphthera eucalypti, Emperor Gum Moth*, Museum Victoria; **139** David Paul, *Phasmatodea, Stick Insect,* Museum Victoria; *Golden Orb Weaver,* © Queensland Museum; Aaron Greenville, *Scorpion (Urodacus armatus)* 2013, NLA, Courtesy Aaron Greenville.

# REFERENCES

## Distribution Maps
Most of the maps are based on those in the list below. The maps are only indicative of the species' distribution range.

Anstis, M., *Tadpoles and Frogs of Australia*. Frenches Forest, NSW: New Holland Publishers, 2013

Pizzey, G. and F. Knight, *The Field Guide to the Birds of Australia*, 9th edn. Sydney: HarperCollins Publishers, 2012

Van Dyck, S. and R. Strahan (eds), *The Mammals of Australia*, 3rd edn. Sydney: New Holland Publishers, 2008

Van Dyck, S., I. Gynther and A. Baker (eds), *Field Companion to the Mammals of Australia*. Sydney: New Holland Publishers, 2013

Wilson, S. and G. Swan, *A Complete Guide to Reptiles of Australia*, 4th edn. Sydney: New Holland, 2013

While some species occur elsewhere, only their distribution in Australia is shown in this book.

Note: All websites listed below were active as of 16 February 2016.

## Websites for Commonwealth, State and Territory Government Departments and Museums
delwp.vic.gov.au/
dpaw.wa.gov.au/
ehp.qld.gov.au/
environment.gov.au/
environment.nsw.gov.au/
environment.sa.gov.au
gbrmpa.gov.au/
lrm.nt.gov.au/
museum.wa.gov.au/
parks.tas.gov.au/
parksandwildlife.nt.gov.au/
qm.qld.gov.au/

## General Websites
A–Z Animals, a-z-animals.com/animals/
Alice Springs Desert Park, www.alicespringsdesertpark.com.au/
Animal Diversity Web, animaldiversity.org/
A–Z Animals: All Animals of the World, atoz.animalstime.com/
Atlas of Living Australia, ala.org.au/
Australia Zoo, australiazoo.com.au
Australian Animal, australiananimallearningzone.com/
Australian Fauna, aussie-info.com/identity/fauna/index.php
Australian Geographic, australiangeographic.com.au/
Australian Museum—Animal Species, australianmuseum.net.au/
Australian Wildlife, australianwildlife.com.au/index.html
Australian Wildlife [Secrets], wildlifesecrets.com.au/
BIRD (Biodiversity Information Resources and Data), bird.net.au/
BUGS@HOME, entomology.edu.au/bugs-home
Climate Watch, climatewatch.org.au/
Encyclopedia of Life, eol.org/
Foundation for National Parks and Wildlife fnpw.org.au/
Kidcyber, kidcyber.com.au/
Museum Victoria, museumvictoria.com.au/discoverycentre/
OzAnimals—Australian Wildlife, ozanimals.com/
The Animal Files, theanimalfiles.com/
Wildscreen Arkive, arkive.org/
WIRES (NSW Wildlife Information Rescue & Education Service) Northern Rivers, wiresnr.org/
Zoos Victoria Healesville Sanctuary, zoo.org.au/Healesville

## Publications and Websites for Animal Types

### Fish and Frogs
ABC Radio Darwin, *Guestroom: Dr Mark Meekan: A Life with the Whale Sharks*, May 2010, abc.net.au/local/audio/2010/05/10/2894737.htm

Anstis, M., *Tadpoles and Frogs of Australia*. Frenches Forest, NSW: New Holland Publishers, 2013

Cogger, H., *Reptiles and Amphibians of Australia*. Melbourne: CSIRO Publishing, 2014

Department of Fisheries WA, *Fisheries Fact Sheet: Whale Shark*, 2011, fish.wa.gov.au/Documents/recreational_fishing/fact_sheets/fact_sheet_whale_shark.pdf

Ecocean, *Whale Shark Fact Sheet*, whaleshark.org.au/education/fact-sheets/

Enchanted Learning, *Whale Shark*, enchantedlearning.com/subjects/sharks/species/Whaleshark.shtml

Frogs of Australia, frogs.org.au/frogs/

Humphries, P., *The Conversation: Australian Endangered Species: Murray Cod*, 2013, theconversation.com/Australian-endangered-species-murray-cod-12555

Prendergast, A., 'Turtle Frogs: A Peculiarity of Australian Amphibians', *Australian Wildlife Secrets*, vol. 2, no. 2, 2012, pp. 34–37

Slater, P. and S. Parish, *Amazing Facts about Australian Frogs and Reptiles*. Queensland: Stephen Parish Publishing, 1997

### Reptiles
ABC Science, *The Baby Blue Tongues Are Coming*, abc.net.au/science/articles/2000/02/01/2662923.htm

Australian Reptile Online Database (AROD), arod.com.au/arod/

Australian Reptile Park, reptilepark.com.au/

Britton, A., *Crocodylus johnstoni*, crocodilian.com/cnhc/csp_cjoh.htm

Chambers Wildlife Lodges, *Boyd's Forest Dragon*, rainforest-australia.com/Boyd's_Forest_Dragon.htm

Chambers Wildlife Lodges, *Northern Leaf-tailed Gecko*, rainforest-australia.com/Northern_Leaf_Tailed_Gecko.htm

*Freshwater Crocodile Crocodylus johnsoni*, learningspark.com.au/shop/nt/fwcroc/

Hollister, J. and J. Fowler, *The Reptiles of Australia*, reptilesofaustralia.com/

Irwin, S., 'Courtship, Mating and Egg Deposition by the Captive Perentie *Varanus giganteus* (Gray, 1845)', *The Vivarium*, vol. 8, no. 4, pp. 27–56, 1997, varanid.us/PDF/SIP.pdf

National Geographic, *Video on Thorny Devil*, video.nationalgeographic.com.au/video/lizard_thornydevil

Science Daily, Australian *Saltwater Crocodiles Are World's Most Powerful Biters*, sciencedaily.com/releases/2012/03/120316093427.htm

Sea Turtle Conservancy, conserveturtles.org/

Slater, P. and S. Parish, *Amazing Facts about Australian Frogs and Reptiles*. Queensland: Stephen Parish Publishing, Queensland, 1997

Sunshine Coast Council, *Turtle Care: Green Turtle*, turtlecare.sunshinecoast.qld.gov.au/green-turtle.php

The Reptiles of Australia, *A Listing of Australian Geckos*, reptilesofaustralia.com/lizards/geckos/geckos.htm

Wilson, S. and G. Swan, *A Complete Guide to Reptiles of Australia*, 4th edn. Sydney: New Holland, 2013

### Birds
*Australian (Maned) Wood Duck*, mdahlem.net/birds/2/austwood.php

Birdlife Australia, birdlife.org.au/

Birds in Backyards, birdsinbackyards.net/

Bouglouan, N., *Crimson Rosella Platycercus elegans*, oiseaux-birds.com/card-crimson-rosella.html

Bouglouan, N., *Purple Swamphen*,
    oiseaux-birds.com/card-purple-swamphen.html
Burke's Backyard, *Fact Sheets: Cockatiels*,
    burkesbackyard.com.au/factsheets/Birds/Cockatiels/624
Burke's Backyard, *Fact Sheets: Wild Budgies*,
    burkesbackyard.com.au/factsheets/Birds/Wild-Budgies/1381
Fennell, P., *Birds of Canberra Gardens*, 2nd edn. Canberra: Canberra Ornithologists Group, 2009
Friends of Queenspark Bushland, *Red Wattlebird*,
    friendsofqueensparkbushland.org.au/red-wattlebird/
Garnett, S.T., J.K. Szabo and G. Dutson, The Action Plan for Australian Birds 2010. Collingwood, Vic.: CSIRO Publishing, 2011
Harrison, F., 'Smash and Grab, Bam, Splat and Bluey', *Australian Wildlife Secrets*, vol. 2, no. 4, 2013, pp. 18–25
National Malleefowl Recovery Team, nationalmalleefowl.com.au/
Olsen, J., *Australian High Country Owls*. Collingwood, Vic.: CSIRO Publishing, 2011
Parish, S. and P. Slater, *Amazing Facts about Australian Birds*. Fortitude Valley, Qld: Steve Parish Publishing, 1997
Parrotlink, *Gang Gang Cockatoo*, parrotlink.com/cms/index.php?page=gang-gang-cockatoo---new
Pizzey, G. and F. Knight, *The Field Guide to the Birds of Australia*, 9th edn. Sydney: HarperCollins Publishers, 2012
Redland City Council, *Bush Stone-curlew*, indigiscapes.redland.qld.gov.au/Animals/Pages/Bush-Stone-curlew.aspx
Rowland, P., *Bowerbirds*. Australian Natural History Series. Collingwood, Vic.: CSIRO, 2008
The Guardian, *It's Official, the Superb Fairy-wren Is Australia's Favourite Bird*, 7 November 2013, theguardian.com/environment/2013/nov/07/superb-fairy-wren-australia-s-favourite-bird
Young, W., *The Fascination of Birds: From the Albatross to the Yellowtail*. USA: Dover Publications, 2014

## Marsupials and Placental Mammals
*A Tale of Two Honey Possums*, honeypossum.com.au/
ABC Science, *The Secret Life of Water Rats*,
    abc.net.au/science/articles/2007/10/04/2185999.htm
AussieInfo.com, *Dingo*, aussie-info.com/identity/fauna/dingo.php
Australian Koala Foundation,
    savethekoala.com/about-koalas/trees-koalas
Benshemesh, J. and K. Johnson, 'Biology and Conservation of Marsupial Moles (Notoryctes)', in M. Jones, C. Dickman and M. Archer (eds), *Predators with Pouches: The Biology of Carnivorous Marsupials*. Melbourne: CSIRO Publishing, 2003, pp. 464–474
The Bilby Appreciation Society, *What Is a Bilby Anyway?*,
    members.optusnet.com.au/bilbies/About_Bilbies.htm
Cronin, L. and M. Westmacott, *Key Guide to Australian Mammals*. Sydney: Reed Books, 1991
Devils@Cradle, *Devil Facts*, devilsatcradle.com/content.php?id=devil-facts
Dolphin Research Institute, dolphinresearch.org.au/
Henderson, N., *Bandicoots: Their Care and Handling*,
    training.ntwc.org.au/PDF/Bandicoots_Care.pdf
Lone Pine Koala Sanctuary, koala.net/
Menkhorst, P., L. Broome and M. Driessen, *Burramys parvus*, 2008, The IUCN Red List of Threatened Species, Version 2014.2, iucnredlist.org/details/3339/0
Morcombe, M., *Australian Marsupials and Other Native Mammals*. Sydney: Summit Books, 1980
Stepnell, K. and D. Newman, *Australian Animals*. Newtown, NSW: Woollahra, 2004
Parish, S. and K. Cox, *Kangaroos and Their Relatives*. Archerfield, Qld: Steve Parish Publishing, 2008
Preservation Society of Wildlife Queensland, *Little Red Flying Fox*,
    wildlife.org.au/wildlife/speciesprofile/mammals/flyingfox/littlered_flyingfox.html
Slater, P. and S. Parish, *Amazing Facts about Australian Mammals*. Fortitude Valley, Qld: Steve Parish Publishing, 1997
Strahan, R. (ed.), *The Mammals of Australia*. Chatswood, NSW: Museum of Australia/Reed Books, 1995
Sullivan, R., ABC Science, *Antechinus Go out with a Bang*, 2011, abc.net.au/science/articles/2011/07/07/3262428.htm
Tree-kangaroo Info: The Tree-kangaroo and Mammal Group Inc., tree-kangaroo.net/tkInfo.html
Vandenbeld, J., *Nature of Australia: A Portrait of the Island Continent*. Sydney: ABC, 2001
Van Dyck, S. and R. Strahan (eds), *The Mammals of Australia*, 3rd edn. Sydney: New Holland Publishers, 2008
Van Dyck, S., I. Gynther and A. Baker (eds), *Field Companion to the Mammals of Australia*. Sydney: New Holland Publishers, 2013
Woinarski, J.C.Z., A.A. Burbidge and P.L. Harrison, The Action Plan for Australian Mammals 2012. Collingwood, Vic.: CSIRO Publishing, 2014

## Little Critters
AntWiki, Australian Ants, antwiki.org/wiki/Australian_ants
Australian National Botanic Gardens, Beetles in the Gardens, anbg.gov.au/gardens/visiting/exploring/fauna/insects/beetles-ANBG.html
Brunet, B., *Spiderwatch: A Guide to Australian Spiders*. Chatswood, NSW: New Holland Publishers, 2000
Butterflies of Australia, lepidoptera.butterflyhouse.com.au/butter.html
Craig, O., *Summer of Singing Cidadas*, 2001, abc.net.au/science/articles/2001/02/17/2822486.htm
CSIRO, Australian Moths Online, www1.ala.org.au/gallery2/main.php
CSIRO, Insect Identification Resources Online, csiro.au/en/Research/Collections/ANIC/ID-Resources
Friends of the Phasmid, friendsofthephasmid.org.au/site/1437587/page/889789
Horne, P.A. and D.J. Crawford, *Backyard Insects*. Carlton, Vic.: Miegunya Press, 2015
Minibeast Wildlife, minibeastwildlife.com.au/resources/
Popple, L.W., *Cicadas of Central Eastern Australia*, 2006, sci-s03.bacs.uq.edu.au/ins-info/cicada.htm
Spiders of Australia, ednieuw.home.xs4all.nl/australian/Spidaus.html
Spiny Leaf Insects, abc.net.au/creaturefeatures/facts/spinyleafinsect.htm
Zborowski, P., *Insects of Australia*. Sydney: New Holland, 2002

# INDEX

**Animals
(by common name)**

**Insects and Arachnids**
ants 136
beetles 137
bugs 137
butterflies 138
cicadas 137
crickets 138
damselflies 138
dragonflies 138
grasshoppers 138
katydids 138
leaf insects 139
moths 138
native bees 136
scorpions 139
spiders 139
stick insects 139
termites 136

**Fish**
Murray Cod 104
Whale Shark 120

**Reptiles**
Black-headed Python 38
Blotched Blue-tongue Lizard 90
Boyd's Forest Dragon 56
Burton's Legless Lizard 15
Common Bearded Dragon 12
Common Blue-tongue Lizard 16
Common Thick-tailed Gecko 36
Crocodile
   Freshwater 105
   Saltwater 121
Dragon
   Boyd's Forest 56
   Common Bearded 12
   Water 106
Eastern Brown Snake 17
Eastern Long-necked Turtle 109
Flatback Turtle 123
Freshwater Crocodile 105
Frill-necked Lizard 13
Gecko
   Common Thick-tailed 36
   Northern Leaf-tailed 57
   Smooth Knob-tailed 71

Green Python 58
Green Turtle 122
Lace Monitor 37
Lizard
   Blotched Blue-tongue 90
   Burton's Legless 15
   Common Blue-tongue 16
   Frill-necked 13
   Shingleback 73
Monitor
   Lace 37
   Yellow-spotted 14
Mulga Snake 74
Northern Leaf-tailed Gecko 57
Perentie 72
Pig-nosed Turtle 108
Python
   Black-headed 38
   Green 58
Red-bellied Black Snake 107
Saltwater Crocodile 121
Shingleback Lizard 73
Smooth Knob-tailed Gecko 71
Snake
   Eastern Brown 17
   Mulga 74
   Red-bellied Black 107
Thorny Devil 70
Turtle
   Eastern Long-necked 109
   Flatback 123
   Green 122
   Pig-nosed 108
Water Dragon 106
Yellow-spotted Monitor 14

**Frogs**
Eastern Banjo Frog 110
Turtle Frog 18
Water-holding Frog 75
Western Banjo Frog 110
White-lipped Tree Frog 59

**Birds**
Australian Barn Owl 24
Australian Magpie 27
Australian Pelican 126
Australian Wood Duck 112
Barking Owl 23

Black Swan 111
Black-Cockatoo
   Red-tailed 39
   Yellow-tailed 39
Black-necked Stork 113
Blue-winged Kookaburra 25
Bowerbird, Satin 42
Budgerigar 79
Bush Stone-curlew 22
Cassowary, Southern 60
Cockatiel 78
Cockatoo
   Gang-gang 92
   Major Mitchell's 77
   Sulphur-crested 40
Crimson Rosella 93
Duck, Australian Wood 112
Eagle, Wedge-tailed 91
Eastern Whipbird 62
Emu 19
Fairy-wren
   Splendid 26
   Superb 26
Frogmouth, Tawny 20
Galah 21
Gang-gang Cockatoo 92
Gull, Silver 125
Hooded Plover 128
Kookaburra
   Laughing 25
   Blue-winged 25
Laughing Kookaburra 25
Little Penguin 124
Lorikeet, Rainbow 41
Lyrebird, Superb 61
Magpie, Australian 27
Major Mitchell's Cockatoo 77
Malleefowl 76
Owl
   Australian Barn 24
   Barking 23
Pelican, Australian 126
Penguin, Little 124
Plover, Hooded 128
Purple Swamphen 114
Rainbow Lorikeet 41
Red Wattlebird 94
Red-tailed Black-Cockatoo 39

Rosella, Crimson 93
Satin Bowerbird 42
Sea-Eagle, White-bellied 127
Silver Gull 125
Southern Cassowary 60
Splendid Fairy-wren 26
Stone-curlew, Bush 22
Stork, Black-necked 113
Sulphur-crested Cockatoo 40
Superb Fairy-wren 26
Superb Lyrebird 61
Swamphen, Purple 114
Swan, Black 111
Tawny Frogmouth 20
Wattlebird, Red 94
Wedge-tailed Eagle 91
Whipbird, Eastern 62
White-bellied Sea-Eagle 127
Yellow-tailed Black-Cockatoo 39

**Monotremes and Marsupials**
Antechinus, Dusky 97
Bandicoot, Long-nosed 45
Bettong, Rufous 30
Bilby 82
Brush-tailed Phascogale 43
Common Brushtail Possum 49
Common Ringtail Possum 48
Common Spotted Cuscus 65
Common Wallaroo 99
Common Wombat 28
Crest-tailed Mulgara 80
Cuscus, Common Spotted 65
Devil, Tasmanian 96
Dusky Antechinus 97
Eastern Grey Kangaroo 32
Echidna, Short-beaked 95
Giles' Planigale 81
Glider, Sugar 47
Hare-wallaby, Spectacled 31
Honey Possum 29
Kangaroo
    Eastern Grey 32
    Western Grey 32
    Red 83
Koala 46
Long-nosed Bandicoot 45
Lumholtz's Tree-kangaroo 67

Marsupial Mole
    Northern 85
    Southern 85
Mountain Pygmy-possum 98
Mulgara, Crest-tailed 80
Musky Rat-kangaroo 66
Northern Marsupial Mole 85
Numbat 44
Pademelon, Tasmanian 50
Phascogale, Brush-tailed 43
Planigale, Giles' 81
Platypus 115
Possum
    Common Ringtail 48
    Common Brushtail 49
    Honey 29
    Striped 64
Pygmy-possum, Mountain 98
Quokka 84
Quoll, Spotted-tailed 63
Rat-kangaroo, Musky 66
Red Kangaroo 83
Rock-wallaby, Yellow-footed 100
Rufous Bettong 30
Short-beaked Echidna 95
Southern Hairy-nosed Wombat 28
Southern Marsupial Mole 85
Spectacled Hare-wallaby 31
Spotted-tailed Quoll 63
Striped Possum 64
Sugar Glider 47
Swamp Wallaby 51
Tasmanian Devil 96
Tasmanian Pademelon 50
Tree-kangaroo, Lumholtz's 67
Wallaby, Swamp 51
Wallaroo, Common 99
Western Grey Kangaroo 32
Wombat
    Common 28
    Southern Hairy-nosed 28
Yellow-footed Rock-wallaby 100

**Placental Mammals**
Australian Fur Seal 134
Australian Sea-lion 133
Australian Water Rat 116
Bat, Gould's Wattled 53

Common Bottlenose Dolphin 131
Dingo 101
Dolphin
    Common Bottlenose 131
    Indo-Pacific Bottlenose 131
Dugong 129
Flying-fox, Little Red 52
Fur Seal, Australian 134
Gould's Wattled Bat 53
Hopping-mouse
    Mitchell's 86
    Spinifex 86
Humpback Whale 130
Indo-Pacific Bottlenose Dolphin 131
Little Red Flying-fox 52
Mitchell's Hopping-mouse 86
Orca 132
Rat, Australian Water 116
Sea-lion, Australian 133
Southern Right Whale 130
Spinifex Hopping-mouse 86
Whale
    Humpback 130
    Southern Right 130

## National Parks (by state and territory)

**Australian Capital Territory**
Namadji National Park 35

**New South Wales**
Blue Mountains NP 88
Dorrigo NP 54
Kinchega NP 69
Kosciuszko NP 89
Oxley Wild Rivers NP 103
Royal NP 119
Sturt Arid Zone NP 68
Warrumbungle NP 11
Wollemi NP 35

**Northern Territory**
Garig Gunak Barlu NP 119
Kakadu NP 103
Judbarra/Gregory NP 35
Litchfield NP 11
Uluru-Kata Tjuta NP 69

**Queensland**
Bowling Green Bay NP 102
Carnarvon NP 10
Crater Lakes NP 55
Cravens Peak Reserve 68
Daintree NP 54
Diamantina NP 69
Great Barrier Reef Marine Park 119
Kutini-Payamu NP 55
Lamington NP 55
Main Range NP 34

**South Australia**
Coorong NP 119
Flinders Chase NP
  (on Kangaroo Island) 119
Flinders Ranges NP 89
Innamincka Regional Reserve 102
Murray River NP 102
Witjira NP 69

**Tasmania**
Cradle Mountain–Lake Saint Clair NP 88
Franklin–Gordon Wild Rivers NP 102
Freycinet NP 34
Mount Field NP 55
Southwest NP 55

**Victoria**
Alpine NP 88
Dandenong Ranges NP 34
Grampians NP 10
Great Otway NP 54
Little Desert NP 68
Port Campbell NP 119
Snowy River NP 103
Wilsons Promontory NP 11
Wyperfeld NP 69

**Western Australia**
Cape Le Grand NP 118
Cape Range NP 118
Karijini NP 10
Nambung NP 68
Ningaloo Marine Park 118
Rottnest Island Authority 69
Stirling Range NP 89
Tone-Perup Nature Reserve 35
Walpole–Nornalup NP 35
Yanchep NP 11

## National Parks (alphabetical order)

Alpine NP (Vic.) 88
Blue Mountains NP (NSW) 88
Bowling Green Bay NP (Qld) 102
Cape Le Grand NP (WA) 118
Cape Range NP (WA) 118
Carnarvon NP (Qld) 10
Coorong NP (SA) 119
Cradle Mountain–Lake Saint Clair NP (Tas.) 88
Crater Lakes NP (Qld) 55
Cravens Peak Reserve (Qld) 68
Daintree NP(Qld) 54
Dandenong Ranges NP (Vic.) 34
Diamantina NP (Qld) 69
Dorrigo NP (NSW) 54
Flinders Chase NP
  (on Kangaroo Island, SA) 119
Flinders Ranges NP (SA) 89
Franklin–Gordon Wild Rivers NP (Tas.) 102
Freycinet NP (Tas.) 34
Garig Gunak Barlu NP (NT) 119
Grampians NP (Vic.) 10
Great Barrier Reef Marine Park (Qld) 119
Great Otway NP (Vic.) 54
Innamincka Regional Reserve (SA) 102
Judbarra/Gregory NP (NT) 35
Kakadu NP (NT) 103
Karijini NP (WA) 10
Kinchega NP (NSW) 69
Kosciuszko NP (NSW) 89
Kutini-Payamu NP (Qld) 55
Lamington NP (Qld) 55
Litchfield NP (NT) 11
Little Desert NP (Vic.) 68
Main Range NP (Qld) 34
Mount Field NP (Tas.) 55
Murray River NP (SA) 102
Namadgi NP (ACT) 35
Nambung NP (WA) 68
Ningaloo Marine Park (WA) 118
Oxley Wild Rivers NP (NSW) 103
Port Campbell NP (Vic.) 119
Rottnest Island Authority (WA) 69
Royal NP (NSW) 119
Snowy River NP (Vic.) 103
Southwest NP (Tas.) 55
Stirling Range NP (WA) 89
Sturt NP (NSW) 68
Tone-Perup Nature Reserve (WA) 35
Uluru-Kata Tjuta NP (NT) 69
Walpole–Nornalup NP (WA) 35
Warrumbungle NP (NSW) 11
Wilsons Promontory NP (Vic.) 11
Witjira NP (SA) 69
Wollemi NP (NSW) 35
Wyperfeld NP (Vic.) 69
Yanchep NP (WA) 11

**NATIONAL LIBRARY OF AUSTRALIA**

Published by the National Library of Australia
Canberra ACT 2600

© National Library of Australia 2016
Text © Gina M. Newton

Books published by the National Library of Australia further the Library's objectives to produce publications that interpret the Library's collection and contribute to the vitality of Australian culture and history.

Every reasonable endeavour has been made to contact the copyright holders. Where this has not been possible, the copyright holders are invited to contact the publisher.

This book is copyright in all countries subscribing to the Berne Convention. Apart from any fair dealing for the purpose of research and study, criticism or review, as permitted under the *Copyright Act 1968*, no part may be reproduced by any process without written permission. Enquiries should be made to the publisher.

National Library of Australia Cataloguing-in-Publication entry

| | |
|---|---|
| Creator: | Newton, Gina M., author. |
| Title: | Amazing animals of Australia's national parks / Gina M. Newton. |
| ISBN: | 9780642278883 (paperback) |
| Notes: | Includes bibliographical references and index. |
| Target Audience: | For children 8–12 years. |
| Subjects: | Animals--Australia--Juvenile literature. |
| | Animals--Australia--Pictorial works. |
| | National parks and reserves--Australia--Juvenile literature. |
| Dewey Number: | 591.994 |

Commissioning Publisher: Susan Hall
Editor: Joanna Karmel
Designers: Elizabeth Faul (concept) and Noel Wendtman (layout)
Image coordinator: Celia Vaughan
Production coordinator: Melissa Bush
Printed in China by Everbest Printing Co Ltd

Find out more about National Library Publishing at publishing.nla.gov.au.
Teachers' notes can be found at publishing.nla.gov.au/pages/teachers-notes.do.

# General Map of Habitats* and Featured National Parks

### Queensland
1 Kutini-Payamu NP
2 Daintree NP
3 Crater Lakes NP
4 Great Barrier Reef MP
5 Bowling Green Bay NP
6 Cravens Peak R
7 Diamantina NP
8 Carnarvon NP
9 Lamington NP
10 Main Range NP

### New South Wales
11 Oxley Wild Rivers NP
12 Dorrigo NP
13 Sturt NP
14 Warrumbungle NP
15 Kinchega NP
16 Wollemi NP
17 Blue Mountains NP
18 Royal NP
19 Kosciuszko NP

### Australian Capital Territory
20 Namadgi NP

### Victoria
21 Wyperfeld NP
22 Little Desert NP
23 Grampians NP
24 Snowy River NP
25 Alpine NP
26 Dandenong Ranges NP
27 Great Otway NP
28 Port Campbell NP
29 Wilsons Promontory NP

### Tasmania
30 Freycinet NP
31 Cradle Mountain–Lake Saint Clair NP
32 Franklin–Gordon Wild Rivers NP
33 Mount Field NP
34 Southwest NP

### South Australia
35 Flinders Chase NP
36 Coorong NP
37 Murray River NP
38 Flinders Ranges NP
39 Innamincka RR
40 Witjira NP

### Western Australia
41 Cape Le Grand NP
42 Stirling Range NP
43 Walpole–Nornalup NP
44 Tone-Perup NR
45 Rottnest Island Authority
46 Yanchep NP
47 Nambung NP
48 Ningaloo MP
49 Cape Range NP
50 Karijini NP

### Northern Territory
51 Judbarra/Gregory NP
52 Litchfield NP
53 Kakadu NP
54 Garig Gunak Barlu NP
55 Uluru-Kata Tjuta NP

---

**NP** National Park
**MP** Marine Park
**R** Reserve
**RR** Regional Reserve
**NR** Nature Reserve

* except mountains